Read this book with enough time to "chew on" the considerable meat that's inside. It is a blueprint for success.
—John H. Zenger, Co-founder, Zenger-Miller Inc.,
and President, Times Mirror Training Group

Being a military officer, I was particularly interested in the thoughts on leadership and management. In my career, I have played both roles; sometimes simultaneously. It is very important to understand the differences and to know when to play each.
—Claude M. Bolton, Jr., Brigadier General, U.S. Air Force

The concept of personal, team, and organizational levels of change is important. Jim Clemmer's sharing of personal experiences in all three areas is powerful . . . and unusual. Many people are not comfortable with personal disclosures as a tool for learning from others.
—Mary-Jo Hall, Professor/Special Assistant for Quality,
Defense Systems Management College, Fort Belvior, VA

Jim Clemmer cuts through the rhetoric of fashionable organization programs and theoretical concepts to navigate the business leader on his journey to high performance and success in his company.
—Roger Staubach, Chairman and CEO,
The Staubach Company

Anyone reading Pathways to Performance must give pause to reflect if he or she has truly made the commitment to be an outstanding leader. The book is a rich review of the many elements that make up effective leadership which—as Jim points out—can be accomplished by anyone who thinks through the process and is willing to make the effort. As I read each chapter our organization's leadership behavior became clear to me and what will be required by our leaders in the months ahead came into focus.
—Gordon Canning, President, Blue Mountain Resorts

Pathways to Performance is an excellent follow up to Firing on All Cylinders. Jim Clemmer provides a challenging and inspirational guide for executives to stay on the path of

improvement in both personal and organizational performance.
—Bernard J. Herman, President,
Mercy Healthcare, Bakersfield, CA

Jim's timely and inspiring book reinforces that managing organizational change and improving quality starts when we decide to change the way we think about ourselves and the impact of what we do on others. **Pathways to Performance** *provides a much needed roadmap for personal quality improvement.*
—J. W. Perry, Vice President, Reimer Express World Corp.,
and Vice President, National Quality Institute

Jim has put his finger on the dark secret of organization change and improvement—most attempts fail because senior managers are unwilling or unable to change their behaviors. His book made me feel uncomfortable (a good sign) because he ruthlessly exposed a number of deficiencies in my leadership style. **Pathways to Performance** *. . . is the most comprehensive guide to leadership skill development that I have read. I will be buying copies for my senior managers and profitably rereading it myself for several years to come.*
—Drew Yallop, President, Canadian Tire Petroleum

Jim Clemmer identifies the indispensable qualities that will define the next decade of exemplary organizations. To read **Pathways to Performance** *is to become captivated by the possibilities for personal and organizational achievement. Entrepreneurs and leaders will be inspired by Jim's very personal challenge.*
—Doug Snetsinger, Executive Director,
Institute of Market Driven Quality

If all you read is the introduction, the book is worth the investment. A bugle call to action.
—Peter Jensen, President, Performance
Coaching Inc., and author of* The Inside Edge

Pathways to Performance *is engaging, challenging, enlightening, inspirational, and (most important!) very entertaining. It* *is an essential playbook for leaders in every field and at every level.*

—Dick Lehrberg, Executive Vice President,
Interplay Productions

Jim Clemmer has written a book for thoughtful leaders who learned long ago that doing more of the same will not bring about sustainable change. He addresses the key issue of our time: that the fundamental and necessary reconstruction of our organizations that will prepare them for the twenty-first century can only be achieved from within, and even then, only one person at a time.

—Lance Secretan, business consultant,
author of *Managerial Moxie* and *The Way of the Tiger*

At a time when managers are common and leaders are at a premium, Jim has woven together the basic principles that provide the foundation for increased personal effectiveness and successful organization change. Regardless of the tools used—total quality management, reengineering, installation of teams, continuous improvement, empowerment—the very practical 'pathways and pitfalls' that Jim provides will help managers successfully lead their organizations in new directions.

—Bob Sherwin, President and CEO, Kaset International

***Pathways to Performance** does a great job of demystifying all the quality and organization improvement buzzwords. This book is an excellent guide to performance improvement for organizations of all sizes and in all sectors whether they be public companies or government services.*

—Tony Johnston, Vice-President, Employee Development and
Quality Improvement, Canadian Airlines International

Jim's approach to vision and values is straight on track and is the highlight of the book. The promise made was fulfilled. It did make me think. It made me reflect on my own approach to leading and the many things I still have room to improve upon.

—Jon Slangerup, Vice President and General Manager,
Federal Express Canada

*Jim, it's been my privilege to recommend your wonderful book **Firing on All Cylinders** to my audiences. It is the best* book on customer service I've ever read. With **Pathways to Performance**, you've done it again. This book is a star in the sky to help lead people and organizations to real change, positive values, and lasting relationships. Thank you for the gift you've given to those of us who care deeply about people and performance.

—Maurice O'Callaghan, professional speaker and former telecommunications executive.

Jim Clemmer's new text is in the forefront of today's thinking about business excellence. His pragmatic approach, based on sound theory, will resonate with thoughtful business leaders everywhere. I would recommend it to anyone whether advanced in the quality journey or beginning to take very first steps. It's an excellent roadmap . . . but more than that, it is illuminated by deep insights into organizational life and the challenge facing leaders in every endeavor.

—John Lynch, President and CEO, North American Life Assurance Company

I found **Pathways to Performance** fascinating reading. The advice, information, and examples really hit home. For me, the book provoked a great deal of thought on continually reviewing the objectives and priorities of a company.

—Sam Poole, President, Maxis

Pathways to Performance provides a valued sense of direction and reference for those struggling to behave differently and lead more effectively. Jim pulls together the many facets of leadership and management and shows how they fit to make the whole. It will become a guide for all our Team Leader/Managers.

—Philip C. Hassen, President, St. Joseph's Health Centre, London, Ontario

Pathways to Performance

Pathways to Performance

*A Guide to
Transforming
Yourself, Your Team,
and Your Organization*

JIM CLEMMER

MACMILLAN CANADA

Toronto

Grateful acknowledgment is made to the following publications for permission to excerpt material: *Punished by Rewards,* by Alfie Kohn. © 1993 Alfie Kohn. Reprinted by permission of Houghton Mifflin Co. All rights reserved. • *The Fifth Discipline,* by Peter M. Senge. Copyright © 1990 by Peter M. Senge. Used by permission of Doubleday, a division of Bantam Doubleday Dell Publishing Group, Inc. • *Benjamin Franklin's the Art of Virtue,* edited by George L. Rogers. Acorn Publishing, Minnesota. • *TNT: The Power within You,* by Claude M. Bristol and Harold Sherman. © 1954, 1982. Reprinted by permission of the publisher, Prentice Hall, a division of Simon & Schuster. • *On Becoming a Leader,* © 1989 by Warren Bennis, Inc. Reprinted by permission of Addison-Wesley Publishing Company, Inc. • Charles Garfield, Ph.D., author of *Peak Performers* and *Second to None.* • "Reengineering the MBA," by Brian O'Reilly. *Fortune,* © 1994 Time Inc. All rights reserved. • *Love, Medicine & Miracles: Lessons Learned about Self-Healing from a Surgeon's Experience with Patients,* by Bernie S. Siegel, M.D. Copyright © 1986 by B. S. Siegel, S. Korman, and A. Schiff, trustees of the Bernard S. Siegel, M.D., Children's Trust. Reprinted by permission of HarperCollins Publishers, Inc. • *Innovation and Entrepreneurship: Practice and Principles,* by Peter F. Drucker. Copyright © 1985 by Peter F. Drucker. Reprinted by permission of HarperCollins Publishers, Inc. • *Learned Optimism,* by Martin E. P. Seligman. Copyright © 1991 by Martin E. P. Seligman. Reprinted by permission of Alfred A. Knopf, Inc. • *Thinking about Management,* by Theodore Levitt. Copyright © 1991 by Theodore Levitt. Reprinted with permission of The Free Press, a division of Simon & Schuster. • *Intelligent Enterprise,* by James Brian Quinn. Copyright © 1992 by James Brian Quinn. Reprinted with permission of The Free Press, a division of Simon & Schuster. • *The Rise and Fall of Strategic Planning,* by Henry Mintzberg. Copyright © by Henry Mintzberg. Reprinted with permission of The Free Press, a division of Simon & Schuster.

Canadian Cataloguing in Publication Data

Clemmer, Jim, date.
     Pathways to performance : a guide to transforming yourself, your team, and your organization

Includes index.
ISBN 0-7715-7327-8

1. Organizational change.   2. Leadership.
I. Title.

HD58.8.C55 1995   658.4'06   C95-930712-5

1 2 3 4 5 FP 99 98 97 96 95

Macmillan Canada wishes to thank the Canada Council, the Ontario Ministry of Culture and Communications and the Ontario Arts Council for supporting its publishing program.

Macmillan Canada
A Division of Canada Publishing Corporation
Toronto, Ontario, Canada

Printed in Canada

To Heather, Christopher, Jennifer, and Vanessa.
Your love, support, and hard work provide
a high-energy home for balancing personal,
family, and business effectiveness.

CONTENTS

FOREWORD

by Scott DeGarmo
EDITOR IN CHIEF AND PUBLISHER,
SUCCESS MAGAZINE

There is an ancient story that has enjoyed endless variations. The one I know involves three wise but sightless men who chance upon an elephant. The first wise man gets hold of one of the elephant's legs and cries out, "Why, it's a magnificent mansion with huge columns!" The next wise man, feeling the elephant's tail, retorts derisively, "It's nothing of the kind. This is but a very strong rope." The last wise man, feeling one of the elephant's tusks, says with equal certainty, "You are both wrong. What we have here are some of the most fearsome sabers you can ever imagine."

I tell you this story because it reminds me of the endless discussions concerning how to build a successful company. There are those who insist that successful organizations come out of personal effectiveness—if your people are effective, then your company will also be. Others insist that it is simply a matter of good leadership—with the right leader, any organization will thrive. Others, however, swear with equal fervor that the measure of a successful company lies in the effectiveness of its organizational structure.

Like the experiences of the three wise men, each of these points of view is right in a limited way and wrong in its incompleteness as a total philosophy for corporate improvement. The truth lies in the fact that these three views combined create the necessary vision to build a successful organization. Here, paradox becomes paradigm!

Jim Clemmer's *Pathways to Performance* is the first book I have read that successfully weaves the high-performance rope out of the strands of organizational improvement, leadership development, and personal effectiveness. Here you'll find no quick fixes; Clemmer correctly believes there are none. Rather, he demonstrates what has taken him years of experience to learn, both as a successful entrepreneur (as you will soon read) and as one of the most brilliant and sought-after consultants in North America.

This is no dry tome. Jim's understated humor permeates every part of this book. The style is breezy and accessible. Yet, he is dead-on accurate in pointing out some of the amazing inanities that underlie the way we go about trying to effect change. He may irritate you, and I know he will challenge and perhaps even madden you. But he will make you think!

So, keep your mind open and your ego in check. You'll be richly rewarded!

ACKNOWLEDGMENTS

*Many times I realize how much my own outer and inner life is
built upon the labors of my fellowmen, both living and dead, and
how earnestly I must exert myself in order to give in return as
much as I have received.*

—Albert Einstein

In recognizing the contributions of specific individuals, there is always the danger that other deserving people will be left out. That possibility looms large as I reflect on the many people who have helped shape the ideas, experiences, actions, and personal learning that have found their way into this book.

The following people and organizations are at the top of my very long appreciation list. Some had a direct impact on this book. Many others contributed indirectly by providing the personal development, insights, research, inspiration, experiences, or ideas woven throughout these pages.

For encouraging, supporting, discussing, or commenting on the first draft of *Pathways to Performance*—Bob Dees and Denise Schon at Macmillan Canada, Ben Dominitz and Jennifer Basye Sander at Prima Publishing, Judy Dick, Owen Griffiths, Pat Henderson, Deb Strong, Kay Marie Wallace, and Jack Zenger.

For their contributions to Achieve's sharp growth and learning curves—the dozens of original "Achievers" and hundreds of Zenger-Miller associates.

For showing me how to condense and more sharply focus my writing into the impossibly small space of a 500-word column— Gordon Pitts, editor of *The Globe & Mail*'s "Change Page."

For writing the books or articles that provided me with especially valuable research, insights, examples, or inspiration in organization improvement, leadership development, or personal effectiveness (here's where hundreds of other authors who've also contributed to my learning get left out)—Warren Bennis, Len Berry, Don Berwick, Richard Bolles, Claude Bristol, Dale Carnegie, Stephen Covey, W. Edwards Deming, Peter Drucker, Charles Garfield, Napoleon Hill, Charles Jones, Joseph Juran, Rosabeth Moss Kanter, John Kotter, Ted Levitt, Ron Lippitt, Og Mandino, Henry Mintzberg, James O'Toole, Norman Vincent Peale, Richard Pascale, Tom Peters, Brian Quinn, Martin Seligman, Peter Senge, Barry Sheehy, Alvin Toffler, Robert Townsend, Bob Waterman, Jack Zenger, and Zig Ziglar.

For providing an endless stream of thought-provoking, highly instructive, and well-written articles—*Fortune* and *Success* magazines and *Harvard Business Review.*

For challenging, suggesting, sharing your experiences with, and applying the concepts of my earlier work and those found in this book—thousands of critics and supporters who've attended seminars, workshops and presentations, readers of my books and columns, and management teams participating in off-site executive retreats.

For developing a deep set of core values and strong work ethic—my mom and now departed dad.

For supporting my endless days of preoccupation and wrestling with creating and writing, my travel, and continually bringing my life back into balance—Heather, Christopher, Jennifer, and Vanessa.

Thanks!

Jim Clemmer

INTRODUCTION

---

*To be good is noble, but to teach others how to be good is nobler—
and less trouble.*

—Mark Twain

A woman was asked why she was wearing her wedding band on the wrong finger. "Because I married the wrong man," she snapped. Before we make a commitment to spend time together, let's make sure this book is the right fit for you. If you're trying to change and improve a team, business, or large organization, then we're off to a good start. *Where you are in the organization is less important than what you are.* You need to be (or strongly aspire to become) a leader. Now that doesn't mean you must have a "leadership" job in the traditional management sense. Rather, it means you are trying to initiate and guide change and improvement in a team, business, or organization.

But before you try to change anyone else, you've got to change yourself. *Self-leadership is at the heart of effectively leading others.* Self-improvement is the beginning point to team or organization improvement. If that sounds as if I've been bungee jumping with a cord that was just a little too long, then we clearly aren't right for each other.

The primary objectives of this book are:

1. *Irritation.* I'll do my best to get under your skin. I want to increase your dissatisfaction with your current approach to and rate of personal and organization change and improvement. I am assuming this book isn't recreational reading for you. You want to make yourself and your team, business, or

organization better. Changes of the magnitude needed to excel in today's world are hard and uncomfortable. So I won't go easy. I will be in your face. I'll be part drill sergeant, part guilty conscience, and part nag (which my wife, Heather, and our kids, Christopher, Jennifer, and Vanessa, can tell you comes very naturally).

2. *Inspiration.* I've tried to select a wide variety of inspiring examples, ideas, quotations, and illustrations. My goal is to energize and inspire you to begin or renew your personal and organization change and improvement process on parallel tracks. Of course, what I find inspiring you may find exasperating, and someone else might find amusing. So highlight, pluck out, or skip to those sections you find the most meaningful.

3. *Instruction.* The road to higher performance is full of traps, pitfalls, and dead ends. I've watched people trying to change and improve themselves, their teams, or their organizations fall into many of them. And I've got the scrapes and bruises to show that I've stumbled into my fair share as well. So I'll point out as many I can along the way. But I've also seen and used many highly effective and very practical improvement tools and techniques. A big part of this book is dedicated to giving you a wide range of personal and organization improvement tools and techniques to choose from. You'll then need to tailor these to your circumstances, personality, and organization culture.

THE BIGGER THEME OF THINGS

What lies behind us and what lies before us are tiny matters compared to what lies within us.

—Ralph Waldo Emerson

This book is a result of my continuing quest to combine, compress, and connect the key principles and practices that lead to ever higher team, business, and organization performance. My first book (written with Art McNeil), *The VIP Strategy: Leadership Skills for Exceptional Performance,* outlined (and explained how to develop) many of the interpersonal communication, coaching, team, and cultural skills used by exceptional leaders to improve their organization's performance. My second book (written with Barry Sheehy), *Firing on All Cylinders: The Service/Quality System for High-Powered Corporate Performance,* outlined the strategic organizational tools and techniques of customer service improvement. After completing my third book, I debated its title with the Canadian (Macmillan of Canada) and U.S. (Irwin Professional Publishing) publishers. We decided to call it *Firing on All Cylinders* since the first edition was never published in the United States and the Implementation Architecture (or "cylinder model") still formed the book's central framework. However, the second edition of *Firing on All Cylinders* was substantially larger and broader than the first edition. It outlined in much greater depth the implementation tools and techniques of service/quality improvement, building a team-based organization, and process management.

Pathways to Performance cuts through the "labelism," jargon, buzzwords, and narrower tools of excellence, customer service, quality, benchmarking, continuous improvement, empowerment, teams, reengineering, process improvement, and the like to identify the underlying performance principles of successful organization change and improvement. The results of those efforts hinge on the leadership skills and personal effectiveness of the people leading and implementing them. So the book draws from and combines the fundamental principles underlying organization improvement, leadership development, and personal effectiveness.

Weaving the High-Performance Rope

Organization Improvement

Leadership Development

Personal Effectivenss

Many of the issues and principles I will touch on throughout *Pathways to Performance* aren't new. In fact, they've been with us for decades, if not centuries. But we continually need to rediscover them for ourselves, repackage them for our time, and make them relevant for today's circumstances or sets of problems. In writing this book, as in most of my work, I am not driven by what's new as much as I am pulled toward what works. When it comes to dealing with personal and people issues, the fundamentals of what works have remained fairly constant through the years.

If we continue to spend time together, you'll be hearing these core themes many times in the pages ahead:

- *Balance, paradox, and dilemmas.* F. Scott Fitzgerald once declared, "The test of a first-rate intelligence is the ability to hold two opposed ideas in the mind at the same time, and still retain the ability to function." One of the reasons highly effective leaders are so effective is because they have well-developed judgment muscles between their ears. The balancing of hard, analytical management skills with those of soft, intuitive leadership is an example of a key theme you'll be hearing.
- *Constant improvement.* You need to keep working *in* your job, team, business, or organization while you also work *on* your job, team, business, or organization. Most people strive hard to get their work done, keep their customers happy, meet their goals and commitments, and keep their business afloat. High performers develop the discipline to continually look at whether they are doing the right things in the best way.
- *Laughter and fun.* You may have missed that recent study showing that suppressed laughter goes back down to spread the hips and produce gas. High performers often have a well-developed sense of humor, fun, and playfulness. I've consistently found that the amount of laughter (Laughter Index) found in a team, organization, or family is a good indicator of its health. So I hope you'll have some laughs in our brief time together.
- *Your true self.* You can't build a team, business, or organization different from you. There must be an alignment between who you are personally and where you're trying to take your

organization or team. An unimproved leader can't produce an improved team or organization. It's possible that some of the changes your organization or team needs to make will pull them closer to your true self. This can be especially true if you've inherited or taken over a group, business, or organization. However, chances are higher that you'll need to make personal changes parallel to the organization or team changes you're trying to make.

- *No quick fixes.* Lasting and effective change and improvement come from moving beyond bolt-on programs to built-in processes. Many people are looking for what's new in quick-fix improvement programs. But what works are fundamental improvement practices that become a habitual way of life.

- *Taking action.* My years of research and work with behavior-based skill development methods clearly show that we act our way into new ways of thinking far more easily than we can think our way into new ways of acting. Throughout this book you may find yourself nodding or thinking "I know that already. When's he going to get to the new stuff?" Whenever that happens, ask yourself "So what I am doing about it?" I'll try to nag, spur, inspire, prod, and otherwise move you beyond knowing to doing.

- *Blazing your own improvement path.* There are as many ways to change and improve as there are people and organizations trying to do so. This is no one right path or approach to higher performance. What works for me may do little for you. What works for one organization may be impossible in yours. That's why I'll present an array of possible pathways, actions, steps, and routes. You need to pick through them and choose the ones that will move you farthest along the personal, team, and organization change and improvement course you're on. The most important thing is that you have an improvement plan or process.

- *Leadership as action not a position.* I've seen outstanding leadership action come from people who weren't in key leadership (management) roles. I've also seen too many key managers fail to act like leaders. Highly effective organizations are brimming over with leaders at all levels and in all positions.

The themes just listed are expanded on in Chapters 1 to 4. Chapter 1 discusses the nature of change and how you might approach, anticipate, and welcome (but not manage) it. Chapter 2 lists the reasons improvement efforts often fail, reasons that reside in the misuse of tools and techniques for improvement. Chapter 3 focuses on leadership—its task of managing paradox—and on performance as a balance of technology, systems and processes, and people. It introduces the management-leadership balance found throughout the rest of this book. Chapter 4 provides the starting point of leadership—self-leadership. Once these themes have been developed, Chapter 5 maps out the path the rest of the book will take.

THREE PATHS CONVERGE

Experience is a comb that nature gives us when we are bald.
—Chinese proverb

Pathways to Performance flows from three paths of my intense study and experience in organization improvement, leadership development, and personal effectiveness. A brief look at these will help you understand "where I'm coming from." You'll also understand the performance and improvement biases I've developed and tried my best to embed in this book.

My Personal Effectiveness Quest

I've often been asked how long it took me to write a particular book. This one has taken more than 20 years. That's when I first began studying and applying the personal effectiveness principles found here.

I was raised on a dairy farm in the 1960s near a town so small that its only heavy industry was a farm equipment welding shop and a 300-pound encyclopedia salesman. My father taught (and especially modeled) the values of hard work and self-sufficiency. He had an eighth-grade education and planned for me to take over the family farm, so learning, personal development, and higher education weren't important. But my mother nurtured in me a deep love of reading. I did well in grade school, but was a C student in high school until I completely lost interest and dropped out at the end of tenth grade, when I was sixteen.

In 1974, after two years of working in a local grocery store, I took a job with Culligan Water Conditioning selling water treatment equipment. I was eighteen, and I discovered an exciting new world. The doors to that world opened when I took a Dale Carnegie improvement course and read Claude Bristol's 1950s bestseller *TNT: The Power Within You.* I began to understand and apply the principles of personal development and visioning and many of the others you'll find in Chapters 4 to 9 and sprinkled through the rest of the book. I started my monthly subscription to *Success* magazine (which I still get today) and began studying personal development books by Napoleon Hill, Dale Carnegie, Zig Ziglar, Og Mandino, Wayne Dyer, and others. I listened to audiotapes by Earl Nightingale (and many others) in my car to and from my office and in between sales calls. I also took every personal effectiveness, communications, sales, and management course Dale Carnegie offered and began to help teach them.

At nineteen I became a Culligan sales manager and began studying and applying many of the leadership and personal development principles introduced in Chapters 3 and 4 and embedded throughout this book. The power of these principles, tools, and skills propelled me rapidly through a successful series of training and general management positions at Culligan. I continued my personal development through evening classes to finish high school and university business, writing, communications, and liberal arts courses.

Developing The Achieve Group

By 1980, I was running one of Culligan's largest company-owned branches with full profit and loss responsibilities in the same way the company's franchised operations were managed by their owners. The organization improvement, leadership development, and personal effectiveness principles I had been studying and applying worked so successfully that I began to look for ways to help others learn and use them. I started by researching the consulting and training field in my university's library. I then began a series of interviewing and exploration discussions with companies in the field.

Early in 1981, I connected with Art McNeil. He had just started a company he called "Achieve Enterprises." One of the first training programs he offered after moving from his basement to a shared office was SUPERVISION from California-based Zenger-Miller, Inc. I found the people skills, values, and practical approach offered by SUPERVISION powerful and exciting. It was a combination of that program, the opportunity to help thousands improve their personal and organizational performance, and the attraction of owning (Art offered to sell me shares in Achieve) and managing a company with such an exciting future that convinced me to get off my fast Culligan career track, take a drop in pay, and join Achieve.

From 1981 to 1991, when Art and I sold The Achieve Group to Zenger-Miller, revenues mushroomed and multiplied many times over. Using the principles and approaches outlined in this book, we had become the largest "strategic consulting/training" company in Canada. Many of our competitors either scaled back or closed down their Canadian operations, and many of their managers applied to us for jobs.

Achieve's growth is modest compared to that of the legendary companies that hit hundreds of millions or even billions of dollars in revenues within their first 10 years. But it was just successful enough to induce me to further develop my personal experiences and applications of the principles that have found their way into this book. We did well and built a strong organization. But during those 10 years we also almost went bankrupt, missed payrolls, lived off our credit cards, invested heavily in products that didn't sell, hired the wrong people, created a bureaucratic maze of interconnected companies, and made a bunch of dumb moves. So I've got just enough entrepreneurial experience to make me dangerous. In the pages ahead, I'll use some of those Achieve experiences to provide a few firsthand illustrations of the agony and ecstasy found in the concepts we'll be exploring.

Living through the sale and merger of Achieve to Zenger-Miller (which is in turn owned by Times-Mirror Training Group) helped me get an up-close and personal understanding of the challenges that mergers, acquisitions, and culture change bring. Watching the company you raised being managed differently by someone else is very difficult. It's probably like trying to live with one of your married kids. The dynamics of your control or influence in their daily decisions and the new life and routines they've developed are now very different. That's one of the key reasons I moved back out on my own and formed The Clemmer Group at the beginning of 1994.

A Student of Organization Change and Improvement

In the early 1980s my attention was focused on establishing Achieve and carving out a presence in the very crowded leadership skill training market. In 1983, Zenger-Miller and Achieve worked with Tom Peters as his and Bob Waterman's book *In Search of Excellence* was gaining momentum. Our work with Tom to develop an executive action planning process built on the excellence principles was another personal turning point. I now had just enough experience with leadership skill development to understand how hard (nearly impossible) it was to sustain new behaviors if the culture didn't encourage or reinforce the new skills. The "Toward Excellence" process that emerged from our work with Tom introduced strategic keys to culture change, participation and involvement, delegating autonomy ("empowerment" later became the popular label), service and quality improvement, innovation, and system alignment. The excellence principles of vision, values, service, participation, and innovation also meshed with what I'd learned from my previous 10 years of work on personal effectiveness.

In 1984, the work with Toward Excellence kicked off an intense period of personal study, writing (dozens of articles, columns, and three books), and speaking on leadership development and organization improvement that continues to this day. I developed an extensive filing system to catalog and easily retrieve the articles I had (and continue to save) from *Fortune, Harvard Business Review, Training,* and many other magazines and newsletters. My expanding library contains hundreds of books I continue to use in the course of this ongoing research. I've given more than 1,200 presentations on leadership development and organization improvement. I've run nearly two hundred senior management retreats (usually two to three days in length), workshops, and seminars to help management teams understand and apply these principles and approaches. I get to see the inside of many cabs, airplanes, airports, meeting rooms, and hotel rooms. And some day I might even have half as much fun on one of these business trips as my family thinks I'm having.

This work is now my full-time job. It's coming dangerously close to being my whole life. But the main reason for telling you all this is to assure you that the principles, concepts, and suggestions contained in this book are well grounded in research and have been rigorously field tested.

HOW TO BEND, MUTILATE, AND OTHERWISE USE THIS BOOK

We know by doing, but we don't always do by knowing.

As you'll soon discover, I've jammed as many "how to" tips and techniques into *Pathways to Performance* as I could without turning it into a tome that you need to put wheels on. But if all you do is read this book, I've failed. So let's start with a few suggestions for how to move this book beyond what I hope is "a good read" to a catalyst for action:

- Like an oyster you can use the irritation this book provides to help you spin a pearl. If you think a section or suggestion is too preachy, impractical, or far-fetched, go ahead and put a heavy X through it. You might even give me a big raspberry (be careful not to get the pages too wet). But come back again later and look at the offending section. If it hit you that negatively, it probably touched an important nerve. There's potential improvement energy there. It could be a good place to start your pearl.
- Read this book with pen and marker in hand. Make notes, underline, and turn down the pages. I once signed a second copy of *Firing on All Cylinders* for a highly effective service/ quality leader who had worn out his first copy. That ap-

proach to learning was one of the reasons he had become a service/quality leader. Of course, the main reason was because he read and applied my book! If you send me your beat-up and worn-out copy of this book I'll gladly send you a complimentary, signed replacement free of charge (see page 298 for my address).

- When I started my personal improvement quest back in 1974 I began by putting inspirational quotes on my car's sun visor and on my office and bathroom mirrors. Later I put them in my day planner on yellow Post-it notes. These have been especially helpful in my darkest times. I have become a serious collector of quotations (with more than 20,000 in a computerized database and dozens of books). That's why they're liberally peppered throughout my books. You may want to pull out the quotes that start each section of this book to inspire your quest for personal, team, or organization improvement.

- Take a chapter or section and review it with your team. The management team of one company held a management retreat that used *Firing on All Cylinders*. Team members each presented a chapter, discussing what they agreed with, what they didn't, and what the team should do to improve in that area. Once each presentation had been made, the team summarized and set priorities for the areas needing attention, identified a champion for each one, and set 30-day action plans.

- There is no quick-and-easy road to outstanding performance. If you're looking for shortcuts or sure-fire formulas, you've got the wrong book. I've tried to make *Pathways to Peformance* easy to read and understand. But it describes a series of transformation and improvement steps and routes that, when added together, take years to turn into habits and routine practices. So *use this as an ongoing guidebook; most of the work described here is never completed.* Keep coming back to this book to review, assess, and renew the endless job of transforming yourself, your team, and your organization.

The turn-of-the-century French philosopher Henri Bergson implored us to "think like someone of action, and act like someone of thought." May this book help you to contemplate and reflect on your approaches to organization improvement, leadership development, and personal effectiveness. But most of all, *may it cause you to act.*

Jim Clemmer
Kitchener, Ontario

CHAPTER 1

Changing, Learning, and Improving

Life is change. Growth is optional. Choose wisely.

In the middle of a meeting with a few Achievers (our name for everyone who worked at The Achieve Group), I caught myself saying, "Once we get through this crazy period and things get back to normal . . ." Then it hit me. I had been saying something like that for at least a year or two. As we scrambled to move into a strong market leadership position, we were initiating endless waves of change and (we hoped) improvement throughout the organization. I interrupted myself with the question, "Do we seem to be consistently talking about change as if it's a temporary condition to be endured until calmer times return?"

"Yeah, it's as if we're battening down the hatches and waiting out the storm."

"But," another Achiever observed, "we've got to learn how to work in the driving rain and high seas because things aren't going to slow down unless we scale back on our vision, goals, and rate of growth."

"And that could be deadly in today's fast-moving market."

"We'd be following and trying to keep up rather than leading and setting the pace."

The discussion went on to mark a turning point for many of us. We began to realize we needed to accept that our frenzied pace of change was the new "normal." Then we had to do a better job of helping other Achievers understand the reasons for this new norm

1

and become energized by the exciting possibilities offered by the changes.

THE CHANGE PARADOX:
SAME TUNE, FRANTIC NEW BEAT

If you can keep your head when all about you are losing theirs, it's just possible that you haven't grasped the situation.

—Jean Kerr, American playwright

When do you think the following statements were made (extra bonus points if you can identify the speakers as well)?

1. "A new factor, that of rapid change, has come into the world. We have not yet learned how to adjust ourselves to its economic and social consequences."
2. "The world is too big for us. There is too much doing, too many crimes, casualties, violence, and excitements. Try as you will, you get behind the race despite yourself. It is an incessant strain to keep pace and still you lose ground. Science empties its discoveries on you so fast that you stagger beneath them in hopeless bewilderment. The political world witnesses new scenes so rapidly that you are out of breath trying to keep up with them."
3. "All is flux, nothing stays still."

Sound familiar? These remarks could have been made last week, couldn't they? Certainly, they might have been uttered within the last decade. The first comment was written in the pages of *Harvard Business Review* by Wallace Donham in 1932. The second one comes from the *Atlantic Journal* of 1837. The last remark was made by the Greek philosopher Heraclitus five hundred years before the birth of Christ.

Down through the centuries many people have believed they were living in times of rapid change. But as timeless as change is, futurists like Alvin Toffler show that we're now in a period of unusually rapid and significant change. In his book *Powershift,* Toffler provides powerful arguments to show that the period of time from the mid-1950s until about the year 2025 is one of those extremely rare pivotal moments in the centuries of Earth's history where everything about the way our world works radically shifts.

He calls it a "hinge of history." And, he's found, "what is emerging is a radical new economic system running at far faster speeds than any in history." So things will settle into a more predictable and calm pace about the time most of us are long gone from our work . . . or just long gone. Speaking at a planning conference, author, researcher, and professor Warren Bennis said, "I can't recall a period of time that was as volatile, complex, ambiguous, and tumultuous." He then quoted Jack Welch, CEO of General Electric: "If you're not confused, you don't know what's going on." See, you do know what's going on!

WHIRLWINDS OF CHANGE

The world is moving so fast these days that anyone who says it can't be done is generally interrupted by someone doing it.
—Elbert Hubbard, nineteenth-century American editor, lecturer, and essayist

My library is full of books chronicling, charting, and categorizing the major changes societies, organizations, and people are going through. My research notes tracking and detailing these changes run to more than four hundred pages. After wading through endless models, "megatrends," "change waves," "powershifts," and "new economies," I've summarized today's most significant changes:

Key Changes	From	To
Economic growth	Steady and predictable	Erratic fluctuations
Financial power source	Physical resources and capital	Information and knowledge
Technological change	Evolutionary	Revolutionary
Markets	Mass	Highly segmented
Communications	Delayed, multistaged, and controlled	Instant, direct, and uncontrollable
Innovation	Important	Critical
Competitive edge	Size	Speed
Customers	Compliant, loyal, and forgiving	Demanding, intolerant, and value-driven
Work ethic	Followership	Shared management
Source of authority	Position	Persuasion

What's Been Wrong with Our Organizations

You can't expect different results if you continue to do the same things.

Most organizations were designed—and managers were trained—for the conditions described in the "From" column of the chart. When economies are expanding, competition is tame, and revenues are growing, it's easy to confuse brilliant management with a bull market. Many entrepreneurs and managers are living proof of Woody Allen's observation that "eighty percent of success is just showing up."

But most traditional organizations and management styles are now about as useful as tail fins, hula hoops, and teletype machines. Here are the all-too-common bad habits, sloppiness, and problems that are seriously impeding the effectiveness of many organizations:

- Up to 50 percent of product features and services don't meet customer needs.
- Departmentalism (vertical management); turf wars; and fragmentation of production, delivery, and support processes limit growth and effectiveness.
- Customers are forced to dance the old familiar bureaucratic shuffle (the highly catchy chorus begins with "No, that's not my department . . .").
- "Me-too" products and services play catch-up to missed market opportunities.
- The organization is composed of layers of coordinators, organizers, error correctors, complaint handlers, auditors, inspectors, approvers, directors, overseers, expeditors, assistants, managers, and "snoopervisors."
- The workforce is disempowered, disconnected, and demoralized.
- Service/quality levels are inconsistent (and generally slipping).
- Production, delivery, and service support costs are stable or rising while revenues slip and other companies are lowering their per unit and per person overhead costs.

What Organization Changes Are Needed

Though forecasting specific events is futile, becoming conversant in the growing technical language and comfortable with the evolving conditions and events that shape the future is an increasingly essential part of what management is and does. Managers who don't make the effort, who don't learn, and who don't get comfortable with what needs to be learned will surely constrain their careers and hurt their companies.

—Ted Levitt, *Thinking About Management*

Predicting the future is a dangerous business. Many economists, futurists, and other seers who have peered into their crystal balls and proclaimed what is to come have then learned to eat ground glass. It's difficult to predict the exact look and approach of those highly successful, twenty-first-century model organizations that we'll be studying in the years ahead. But the key elements of top-performing organizations in today's environment are clearly emerging. When you scratch below the surface, you'll notice that the same characteristics have described many of our best-run companies for decades:

- Clear identification and segmentation of key customer groups and their expectations. This is followed by rigorous measurements to provide feedback on progress toward meeting those needs.
- Permanent and continuous structural and overhead reductions that lower per unit and per person costs (rather than just "bad times budgets").
- Seamless structure and flow of work, information, products, services, and customers across the organization (horizontal management).
- A highly involved, team-based organization with few management and administrative levels.
- A sharp strategic focus (where we're going, what we believe in, what business we're in) and disciplined priority and objectives setting.
- Continuous streams of innovative new products, services, and extensions that expand and add new value or use existing products and services in new ways.
- Creating and leading new markets and exploiting growth opportunities.

"CHANGE MANAGEMENT" IS
AN OXYMORON

Maturity of mind is the capacity to endure uncertainty.
—John Finlay, nineteenth-century Irish poet

A dubious consulting industry and "profession" claims to provide "change management" services. Those two words make about as much sense together as "holy war," "nonworking mother," "mandatory option," and "political principles." Many of the books, models, theories, and "processes" on change have come from staff support people, consultants, or academics who have never built a business or led an organization. "Change management" comes from the same dangerously seductive reasoning as strategic planning (we'll look further at this area in the chapters ahead). Both are based on the shaky assumption that an orderly thinking and implementation process can be used to objectively plot a course of action, as Jean Luc Piccard does on the starship *Enterprise,* and then "make it so." But if that ever was possible, it certainly isn't in today's world of high-velocity change.

But even worse than the need for control manifested by some "change agents" is how frequently their approaches are used in a vacuum. The means become the ends, and everybody gets confused and off track. For example, vision, mission, or values exercises are prized for their own sake. Or participation, empowerment, employee involvement, quality of work life, teams, and the like become goals in themselves. General techniques and knowledge of the "change process" are useful only as supplements to the larger organization, career, or life issues.

BEHIND SUCCESSFUL CHANGE:
GROWTH, LEARNING, AND IMPROVEMENT

When you're through changing, you're through.
—Bruce Barton, American advertising executive, author, and politician

Let's look at change on a deeper, more fundamental level. *To master or thrive on change, we need to embrace perpetual growth and development, continuous learning, and constant improvement.* That's the stuff true change management is made of. Rate and type of change are only surface issues. The deeper issue is whether we are learning and improving so that change is another step forward in our progress to a brighter future. Are we steadily striving to build a better self, team, organization, and world? I've seen very few effective, and especially lasting, "change programs." But I have seen and personally experienced, the power and payoffs of constant and habitual personal, team, and organization learning and improvement.

When change represents learning, growth, and improvement, it generates energy and is often eagerly embraced. When change is just change or appears to make things worse—and especially if it makes things worse for us—it's something to be avoided. At worst, some people are neutral or somewhat resistant to change that they believe will eventually be for the better. At best, most people (and especially high performers) welcome and embrace that kind of beneficial change. A bigger barrier is failure to develop the discipline and follow-through to improve ourselves and enjoy the benefits of the change. Most of us clearly hate and strongly resist *being changed.*

The ideas of change, learning, and improvement bring us to the very core of this book. Developing and improving our organizations, teams, or selves to ride the waves of change means:

- Balancing "hard" analytical management systems and techniques, quickly changing technical and technological tools, with "soft" human leadership issues
- Strengthening our self-leadership and self-determination as a base for leading others
- Establishing a clear focus and "big picture" context. This encompasses the Three P's—picture of our preferred future (or vision), principles (values or beliefs), and purpose (mission, niche, or why we exist)
- Identifying whom we've chosen to serve, understanding what they want, and analyzing how we're doing at meeting their needs
- Digging below our current customers' needs and expectations to reveal latent and unmet needs that lead to new markets, customers, products and services, or extensions

- Nurturing experiments, pilots, and "clumsy tries" as we muddle (and learn) our way to new products, services, markets, methods, and such
- Setting clear priorities and strategic goals to provide tighter discipline in our use of limited time and organizational resources
- Developing improvement plans that encompass our key production, delivery, and support processes, operational and improvement teams, skill development, measurement and feedback, structure and system alignment, education and communication strategies, as well as reward and recognition programs and practices
- Developing change champions and supporting local improvement initiatives
- Regularly reviewing, assessing, celebrating, and refocusing our improvement progress

PATHWAYS AND PITFALLS

Destiny is not a matter of chance, it is a matter of choice. It is not something to be waited for, but rather something to be achieved.
—William Jennings Bryan

- Don't let a consultant loose with a "change management program" or unleash improvement teams in a vacuum. (Beware of this type of consultant—"It's worse than I thought. Your organization change program is going to put me in a higher tax bracket.") Make sure all changes are driven by very clear business goals (quality, service, innovation, etc.), come from your organization's Focus and Context (picture of the future, principles, and purpose), and are managed by line management and performance teams.
- Use the "What's Been Wrong with Our Organizations" and the "What Organization Changes Are Needed" lists from this chapter to check the changes needed in your organization. Have each team member do assessments individually and then compare views.

- Use a painful crisis (or even project a small one into a potential future catastrophe) to smash existing mind-sets and complacency. But once that's done, keep everyone focused on the gain rather than the pain of change and improvement.
- Involve everyone in understanding (why should we change?), diagnosing (what's not working well now?), visioning (what would our ideal future look like?), and planning (what improvement route are we following?) for the changes needed.
- Keep communication channels wide open and information flowing on progress, what's being learned, and changes to the improvement effort. And make sure feedback and measurement loops are strong.
- Stay tuned to this channel for lots more Pathways and Pitfalls on change and improvement. That's what this book is all about.

To better understand what helps us develop learning and improving organizations, teams, and selves we need to understand what can hinder our progress. That's the focus of the next chapter.

CHAPTER 2

Wandering Off the Improvement Trail: The Deadly Dozen Failure Factors

---

I can't say I was ever lost, but I was bewildered once for three days.
—Daniel Boone

Many team and organization change-and-improvement efforts are lost or badly bewildered. There are as many reasons that improvement endeavors lose their way as there are people, teams, and organizations trying to improve. Besides riding in smelly cabs, eating rubber chicken (or guessing the day's mystery meat), and racing through crowded airports to catch a flight, another benefit of my occupation is the opportunity I've had to work with hundreds of leadership teams trying to improve themselves and their organizations. Some have been hugely successful. They've seen increases in response times, cycle times, customer service, quality, teamwork, morale, productivity, innovation, cost effectiveness, and the like that range from 25 to 300 percent or more. Others have been somewhat successful in some areas of their improvement activities. And some ended up in the swamp.

I've spent years studying, researching, analyzing, and writing about why some improvement efforts are wildly successful in one organization and failures (or only modest successes) in others. Since the early 1980s, many organization improvement tools, techniques, and approaches have passed in and out of fashion. The five that stand out the sharpest for me (because of my close involvement in each one) are quality circles, excellence, service/ quality, teams, and reengineering. In all the studies I reviewed or personal experiences I've had with thousands of organizations using these approaches, it's clear that their leadership teams all had access to or used the same basic tools, techniques, or philosophies. *The wide gap in results came from how they were used.* In reviewing this research, it also becomes clear that a core number of execution problems or failure factors are common to all of the team, organization, and individual improvement efforts.

THE DEADLY DOZEN FAILURE FACTORS

Our tendency is to try things out capriciously . . . without an in-depth grasp of their underlying foundation, and without the commitment necessary to sustain them. When a new idea fails, we give up instead of investigating the causes of failure and addressing them systematically.

—Richard Tanner Pascale, *Managing on the Edge*

Like a gnarled old root system, the following twelve causes (presented in no special order) of improvement shortfalls are interconnected and tangled together. It's hard to tell exactly which area, or combination of problem areas, dozens of other problem offshoots are growing from. These core failure factors and their kin will be addressed in a variety of ways throughout the rest of this book.

Leadership Lip Service

The single most critical variable to the success of a team or organization improvement effort is the behavior of those leading it. Successful improvement efforts are led by people who are highly involved leaders. They model, use, and live the approaches they are asking their team or organization to use. Unsuccessful team or organization improvement efforts are headed up by managers who have done little more than give permission and then delegated the details to others to take care of. Often they pay lip service, perhaps even passionate lip service, to the importance of customers, quality, teams, innovation, reengineering, new technologies, discipline, training, and the like. Although their words declare otherwise, their actions loudly shout, "You ought to improve in these areas. But I am too busy, already skilled enough, or have more important things to do."

Fuzzy Focus

Too many organization improvement efforts are not connected to the burning issues that keep senior managers awake at night. Improvement for the sake of "making things better," getting people involved, forming teams and fostering teamwork ("teaminess"), and other equally noble but vague goals is too diffused and unfocused. A team or organization's ultimate customers and external partners are often lost in the improvement haze as well. Their needs and expectations should be—but aren't—driving all improvement activities. And the improvement work isn't framed within the larger context of a personal, team, or organizational picture of the preferred future, principles, and purpose.

Priority Overload

Many managers confuse motion with direction and "busy-work" activity with meaningful results. They are like the pilot who announced, "I have some good news and some bad news. The bad news is we're lost. The good news is we're making great time." A big part of the problem is that many people measure their effectiveness by volume (quantity) rather than by whether real value is being added (quality). Many organization improvement efforts have about as much impact on performance as does having all the passengers in a jet flap their arms to help the plane fly. A management group of a struggling administrative section in a large bureaucratic organization was discussing how well they had done in moving "dockets" through their organization. "Let's not forget how much work we've moved through our sector in the last year," they reminded each other. Yeah, but . . . how much of it really mattered? I later discovered they had a list of thirty-seven urgent goals and objectives. Little meaningful progress was being made because everything needed to be done—now.

People who get little done often work a great deal harder. They seem to live by the French Cavalry's motto, "When in doubt, gallop." How hard you work is less important than how much you get done.

Partial and Piecemeal Efforts

The senior management team of a large national retailer that had enjoyed a dominant position in its markets realized that radical changes were needed to drive down overhead costs while boosting customer service. They hired consultants and launched a series of major reengineering and improvement projects in warehouse and shipping logistics, market positioning, store renovation, product-line revamping, customer service training, information technology, and the like. Besides the fuzzy focus, the efforts were not well co-ordinated. Each group fiercely protected and isolated its own initiative or project. Most of the projects floundered amid political infighting, segmentation, and confusion. The company is now being mauled by new competitors with higher performance.

Unfortunately this is not an isolated story. My files are full of similar examples from health care, financial services, and other sectors. *Many improvement efforts are too narrow and segmented.* Broad, system-wide cause-and-effect issues aren't identified and addressed. Improvement teams work with bits and pieces of processes and systems. For example, much of what's called TQM (total quality management) is really PQM—partial quality management. Effective quality improvement knocks the "Q" out of TQM programs and turns the effort into a total management process.

Confusion Between Knowing and Doing

Years ago I met a manager who was trying to get his company's senior management group to put into action the concepts of Tom Peters and Bob Waterman's runaway bestseller *In Search of Excellence*. Once the senior managers read the book, they not only concluded that they didn't need to learn how to apply these principles, but also became indignant that their company hadn't been one of the "excellent" ones described in the book. "I don't know whether to laugh or cry," reported the manager. "Sure they use all the latest buzzwords like 'values-driven,' 'close to the customer,' 'productivity through people,' and 'a bias for action.' But their video isn't in sync with their audio. What they're doing and what they're saying are two different things. The scariest part is that they really do believe we're already an excellent company." Today the company is struggling for survival. Most of those "excellent managers" left or were fired.

Many people confuse understanding improvement or effectiveness concepts with actually using them. They continue to confuse strategy formulation with its execution. No matter how brilliant the plan or technique, no matter how well it has worked elsewhere, or how well it is understood, if it's not implemented effectively, it's all a waste of time. If a little knowledge is dangerous, managers of half-baked improvement efforts are positively deadly.

Flimsy Feedback

A key reason knowing is confused with doing is lack of feedback. Whether parenting, coaching, teaching, or leading others, a major part of our learning and improvement comes from finding out how we're doing. But, ironically, those people who need the improvement feedback the most are usually the ones least receptive to it. They're too busy ignoring or denying their mistakes and correcting everyone else. They don't realize that their biggest fault is their lack of awareness and sensitivity to the impact of their behavior. So they end up with a serious learning disability that stunts their personal growth and development.

This aversion to feedback contributes to the pitifully meager measurements of softer issues found in most teams and organizations. For example, customers' perceptions of value, team members' perceptions of team effectiveness, organization morale, leadership skill levels, and cultural effectiveness aren't measured in a regular, rigorous, and meaningful way. Yet it's very tough to have real behavior change and constant improvement without this feedback.

Technomanagement Tools

Many organization improvement efforts are overly dependent on hard analytical management tools and/or technology and technical expertise. Most do a terrible job of dealing with the "soft, people stuff." So improvement tools and technologies remain cold and sterile. People don't feel energized and enthusiastic about using them to move toward an exciting future where they can really make a difference. This bureaucratic "technomanagement" (more on this in the next chapter) approach also results in overly rigid planning. Thoughtful planning is not well balanced with the experimentation, pilots, and "clumsy tries" that help a team or organization capitalize on the unexpected and unpredictable opportunities that quietly emerge.

Misaligned Systems and Processes

A life insurance company put an intensive effort into training its customer service representatives, field support offices, and other head office support staff in "service excellence." In the second year of the effort, morale and service levels rose. Then they "hit the wall." Frustration levels rose and performance fell as communication problems, interdepartmental conflicts, costly error rates, and complaints from field agents and customers increased. Senior management began to look for ways to get the improvement effort back on track. Analysis showed that the problem was not in people's motivation, understanding, or carefulness. The roots of the problems were much deeper. They were in organizational systems (such as information technology, compensation, planning, performance feedback, measurements, etc.) and the organization-wide processes carrying services, customer interactions, and field support across many departments.

This type of experience became so common in the 1980s that it became a truism in the quality improvement movement called the 85/15 Rule. The "rule" reflects evidence clearly showing that only about 15 percent or less of the time is an error, complaint, or problem rooted in people problems. Over 85 percent of the time the root cause is found in organizational systems, processes, or structure.

Failure to Connect to Customers

There's nothing more useless than putting a lot of time and effort into making improvements that your customers don't care about.

Yet that's the very trap that many teams and organizations fall into. Because they don't have good feedback and customer research, they end up developing new products or services, or improving existing ones in areas that don't matter much to customers. As a result, issues or features that customers care deeply about are passed over or not given enough attention.

Impotent Improvement Process

Developing a rigorous improvement process with a highly disciplined follow-through is a big problem for many less successful organization and personal improvement efforts. As with New Year's resolutions, a burst of energy and good intentions may get things started. *But not enough time is invested in developing ongoing improvement plans, habits, or approaches.* Even less time is devoted to reviewing, assessing, and reflecting on successes, problems, and lessons learned. And so opportunities to reenergize yourself and others on your team or in your organization are missed.

An improvement process is also liable to fail when those who will ultimately try to make it work are not involved in planning the effort (and sometimes don't even understand why, how, what, and who). Poor communication skills and processes then compound the problem.

Passing Programs

A few years ago I wanted to take off 20 pounds. I dieted religiously (yes, I did quit eating in church) and got my weight down. But I still loved my weekends of junk food and rich desserts. So I pigged out on the weekends and then cut back during the week. I was attempting to use "the rhythm method of girth control." Because I didn't change my lifestyle, I eventually found many of the pounds I thought I'd lost.

The CEO of a service company announced "spring cleaning" one April. Those who found a way to save money would have their names put in a drawing to share a pot of money. This improvement program was unconnected to customers, bigger processes, systems, organizational priorities, or anything else.

Both of these examples illustrate the all-too-common problem of temporary, short-term change. Binging and purging on change and improvement programs won't keep the weight off. We have to learn how to change our lifestyle by choosing whether to approach improvement as a series of programs to be bolted on to the side of our lives, teams, and organizations or as a lifestyle and cultural change to be built in to our very being.

Asinine Improvement Attitudes

Many people seem to have trouble getting ready for distant change when things are going well today. So they let their skills atrophy, don't stay on top of new developments in their field, and generally fail to build regular and disciplined improvement habits. Then, when the accumulated consequences of choices from past years suddenly explode in a performance crisis, they're unprepared. Suddenly they're scrambling for novel, quick fixes to long-term, festering problems.

Another asinine attitude is "victimitis." This is a terminal case of "it's all their fault." Victims act as if they're corks bobbing helplessly on the ocean waves. They believe their fate is "in the stars" or anywhere else except their own hands. They'll blame the economy, unions, politicians, management, customers, suppliers, the industry, a declining work ethic, shareholders, competitors, or anyone else except themselves for their performance problems.

FOCUSING YOUR IMPROVEMENT ACTIVITIES

Don't waste your time searching for a secret of success.
Work instead to develop your own system of success.

Each of these failure factors is bad enough on its own, but the more of them you combine, the deadlier they become. Throughout the rest of this book you'll find many strategies, techniques, tips, and suggestions for overcoming these common problems. To better focus your improvement activities you may want to:

- Get your team to review the Deadly Dozen, assess your improvement approaches and then discuss the top five factors everyone feels are least problematical for you and the ones that are hindering your improvement effort the most. Try to get to the root causes of your low-scoring factors.
- Have those people your team is serving and partnering with give you the same assessment.
- Gather the same personal feedback from colleagues, people you are leading, and significant others in your life (such as a spouse or immediate family members).

CHAPTER **3**

The High-Performance Balance: Managing Things, Leading People

> *Fine art is that in which the hand, the head, and the heart go together.*
>
> —John Ruskin

Too often, we see the world in narrow, binary, either/or terms. Odd or even, closed or open, introverted or extroverted, individual or group, profitable or unprofitable, rational or irrational, right or wrong, real or imagined, hard or soft, emotional or dispassionate, and vertical or horizontal are common pairs of contradictory opposites. But top performers look beyond either/or to and/also. Instead of seeing just polarization, the contradictions that limit most people, they're able to manage the third position that emerges from balancing the two opposites. As professor, consultant, and author Charles Handy points out in his book *The Age of Paradox,* "paradox does not have to be resolved, only managed."

Five thousand years ago in ancient China, Fu Hsi developed an "and/also philosophy" that is still with us today. His concept of yin and yang taught that much of life consists of two opposite and sometimes opposing forces. As with male and female, the very existence of each may depend on its opposite. In other cases, one may transform or kill the other, as with fire and water, darkness and light, or cold and hot. Samuel Johnson, the eighteenth-century poet, essayist, and journalist, captured this interdependence of contrasting forces when he wrote, "The lustre of diamonds is invigorated by the interposition of darker bodies; the lights of a picture are created by the shades; the highest pleasure which nature has indulged to sensitive perception is that of rest after fatigue."

Finding the Right Balance

Improvement Efforts Must . . .	And Also . . .
Produce quick, short-term results	Change long-term personal habits and organization culture
Expect the best	Be prepared for the worst
Build consistency, discipline, and a systematic approach	Constantly change, experiment, and learn by "mucking around"
Respond to and serve existing customers	Develop new customers and markets by uncovering unmet needs
Amplify the potential pain	Focus on the gain
Continuously improve in small increments wherever possible	Make breakthrough changes

The key lesson of the yin and yang philosophy or of managing paradox is that it's necessary to find a balance that's right for the conditions and circumstances (see chart). That means we need to learn how to deal with the ambiguity and uncertainty of and/also. Although many of those balances have always been dynamic and changing, the hyperspeed of change today makes them all the more so. The words of Voltaire ring even truer today than they did in eighteenth-century France: "Doubt is not a pleasant condition, but certainty is an absurd one."

THE PERFORMANCE TRIANGLE

The art of progress is to preserve order amid change and to preserve change amid order.

—Alfred North Whitehead, nineteenth-century British mathematician and philosopher

As Achieve was working with clients to implement Toward Excellence (the cultural change process developed in conjunction with Tom Peters), I was growing increasingly uneasy. Something didn't feel right. In *In Search of Excellence*, Peters and Waterman presented a powerful case against "the rational model" of management. They forcefully argued (among other things) for focusing on people (customers and those serving them) rather than processes, for acting instead of analyzing, and for being driven by values rather than numbers. Sure, there was a strong need for managers to move away from the overstuffed bureaucratic, controlling, and hierarchical approach many companies had fallen into. But I also knew of companies that were entrepreneurial, exciting, people-oriented, customer-driven—and they were struggling or even going down the tubes because they used a shoe box for an accounting system and depended upon yesterday's technology. Some of their managers came from the we-must-still-have-money-because-we-still-have-checks-left school of business mismanagement.

It seemed to me the real issue was balance. So as I went to work on my first book, *The VIP Strategy*, I developed an early version of the "triangle model." After using it with numerous management teams to frame key organization improvement issues and after continuing to study, speak, and write about performance balance, I have since further refined the model. The three sides of the triangle represent three areas that must be kept in balance for high performance.

The Performance Balance Triangle

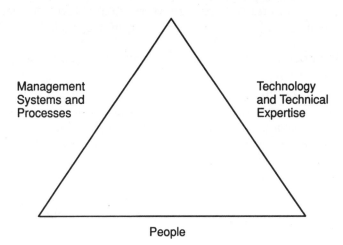

Management Systems and Processes

Technology and Technical Expertise

People

- *Technology and Technical Expertise.* Your organization's core technology is the expertise and/or equipment that produces the products or services your customers buy. Supporting technology may include computers, telecommunications, robotics, production equipment, and the like to produce, deliver, or support your organization's core technology. Your personal technology is the technical expertise you bring to the production, delivery, or support of either core or supporting technologies.
- *Managment Systems and Processes.* Organizational processes are the flow of materials, work activities, customer interactions, or information across your organization to produce, deliver, or support the products or services your customers buy. Organizational systems are the underlying feedback and measurements loops, performance improvement methods, and organization structure. Your personal systems and processes are the methods, habits, and approaches you use to get things done.
- *People.* The base of the triangle includes those people your organization serves, the people you would like to serve, people in your organization doing the producing and serving, your key external partners (such as distributors, strategic alliances, suppliers, etc.), everyone in your organization supporting the producers and serving the servers, shareholders or funding partners, and (very deliberately last) management.

In high-performing organizations, each area is strong and constantly improving. For example, in our technological age, you and your organization need to ensure that you're constantly upgrading your technical expertise and technological tools. You can't afford to fall behind. And if you're not personally using a computer, get one (preferably a notebook you can carry around with you) now. My notebook computer has been a huge help in communicating (sending and receiving faxes and electronic mail, writing, etc.), managing my time, storing and easily retrieving information, keeping contact and project records, maintaining mailing and contact lists, developing overheads and slides for presentations and workshops, and accessing a multitude of information and research through on-line data services. Without it, I'd be 30–40 percent less productive and would need much more administrative help. But as with any technology, if you just automate sloppy personal habits and disorganized files, you'll just mess things up faster.

The area of systems and processes is also extremely important. You and your organization can be using the latest technologies and be highly people-focused, but if the methods and approaches you're using to structure and organize your work are weak, your performance will suffer badly. People in your organization can be empowered, energized, and enlightened; but if your systems and processes (and technologies) don't enable them to perform well, they won't. Developing discipline and using the most effective tools and techniques of personal and organization systems and processes is a critical element of high performance. We'll look at this further in the chapters that lie ahead.

The Performance Balance triangle has people at its base. That's very deliberate. *In well-balanced, high-performing teams or organizations, technology, systems, and processes serve people.* For example, as information technology specialists study why so many huge investments in equipment and software haven't paid off, they find the problem comes back to how the technology is designed and used, by whom, and for whom. An executive in California's Silicon Valley summed up an important new perspective making the rounds there: "We used to say people need to be more computer-literate. Now we say that computers need to become more people-literate." And if your understanding of customer expectations is only partially accurate, expensive technology and "reengineered" processes will deliver only partial results. If people in your organization can't communicate face-to-face, electronic communications won't improve communications very much. If you haven't established the discipline of setting priorities for your time and organizing your desk, a notebook computer won't do it for you.

SIGNS OF TECHNOMANAGEMENT

The practice of management is badly misunderstood by management scientists who confuse thinking with merely being logical.
—Ted Levitt, *Thinking About Management*

Far too many organizations are ruled by bureaucrats and technocrats in either management or staff support roles. One of their (often unconscious) driving motives is to "eliminate the human factor." They feel that their technology, systems, and processes would work much better if it weren't for all the people always messing things up. Technomanaged organizations have the Performance Balance triangle upside down. People serve the systems or processes. Customers are made to fit the organization. Technology drives behavior.

Here are some telltale signs and examples of technomanagement:

- Bureaucratic language is a dead giveaway of a technomanager. In talking about cross-training and moving people around, one bureaucrat called it "rotationality." He said it with a straight face, and everyone in the room nodded knowingly.

  Hierarchical language also shows where many technomanagers are coming from. Phrases and terms like "people who work *for* me," "subordinates" (and its especially repulsive companion "superiors"), "staying on top of things," "my people," and "down the organization" show the need many technomanagers have to dominate and control.

- A senior manager in a professional services company assigned a staff support person to fix the marketing efforts of the company's divisions. It didn't work. The failed effort sprang from an all-too-typical view of the organization as being composed of segmented and separate functions and divisions. But marketing couldn't be separated from running the business. Business development (sales) people weren't effectively trained and supported to sell within the larger strategy or new market position (they got a one-day information session and a few updates). A key division that provided the umbrella strategic services to position and pull through the core business services was forced to continually justify itself as a stand-alone, profitable business to the accountants running the company. So the structure of the organization couldn't support working across a broader market that called for integrated divisions serving customers through regional (rather than head office) management.

- Management's needs, goals, and perspectives are the starting point for all activities. Managers and their staff professionals are the brains, and employees are the hands. Employees serve their managerial masters and do as they are told. Broad business perspectives and strategies, operational performance data, problem-solving and decision-making authority, and cross-functional skills are kept by management.

- In a financial crunch, technomanagers often "cut heads," "trim the fat," and "tighten belts" in short-term attempts to bring costs down. Although wholesale slashing and burning can be a short-term success, it's often a long-term disaster. Not only is the organization weakened and demoralized—while customer service plummets—but, in addition, the fundamental cost structure hasn't really been changed. So costs creep back up.

- Technomanaged companies are head-office-driven. Field professionals have little say in product development priorities, marketing focus, accounting systems, etc. Their only means of providing input is through committees (which take months to meet and decide anything), by screaming the loudest (or to the right political player), or by working through the entrenched hierarchy. There are few mechanisms or channels to systematically collect field input on emerging or latent market needs/trends. Accountants aren't out in the real world looking behind and beneath the numbers and learning how revenues are built.

- The quality movement has given rise to a new breed of technomanager—the qualicrat. These support professionals see the world strictly through data and analysis and their quality improvement tools and techniques. Although they work hard to quantify the "voice of the customer," the faces of current customers (and especially potential new customers) are often lost. Having researched, consulted, and written extensively on quality improvement, I am a big convert to and evangelist for the cause. But some efforts are badly skewed as customers, partners, and team members are reduced to numbers, charts, and graphs.

- In his book *Organizational Culture and Leadership,* Edgar Schein, professor of management at the Sloan School of Management, Massachusetts Institute of Technology, discusses the results of a study on IT (information technology) assumptions about people and learning. Some of his most deadly findings include "technology leads and people adapt," "all people can and should learn whatever is required to use the technology," and "people already know how to communicate and manage; therefore, IT needs only to enhance these processes."

MANAGING THINGS, LEADING PEOPLE

Too many managers treat "their people" as assets with skin wrapped around them.

Do you like to be managed or led? You're not alone. Very few people want to work for a manager. Most of us would much rather be led by a leader. To manage is to control, handle, or manipulate. To lead is to guide, influence, or persuade. *You manage things*—systems, processes, and technology. *You lead people.* The roots of the rampant morale, energy, and performance problems found in many organizations are technomanagers who treat people as "human resources" to be managed. If you want to manage someone, manage yourself. Once you master that, you'll be a much more effective leaders of others.

High-performing teams and organizations balance the discipline of systems, processes, and technology management on a base of effective people leadership. The Management-Leadership Balance chart lists some key distinctions between the two.

Both management and leadership skills are needed at the organizational, team, and personal levels. It's not a case of either/or, but of and/also. Futurist Joel Barker provides another helpful distinction between the two roles: "Managers manage within paradigms, leaders lead between paradigms." Both are needed. Trying to run an organization with only leadership or management is like trying to cut a page with half a pair of scissors. *Leadership and management are a matched set; both are needed to be effective.*

For example, in the early 1980s, fueled by the leadership of the charismatic and highly people-oriented Donald Burr, People's Express airlines blasted into the upper atmosphere of new business success only to self-destruct like many of the earlier rockets launched from Cape Canaveral. In *Intelligent Enterprise,* Profes-

The Management-Leadership Balance

Management	Leadership
Systems, processes, and technology	People—context and culture
Goals, standards, and measurements	Preferred future, principles, and purpose
Control	Commitment
Strategic planning	Strategic opportunism
A way of doing	A way of being
Directing	Serving
Responding and reacting	Initiating and originating
Continuous improvement of what is	Innovative breakthroughs to what could be

sor James Brian Quinn explains that much of the reason for the failure was Don Burr's "disdain, if not dislike for technology" and lack of effective infrastructure, systems, and operating processes. "Morale began to lag and fail because of the frustrations of operating in confusion, costs flew out of control, and customers abandoned the airline," he concludes.

OVERMANAGED AND UNDERLED

People and culture—the human systems of a company—are what make or break any change initiative.
—Thomas Stewart, "Rate Your Readiness to Change," *Fortune*

Some of the best research and thinking on leadership comes from USC professor Warren Bennis. His books, *Leaders* and *On Becoming a Leader,* are among those rare works that are short, readable, and insightful. One of Bennis's long-standing arguments has been that our organizations are "overmanaged and underled." I heartily agree. And many improvement efforts are perpetuating that imbalance. For example, the quality and reengineering movements have been long on management methods and technologies, but pitifully short on effective leadership actions (although some of the right words are mouthed). One area that has been undermanaged, however, is self-management. But, then, a lot more

Downsizing Choices

Traditional Management Approach	Leadership-Based Approach
Focusing on pain (problems)	Focusing on positive possibilities
Helpless victim	Hopeful victor
Across-the-board cuts	Strategic redesign
Top-down cost-reduction directives	Involving everyone in finding savings
Guarding turf	Collaboration and redesign

self-leadership is needed too (more about both of these critical topics in the next chapter).

Downsizing is a classic example of an activity that's continually overmanaged and underled. If you need to reduce or restructure a team, unit, or organization, the Downsizing Choices chart illustrates the management-leadership choices you have.

LEADERSHIP: AN ACTION, NOT A POSITION

The world bestows its big prizes both in money and honors for but one thing. And that is initiative. And what is initiative? I'll tell you: it is doing the right thing without being told.

—Elbert Hubbard, turn-of-the-century editor, publisher, and author

Many people in so-called leadership positions aren't leaders. They're managers, bureaucrats, technocrats, bosses, administrators, department heads, and the like; but they aren't leaders. On the other hand, some people in individual contributor roles are powerful leaders. Leadership is an action, not a position. A leader doesn't just react and respond, but rather takes the initiative and generates action. A leader doesn't say "something should be done," but ensures that something is done. An effective leader is a "people person." Effective leaders connect, stay in contact with, and are highly visible to everyone on their team and in their organization. Leaders have developed the skills of supercharging logic, data, and analysis with emotion, pride, and the will to win. Their passion and enthusiasm for the team or organization's vision and purpose is highly contagious. They fire the imaginations, develop the capabilities, and build the confidence of people to "go for it." Leaders help people believe the impossible is possible, which makes it highly probable.

The people we are attempting to lead empower and entrust us with a leadership role—if and when we earn it. A key element of earning leadership is building credibility with the people we're leading. Consultant Jim Kouzes and Professor Barry Posner have run a series of studies and research on the "key characteristics of admired leaders." In their practical and useful book, *Credibility: How Leaders Gain and Lose It, Why People Demand It,* they write, "The results of our surveys over the last decade have been strikingly consistent . . . the majority of us look for and admire leaders who are honest, forward-looking, inspiring, and competent." Many of the leadership approaches and skills we'll be covering throughout this book will deal with these four (and many other) characteristics of effective leaders. But this is a good time to take a quick look at inspiration.

INSPIRING, ENERGIZING, AND AROUSING: A CORE LEADERSHIP SKILL

Half the world is composed of people who have something to say and can't, and the other half who have nothing to say and keep saying it.
—Robert Frost

You don't inspire and energize people with memos, mission statements, data and analysis, Pareto charts, goals and objectives, measurements, systems, or processes. These are important factors in improving performance. But that's management, not leadership. People are inspired and aroused by exciting images of a preferred future, principles or values that ring true, and being part of a higher cause or purpose that helps them feel they're making a difference. I call these Focus and Context. We'll be looking at each of these key leadership areas in Chapters 6 to 9.

Highly interconnected with and dependent upon your ability to provide Focus and Context are your communication skills, especially your verbal skills. When I was eighteen and starting my Culligan career, I took a Dale Carnegie sales course. I followed that with Carnegie's public speaking course. Both had a major impact on my leadership performance. Learning the basic persuasion skills of clarifying and simplifying what you're trying to say, tuning in to your audience, and grabbing them by the handles of their emotions is critical to effective leadership. The effective leaders I've met that inspire, energize, and arouse people to improved performance are all effective speakers. Some are charismatic and dynamic orators. Others are soft-spoken and almost shy. But without exception, they can stand in front of a large or small group and express themselves with a clarity, conviction, and credibility that stirs their audience or group members' feelings and emotions.

If you want to be an effective leader, continually improve your verbal skills. If you're not convinced it's that important, I hope some of these observations will move you to action:

- "Recent research at the University of Southern California suggests that students with high verbal scores may be better at coping with ambiguity and uncertainty. . . . They tend to be open-minded, analytic, nonjudgmental, and better at integrative thinking—using scattered bits of information to develop a big picture." —Brian O'Reilly, "Reengineering the MBA," *Fortune*
- "It is not enough for leaders to have dreams of the future. They must be able to communicate these in ways that encourage us to sign on for the duration and to work hard toward the objective. . . . Of executives surveyed, 91 percent said that by the year 2000 it will be very important that CEOs be inspiring. This quality is rated as more important than 'analytical,' 'organized,' and 'tough.'" —James Kouzes and Barry Posner, *Credibility*
- Studies commissioned by Robert Half International "prove conclusively that there is a strong link between success and the ability to communicate."
- "Without exception, visionary leaders are able to communicate their visions to others so they are thoroughly understood and accepted." —Burt Nanus, *Visionary Leadership*

- "The ability to express an idea is well nigh as important as the idea itself." —Bernard Baruch, American financier and presidential advisor
- "Charles de Gaulle did not call in 'writers.' The very idea is grotesque. The leader who allows others to speak for him is abdicating." —May Sarton, American poet and writer

PATHWAYS AND PITFALLS

You are more than a human being, you are a human becoming.
—Og Mandino, *The Greatest Miracle in the World*

- Get feedback on the management (technology, systems and processes) and leadership (people) strengths and weaknesses of your team or organization from organization and team members, customers, suppliers, and other key partners. Compare that to your own perceptions.
- Determine which areas are weakest for you and develop a plan to improve them. In some cases, you need to have weaker areas covered by adding others to your team. If you operate an entrepreneurial business you might assemble an advisory board that brings some of the management skill (and forces the discipline of regular management reviews and planning) to your organization. You can (and often should) develop new team members or bring in management expertise in many technical, systems, and process areas. But if you're the head of your team or organization, you can't delegate leadership. You need to build your leadership skills.
- Identify and discuss the and/also paradoxes to be balanced and managed within your team. Develop some guidelines or general approaches for dealing with some of these contradictory demands and reaching a better balance.
- Join Toastmasters, take a Dale Carnegie course, get personal video-based speaking feedback, take a speaking course at your college, get interpersonal skills training, get training on facilitating meetings, take a sales course, give speeches at

service clubs—do whatever you can and as often as you can to continually improve your ability to speak to groups, and persuade others to follow your lead.

Effective leadership of others is critical to high performance. That pathway begins with strong self-leadership.

CHAPTER 4

Self-Leadership:
It All Starts with You

To master one's self is the greatest mastery.
—Seneca, Roman philosopher,
moralist, and dramatist

A sociologist researching the long-term effects of family violence interviewed two sons of an alcoholic and highly abusive father. Both brothers were now in their sixties. One son looked back on a life of alcoholism, violence, failed marriages, joblessness, prison terms, suicide attempts, and poverty. The other son was a successful lawyer with a close, loving family. He was a teetotaler who kept himself in top physical shape. In separate interviews, the researcher asked each son how he explained the direction his life had taken. Each gave essentially the same answer: "You'd turn out this way too if you had a father like mine."

FATE: A MATTER OF CHOICE, NOT CHANCE

Remember this also, and be well persuaded of its truth: the future is not in the hands of Fate, but in ours.
—Jean Jules Jusserand, French scholar and
ambassador to the United States

Choice is key theme of this chapter (and book). Successful leaders face the same confusing and changing circumstances as everyone else. But a leader doesn't just follow the crowd drifting down the road of discouragement and mediocrity. *Leaders*

choose where they want to go and then blaze a trail to get there.
This is something I've come to call "self-determination." The
thousands of choices and daily decisions of our yesterdays have
accumulated and determined where we are today. If we want to
change where we'll be tomorrow, we'll have to make different
choices today.

Successful leaders recognized that before they could change the
direction of their team or organization, they had to change themselves. Highly effective leadership begins with self-leadership. If
you're not improving, you can't be an effective team or organization improvement leader.

Have You Chosen to Be a Thermometer
Manager or Thermostat Leader?

Accusing the times is but excusing ourselves.
—Thomas Fuller, seventeenth-century
English historical and religious writer

The late-nineteenth-century Irish playwright, critic, and social reformer George Bernard Shaw had a lot of useful things to say
about personal effectiveness. A few of his comments have hung on
my mirror or been posted in my day planner over the years. This
one speaks to a core management-leadership choice we all have:
"The reasonable man adapts himself to the world; the unreasonable one persists in trying to adapt the world to himself. Therefore
all progress depends upon the unreasonable man." Leaders are
"unreasonable" enough to believe they can make a difference.
Like thermostats they try to set the temperature of their environment. Thermostat leaders work to define and create what could
be rather than just reflecting what is. Now if the furnace or air
conditioner isn't working or all the windows have been left open,
a thermostat might not be able to change the room's temperature.
But it still tries.

The most useful and inspiring of Shaw's comments on self-
leadership was "People are always blaming their circumstances
for what they are. I don't believe in circumstances. The people

who get on in this world are the people who get up and look for the circumstances they want, and, if they can't find them, make them." Thermometer managers blame their circumstances for poor results. Their list of excuses include (but aren't limited to) the economy, declining work ethic, competition, their business partner, their spouse, an uneven playing field, government, politicians, the bureaucracy, their organization's culture, unreasonable customers, their boss, the head office, the field, unions, management, shareholders, and so on. As our daughter Jennifer would say, "Would you like some cheese with your whine?"

Sure, those circumstances are real. And, yes, they can have a negative impact on performance. But I have yet to find an industry where there isn't at least one leader who has refused to be boxed in by the circumstances that had everyone else drifting down the "me-too" road. Somewhere in every hopeless bureaucracy there are always a few leaders with little or no formal power who improve themselves and parts of the organization despite the odds stacked against them. One of my favorite posters is an aerial view of a group of people trying to find their way through a neatly trimmed cedar hedge maze. And going right through the middle of the maze is a leader with a chain saw. As a gardener, the destruction makes me grimace. But the image of someone's refusal to stumble around on the conventional path and play by the rules is a powerful one.

A key rallying cry in Achieve's early years was "changing the rules of the game in the consulting and training business." I tried very hard to provide thermostat leadership to myself and fellow Achievers. During our most difficult times it was a real struggle to keep remembering that when we pointed a finger at the economy, time of year, or each other, the hand we used to point had three times as many fingers pointing backward at the source of our circumstances. To prove this point, I once charted our 10-year sales growth. The dips and surges correlated to things we had or hadn't done with new products, marketing, internal training, repositioning the business, and so on. There was little correlation to the economy, competition, and other external factors. Of course, if we believed and behaved as if those factors determined our fate (thermometer management), they would have.

LUCK RUNNING AMOK

Man who waits for roast duck to fly into mouth must wait very, very long time.

—Chinese proverb

One of the core assumptions determining whether you behave like a thermometer manager or "unreasonable" thermostat leader has to do with luck. Some people and organizations get lucky. They happen to be in the right place at the right time. Just showing up made them successful. The rising tide of economic growth or their industry's expansion raised their boats high in the water. Or they developed a technology, product, or expertise that has the world beating a path to their door (at least until other mousetraps become available). Many of these one-dimensional organizations succeed (for a while) despite themselves. The people heading these organizations then go on to confuse their good luck with good leadership.

Uncontrolled luck does play a part. However, as the "father of modern management," Peter Drucker, once put it, "miracles are great but they are so unpredictable." The kind of luck effective leaders depend upon was well described by Canadian humorist Stephen Leacock: "I am a great believer in luck, and I find the harder I work the more I have of it." I found that the harder I worked at developing people, the luckier I got at finding a committed, motivated team. The harder we worked at serving our clients, the luckier we got with repeat business and referrals. The harder I work at loving Heather, the luckier I am in falling into a great marriage. The harder I work at growing up with our kids, the luckier I am at getting their respect and trust. The harder I work at defining and working toward my life vision, principles, and purpose, the more lucky breaks come my way. The harder I work at community involvement, the luckier I am in happening into a great town. The harder I work to enrich and develop myself, the luckier I am in having a fulfilling life. The more I look after my body with good food, exercise, and rest, the luckier my health seems to be.

Every effective leader became one through luck. All that was required was to work long hours, pay attention to customers, set and maintain a strong personal and organizational vision and purpose, be passionate about one's work, build partnerships with people and treat them like trusted adults, set and follow an aggressive personal and organization improvement plan, align systems and processes, keep developing one's skills, set clear priorities and use time well, discipline oneself to follow through, stay flexible and look for innovative new breakthroughs, celebrate and reward success along the way, make the rules rather than play by them, and learn how to communicate. After that, success was just luck.

Our Fate Is in Our Own Hands

> *People who want milk should not seat themselves in the middle of a field in hope that a cow will back up to them.*
>
> —Elbert Hubbard

A few years ago a friend had Ned, a small independent contractor, do extensive renovations to his home. Being a very fussy craftsman and cabinet maker, Ned did an especially superb job on the extensive woodwork involved in the renovation. About a year after completing the renovations, Ned bumped into my friend at the local hardware store. "The recession finally caught up to me," Ned told my friend. "I've had to lay off my crew and try to wait out this slow period." Yet, other neighbors were in the midst of major renovations. They hired another contractor because Ned never got back to them with a firm quote after he had been out to estimate the job. Their repeated phone calls would go unanswered. Many wanted to hire Ned because of the high-quality work he had done at my friend's place. But Ned was disorganized. When he was working on one job, it was all he could do to keep things together there. He became too preoccupied to do all the additional drafting and estimating work to needed to firm up a bid on another job. Besides, when he had a big job, he didn't feel much pressure to get more work. But once that job was finished, he had to scurry desperately to find another construction project. It wasn't the recession that got to Ned; it was his lack of follow-through. In fact, my friend had shown many neighbors who were in the market for renovations through his house. Most were very impressed. But he stopped recommending Ned because of Ned's embarrassing disorganization and failure to follow up.

I've often reflected on the truth and paradoxes found in Reinhold Niebuhr's popular Serenity Prayer: "God, grant me the serenity to accept the things I cannot change, the courage to change the things I can, and the wisdom to know the difference." There are many circumstances we can't control (but we can control how we deal with the uncontrollable). However, we tend to easily become confused by what we can and can't control. Before the "courage to change the things I can" is of any use, *we need to learn how to recognize just what we can change*. Like Ned, most people rarely examine their own assumptions, beliefs, skills, behaviors, and learning levels to see how they created their own circumstances. Instead, they develop a full-blown case of victimitis—the poor-little-helpless-me syndrome.

Twenty years ago I came across a story (I don't know who wrote it) that impressed this fact very deeply on me. Whenever I caught myself pointing "out there" to explain my poor performance, I would pull out this story and read it again. I have since used it with many groups to make the same point.

The Man Who Sold Hot Dogs

There was a man who lived by the side of the road and sold hot dogs. He was hard of hearing so he had no radio. He had trouble with his eyes so he read no newspapers. But he sold good hot dogs. He put up signs on the highway telling people how good the hot dogs were. He stood by the side of the road and cried, "Buy a hot dog mister?" And people bought.

He increased his meat and bun orders. He bought a bigger stove to take care of his trade. He finally got his son home from college to help him out.

But then something happened.

His son said, "Father, haven't you been listening to the radio? Haven't you been reading the newspapers? There's a big recession. The European situation is terrible. The domestic situation is worse."

Whereupon the father thought, "Well, my son's been to college, he reads the newspapers and he listens to the radio. He ought to know."

So the father cut down on his bun orders, took down his advertising signs, and no longer bothered to stand out on the highway selling hot dogs. And his hot dog sales fell almost overnight.

"You're right, son," the old man said to his boy. "We're certainly in the middle of a great recession."

As CEO, Jack Welch has led a remarkable turnaround of General Electric. One of his books has one of my all-time favorite titles. It sums up the self-determination concepts we've been talking about here and explains what has made Jack so successful. The book is called *Control Your Destiny or Someone Else Will*. Exactly.

What's Your Explanatory Style?

People often say that this or that person has not found himself. But the self is not something that one finds. It is something one creates.
—Thomas Szasz, twentieth-century American psychoanalyst who founded the "anti-psychiatry" movement

Effective leaders are unreasonable optimists. Optimists refuse to live in "the real world." They live in a world of hope and possibilities. They see opportunity in every calamity. The pessimist sees calamity in every opportunity. Optimists excite and arouse others to action by helping them see, believe in, and reach for what could be.

If you haven't already read *Learned Optimism*, put it at the top of your reading list (but finish this book first). *Learned Optimism*, written by Martin Seligman, professor of social science and director of clinical training in psychology at the University of Pennsylvania, reports on more than twenty years of pioneering research on the effects of pessimism and optimism, ways to assess the degrees of either, and how to change a pessimistic style to an optimistic one. Seligman's work adds an important new twist and depth to what we have been discussing here. He writes, "The defining characteristic of pessimists is that they tend to believe bad events will last a long time, will undermine everything they do, and are their own fault. The optimists, who are confronted with the same hard knocks of this world, think about misfortune in the opposite way. They tend to believe defeat is just a temporary setback, that its causes are confined to this one case. The optimists believe defeat is not their fault: Circumstances, bad luck, or other people brought it about. Such people are unfazed by defeat. Confronted by a bad situation, they perceive it as a challenge and try harder."

At the core of Seligman's findings are the interconnected concepts of "learned helplessness" and "explanatory style." Seligman explains, "Learned helplessness is the giving-up reaction, the quitting response that follows from the belief that whatever you do doesn't matter. Explanatory style is the manner in which you habitually explain to yourself why events happen. It is the great modulator of learned helplessness. An optimistic explanatory style stops helplessness, whereas a pessimistic explanatory style spreads helplessness." He goes on to cite research that shows pessimism is a major cause of depression, inaction and inertia, worry, and much poorer physical health (including earlier death). He has also found, "Pessimism is self-fulfilling. Pessimists don't persist in the face of challenges, and therefore fail more frequently—even when success is attainable . . . their explanatory style now converts the predicted setback into a disaster, and disaster into a catastrophe."

YOU CAN'T BUILD A TEAM OR ORGANIZATION DIFFERENT FROM YOU

The management of self is critical. Without it, leaders may do more harm than good. Like incompetent physicians, incompetent managers make people sicker and less vital.

—Warren Bennis and Burt Nanus, *Leaders*
(in a chapter titled "Leading Others, Managing Yourself")

Too many managers who aspire to lead and develop others haven't learned how to lead and develop themselves. They are trying to build organizations or provide services that are different from them. These well intentioned managers are trying to improve their teams or organizations without improving themselves. Many seem to be echoing Mark Twain's observation, "Nothing so needs reforming as other people's habits."

Here are some examples of these all-too-common disconnects between organization and personal performance:

- Pessimistic managers push their companies to be market and industry leaders, while blaming external factors like the economy for their poor performance.

- Managers with stunted personal growth set strategies to build a "Learning Organization."
- Managers produce team and organization vision, values, and mission statements without having clarified and aligned their own personal preferred future, principles, and purpose.
- A major program to improve customer service is initiated by managers who boss, direct, and control rather than serve their organization's servers.
- Continuous quality improvement programs are implemented by managers with weak levels of continuous personal improvement.
- Strict technomanagers who oversee rigid systems and processes talk about risk taking and innovation.
- Management groups composed of turf-protecting departmental managers, fighting like our three kids in the back seat on a long, hot drive, try to build a team-based organization.
- Disorganized managers with poor time management habits are setting goals, priorities, and disciplined processes for everyone else.
- Although they have no personal improvement plan, process, or habits, managers develop extensive organization transformation and improvement plans.
- While avoiding (and shooting messengers of) personal feedback, managers construct extensive performance appraisal systems and measurements for everyone else.

A Team or Organization Can't Rise Above the Level of Its Leadership

Organizational change begins with leaders who walk the talk by transforming themselves.

—Stratford Sherman, "Leaders Learn to Heed the Voice Within," *Fortune*

It just doesn't work. *You can't build a team or organization that's different from you.* You can't make them into something you're not. But I've watched countless managers and management teams try. This disconnected approach doesn't work. First, unless you're a superb actor, you can't be a split personality and teach or lead others to do something that's out of basic alignment with your own habits, skills, and characteristics.

Second, everyone's "phoniness radar" and "BS meters" are getting ever more sensitive (from overuse). We're fed up with sanctimonious church leaders charged with sexual abuse, fat doctors telling us to get into shape, politicians making retractable promises to get elected, executives drawing big salaries and bonuses while their company's financial value declines, municipal transit managers who don't take their own buses to work, training and consulting companies who don't practice what they teach, and the like. I once wrote a scathing note (which was never answered) and quit a speakers' association because I kept hearing "the old pros" telling people who wanted to get on speaking platforms and tell others how to be successful to "fake 'til you make it." (The personal and organization improvement field is full of phonies who haven't earned the right to even be in the same room as the people they're trying to advise.) One of those speakers also asked me to provide an endorsement for the jacket of a "motivational book" he bragged he'd written "on a six-hour airplane flight." And that's about how much research and thought the warmed-over platitudes, old jokes, and generalities he'd pieced together obviously had. I declined his invitation.

We loathe phoniness and crave genuineness in our leaders. If you aspire to be a leader, the authenticity (being the real thing) that stems from aligning who you are with where you're trying to take your team or organization will inspire trust, cooperation, and forgiveness in the people who'll help take you there. Nobody expects you to be the perfect role model. But they do expect to see a close connection between who you are and the direction you're pointing the team or organization toward. Or they at least need to see that you recognize your shortcomings and are working hard to improve yourself so you can close the organization–personal performance gap. Otherwise, they'll shrug off all your team and organization improvement rhetoric and planning with a sense that this is just "kidney stone management"—it will hurt for a while, but this too shall pass. "Watch out, (your name here) has been off to another seminar (or read another book). If we lay low long enough, he/she will move on to the next fad."

Successful team or organization leadership begins with successful self-leadership. The first step in improving your team or organization is improving yourself.

CONTINUOUS PERSONAL IMPROVEMENT: LEADERS ARE MADE, NOT BORN

> *You think me the child of circumstances; I make my circumstances.*
> —Ralph Waldo Emerson

Imagine picking up your newspaper and finding these announcements in the Births section:

BIRTHS

Mr. and Mrs. Blue Collar proudly announce the birth of Jack, a construction foreman. At 13 lbs., 12 oz., he arrived with a bellowing cry and tattoos, and began whistling rudely at the nurses.

Wilma and Sam Klutz are sad to announce the arrival of an underachiever. Mia Klutz came complete with slumped shoulders, listless eyes, and a whiny cry. Birth was by cesarean section.

Mr. and Mrs. Weir Skilled happily announce the birth of their daughter Heidi, a highly effective leader. Heidi Skilled arrived full of confidence and energy. Her vibrant vision and well-grounded values inspired and energized everyone in the delivery room. She immediately put her natural leadership skills into

```
action by pulling the team together
to map out processes for ongoing
personal, group, and organization
improvements.

Tomorrow the maturity pool has bets
on the arrival of a genetic scien-
tist, a space station entrepreneur,
an intergalactic pilot, a break-
and-enter artist, and a Secretary
for Tax Complication and Deficit
Financing.
```

These "births" are clearly ridiculous fiction. You'll never see anything like them in your newspaper. Yet they reflect an equally ridiculous view a lot of people have about leadership development. Many people believe that they just weren't born leaders (speakers, writers, negotiators, strategists, facilitators, etc.) and that there's not much they can do about it. They feel that the leadership skills, attributions, and characteristics they now have are pretty much what they're stuck (or blessed) with.

If you're not working hard to continually improve your leadership skills because you weren't "born with natural talent," then you're either copping out, misinformed, or both. You are unknowingly or knowingly choosing to be a "reasonable" thermometer manager who follows the crowd rather than an "unreasonable" thermostat leader making your own trail. You've decided to let your luck run amok (in the words of that noxious song, "whatever will be will be"). You're choosing not to control your own destiny, and so somebody else probably will. You've decided not to immunize yourself against the deadly victimitis virus. You choosing to raise your levels of pessimism and helplessness. And you're decided to leave your team or organization's improvement levels as low as your personal improvement standards are. As Zig Ziglar, the personal effectiveness speaker and author, puts it, "All of life is a series of choices, and what you choose to give life today will determine what life will give you tomorrow."

Leadership and Learning

Leadership and learning are indispensable to each other.
—John F. Kennedy

The American founding father, author, and statesman Benjamin Franklin was devoted to lifelong learning and continual personal improvement. His book *The Art of Virtue* (edited by George Rogers) is an inspiring account of Franklin's life and an instructive guide to his improvement process and personal effectiveness system. Franklin once said, "If you empty your purse in your head, no one can take it away from you. An investment in knowledge always pays the best interest." Modern research shows that Franklin's advice on learning is as valid today as it was two hundred years ago:

- Doug Snetsinger, executive director, the Institute of Market Driven Quality (part of the Faculty of Management at the University of Toronto) surveyed 326 Canadian CEOs to see if there were any connections between the senior executive's personal development and the organization's performance. The organization performance indicators he used were profit, market share, customer satisfaction, quality goals, and costs. The "Learning Leaders" study found, "regardless of the size of the business or the industry in which it competes, organizations headed by learning leaders are far more likely to be achieving their operational goals than those that do not have that leadership. . . . the higher the learning effectiveness of the senior team, the more likely that the firm is prospering." Snetsinger concludes, "The CEO's personal development is not personal. It is fundamental to sustaining and rejuvenating the health of the organization."
- At the end of his lengthy and highly researched book *Organization Culture and Leadership,* Sloan School of Management (MIT) Professor Edgar Schein writes, "It seems clear that the leaders of the future will have to be perpetual learners. This will require (1) new levels of perception and insight into the realities of the world and also into themselves;

(2) extraordinary levels of motivation to go through the inevitable pain of learning and change . . . ; (3) the emotional strength to manage their own and others' anxiety as learning and change become more and more a way of life; (4) new skills in analyzing and changing cultural assumptions; (5) the willingness and ability to involve others and elicit their participation; and (6) the ability to learn the assumptions of a whole new organizational culture."

- Psychologist and author Charles Garfield has been conducting a study of hundreds of "peak performers" in every major field and profession for over twenty-five years. His book *Peak Performers* is an insightful look into the performance processes and improvement systems of many of today's most effective people. Here's a fascinating story and an important conclusion I picked up from a presentation he gave some years ago: "The great Italian opera tenor Luciano Pavarotti was an average singer in the boys' choir in Italy when he was a teenager. They only reason they let him in the choir was because his father ran it . . . he wanted to be spoken of with the same reverence and respect as his fellow countryman Enrico Caruso. He studied and he practiced and he trained and he studied and he practiced and he trained and slowly, slowly he got there." Garfield's research made him highly disdainful of the very idea of anyone's being a born anything. He finds, "It's not always the person with greatest genetic talent or it's not always the person who has the greatest gift. It's sometimes the people who, flat out, are the most determined to get there."

- Researchers at the University of Virginia's Colgate Darden Graduate School of Business Administration found that "learning managers approach key events as opportunities to learn rather than simple checkpoints in the march forward." They found that *only 10 percent of executives interviewed had this "learning mind-set"* [my emphasis], and this group "received the highest job performance ratings of the entire group." The learners in their study demonstrated "agility of thought . . . focused on learning from many sources . . . communicated readily in metaphors and analogies, and conducted discussions in a nonlinear manner—characteristics that were rare among other managers" (there's the importance of those verbal skills again). The research also looked at strategic alliances and found "the learning mind-set to be critical to getting these alliances started and to weathering difficult times during their evolution."

- Reporting on his continuing leadership research, Warren Bennis writes in *On Becoming a Leader,* "They [leaders he's interviewed] all agree that leaders are made, not born, and made more by themselves than by any external means . . . each of these individuals has continued to grow and develop throughout life. This is the best tradition of leadership. . . . Becoming a leader isn't easy, just as becoming a doctor or a poet isn't easy, and anyone who claims otherwise is fooling himself. But learning to lead is a lot easier than most of us think it is, because each of us contains the capacity for leadership."

Are You Interested in Leadership or Committed to Becoming a Leader?

Nothing is impossible; there are ways that lead to everything, and if we had sufficient will we should always have sufficient means. It is often merely for an excuse that we say things are impossible.

—François de La Rochefoucauld,
seventeenth-century French courtier and writer

I should be used to it by now. But I continue to be stunned by the stunted personal growth of so many managers who are supposed to be in "leadership roles." Their "years of leadership experience and learning" consist of formal education (usually technical and/or management) followed by a year or two of experience multiplied twenty or thirty times. Here's an all-too-typical dinner conversation I had with a senior manager in the middle of a two-day improvement workshop I was running with a senior management team. The company was in crisis. It was struggling just to stay even in its industry.

"What do you do to personally improve the leadership skills we discussed today?"

"I am afraid I don't get much time to do anything."

"How many leadership or organization effectiveness books do you read a year?"

"One or two if I'm lucky."

"What about seminars, workshops, or executive learning forums?"

"Well, I did get to one. . . . No, that was two years ago."

"Do you listen to audiotapes in your car?"

"No, I'm either winding down, gearing up, or talking on the phone."

"How often does your management team meet to review progress, reflect on its performance, and plan for improvements?"

"This is the first meeting we've had in a few years."

The twentieth-century American critic and novelist John Gardner once said, "All excellence involves discipline and tenacity of purpose." Both are critical elements in leadership development and personal effectiveness. Our tenacity and clarity of purpose and vision can help to spin the daily, weekly, and monthly disciplined habit strands. These become the cables that will either raise our performance up or drag us down. To "pay the price" of personal improvement means dwelling on the pain and sacrifice. I've found instead that focusing on the gains by keeping my preferred future and purpose firmly in mind has been my biggest improvement habit booster.

It's impossible to put an exact number of hours on the time that effective leaders invest in their own personal improvement. But I would peg the minimum at around 10 percent. So, if you work 50 hours per week, that's about 20 hours, or 2 to 3 days per month. The type of personal development varies widely. Reading is my single biggest personal development catalyst. More than 15 years ago, I started getting up 45 minutes earlier each day to exercise and then read personal development or spiritual material, pray, and meditate. It's proven to be one of the best habits I ever developed for starting my day with more energy and a constant refocus on my life's highest priorities. I read organization improvement and leadership development material in the evenings when I am at home or on airplanes (it constantly amazes me how many people dribble away this wonderfully rich, uninterrupted reading and thinking time on movies, airline magazines, or sleeping) and in hotel rooms when I travel. I find reading with a highlighter pen and my notebook computer nearby especially beneficial. I've also found that listening to audiocassettes in my car is a terrific way to catch up on speakers or authors I want to hear and listen to conference presentations I've missed.

There are as many learning styles and pathways to personal development as there are leaders using them. A partial list includes books, magazines, newspapers, and newsletters; special education or business television programs; customer research; pilots, experiments, and "clumsy tries"; personal coaching and mentoring; benchmarking internal and external "best practices"; seminars, workshops, and skill development sessions; performance review, assessment, celebration, and refocus; operational planning and strategy development sessions; customer, supplier, and internal team/organization member feedback; system and process measurement systems; audio- and videotapes; computer and multimedia (CD-ROM based) programs; peer groups and networks outside your organization; teaching and training others; industry conferences and trade shows; university or college courses; keeping a personal journal; self-evaluation, reflection, and improvement planning; consultants; and study tours. Throughout the rest of this book, we'll look at a wide variety of strategies, tips, traps, and techniques for incorporating and integrating many of these approaches to transforming yourself, your team, and your organization.

PATHWAYS AND PITFALLS

He worked by day, And toiled by night; He gave up play, And some delight; Dry books he read, New things to learn; And forged ahead, Success to earn; He plodded on, With faith and pluck; And when he won, They called it luck.

—Jacob Braude, "Rhyme and Verse"

- Follow Martin Seligman's ABC's to assess your explanatory style: any *Adversity* we encounter triggers our habitual *Beliefs*, which determine the *Consequences* of that situation or those circumstances. *Learned Optimism* has many useful assessment tools to help you understand whether you tend to pessimism or optimism and suggestions on how to become more optimistic.

- Work with your team or by yourself to "reframe" negative situations and problems by looking for improvement opportunities buried in them.
- Identify which excuses you and your team use to explain away performance problems.
- Begin making a list of the personal habits and team/organizational characteristics you and/or your team want to develop. (We'll be working on an improvement plan and process in Chapters 14 and 15.) You might start this by reviewing those things you admire most in successful leaders or highly effective teams/organizations.
- Use the organization-personal improvement disconnects list (pages 40 and 41) to assess where you and your team need work.
- Don't try to change everything at once. Your habits and team or organizational culture took years to evolve and develop. You won't change them quickly. Begin the change process one step at a time.
- Keep a journal of your thoughts, ideas, and/or improvement efforts. Learn more about yourself by looking back for major themes and issues. A year after we sold Achieve, my father died unexpectedly of a heart attack, *Firing on All Cylinders* was launched in the United States, we were in the midst of a major home renovation, and my career direction was becoming increasingly unclear. I found that writing and reflecting on my feelings brought my churning emotions to the surface where I could examine them and better understand what was eating at me. This proved to be a big help in reviewing and renewing my vision and purpose. And my career direction gradually came more sharply into focus.
- Manage your wealth by living below your means. Pay yourself at least 10 percent of your income (into a savings and investment plan) first before you pay for all your other needs and wants. This is either your "drop dead pot of career options money" or an early retirement fund. Having it will increase your confidence and help you assess whether what

you're doing is what you really want to be doing. Dave Chilton's fictionalized money management book, *The Wealthy Barber,* is a highly entertaining guide to the basics of financial planning.

- Add to your confidence (and leadership abilities) by developing your public speaking and interpersonal skills. Draw up a list of all your personal strengths and achievements, no matter how small. During those dark times of defeat and discouragement, this helped me put things back in perspective and renewed my energy to push on toward my preferred future.
- Ask others for advice and their help. It's a sign of healthy self-confidence and strength, not weakness.
- Be wary of advice from those who haven't done what you're about to do or paid the price you're about to pay (unless you want to use them as bad examples to avoid). Seek out and learn from those who've been there—those who lead by example.

Is this what it takes to be a leader? Well, it's a good start. The rest of this book will look at balancing both management and leadership on parallel organization and personal improvement tracks to dramatically increase performance.

While my fictional "birth announcements" were ridiculous and far-fetched, this fictional "death notice" of a manager who succumbed to the victimitis virus could be closer to the truth:

> He died a penniless man. He blamed his bankrupt business on high taxes, low tariff protection, a nonsupportive wife, unfair competition, militant unions, lazy and dishonest workers, a weak economy, unlucky timing, high interest rates, conservative bankers, bureaucratic regulators, weak managers, poor consulting advice, and general bad luck. He died of malnutrition buying lottery tickets, four-leaf clovers, and rabbit's feet.

CHAPTER 5

The Big Picture:
A Map to Improvement
Pathways and Passages

---

*You should keep on learning as long as there is something
you do not know.*

—Seneca, Roman philosopher, moralist, and dramatist

Diagrams, maps, and models are very helpful in visualizing the
ground to be covered in an improvement effort. Many groups I've
worked with over the years find a planning chart helps them to see
the big picture as they begin, or renew, the tough job of figuring out
how to move from where they are to where they want to be. However, many change and improvement models are far too detailed
and complex to be practical. In some cases, the "paradigms" were
developed by fuzzy-thinking intellectuals who've found something
that works in practice and wonder if it will work in theory. In other
cases, academics develop complex, theoretical models that most
leaders don't have the time to understand, much less try to actually
use (fortunately, most of this work is kept safely out of harm's way
in scholarly journals). The degree of complexity of a change and
improvement theory is usually in inverse proportion to its useful-
ness. Too many theories are where the rubber meets the sky.

The VIP Strategy was constructed and written around an eight-
part "Vision Integrated Performance" organization and team
leadership model. *Firing on All Cylinders* was structured around
a "twelve-cylinder" organization improvement model. It pulls together some of the leadership and many of the management issues
involved in improving service/quality, building a team-based organization, and improving and/or reengineering processes.

This chapter will give you an overview of the central improvement
map that the rest of this book is built around. This model moves one

level deeper than my earlier books to uncover the three-part foundation of successful improvement efforts. One part of that foundation is organization improvement. Here I've dug below the labels and jargon of service/quality, teams, reengineering, and the like to unearth the successful management systems and processes that underpin these approaches. The second major component of the model is leadership development. As introduced in Chapter 3, these are the skills and approaches that counterbalance management systems and processes. The third element of the model is personal effectiveness: self-leadership and continuous personal improvement.

ESSENTIAL IMPROVEMENT PATHWAYS AND PASSAGES

If there's a way to do it better . . . find it.
—Thomas Alva Edison

The improvement map (see illustration) that the rest of this book is structured around has two main balance points: what and how.

Improvement Pathways and Passages

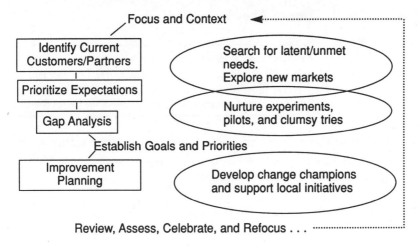

© The Clemmer Group Inc.

The "what" balance is the melding of organization, team, and personal performance improvement into parallel and combined tracks. This is what's to be accomplished. The "how" balance consists of the parallel management and leadership tracks that work together to blend and complement each other. The hard boxes on the left side of the improvement map represent management systems and approaches. The paths on this side of the model coincide with the Management column of the chart on page 27. The softer bubbles on the right side of the improvement map represent leadership issues and activities. These paths correspond to the Leadership column of the chart on page 27. And down the middle of the improvement map are three central activities that head, anchor, or reinforce both management and leadership.

The improvement map is full of and/also paradoxes to be managed. It's made up of linear pathways that are also fluid and circular and unending. Some of these passages are both conflicting and complementary. Although the map has a logical order and flow, many groups and individuals have used it to pinpoint their strengths or current areas of improvement focus. This becomes their starting point for renewing and expanding their team, organization, and personal improvement efforts.

A Tour of the Terrain Ahead

Never look down to test the ground before taking your next step; only he who keeps his eye fixed on the far horizon will find the right road.
—Dag Hammarskjöld, Nobel Prize–winning Swedish economist
and statesman, Secretary-General of the United Nations

Throughout the rest of this book, chapters or entire sections are built around each area or section in the improvement map. Here's a quick overview of what's to come:

Focus and Context. Your team, organization, and personal Focus and Context define who you are, who you want to be, and where you want to go. Focus and Context are core people issues (starting with yourself) that call for strong leadership. *This area is* *critical to continual improvement and high performance.* It's also an area that's notoriously weak in practice even when many of the right words are used. That's why I've devoted four chapters to it. First, Chapter 6 gives you a "big picture" overview of Focus and Context; the next three chapters are then built around a set of basic questions: Where are you going (your vision or picture of your *preferred* future)? What do you believe in (your principles or values)? Why do you exist (your purpose or niche)?

Current Customers/Partners. Improvement in this area requires identifying your current customers or external partners (like distributors, agents, alliances, suppliers, etc.), prioritizing their expectations, and analyzing performance gaps. Because you're likely among the smarter and better informed readers of this book, you no doubt have a copy of *Firing on All Cylinders.* (There are two groups of people in this world: astute, intelligent readers of my books and everybody else!) *Firing on All Cylinders* outlines many tools, techniques, and approaches for customer research. I won't repeat that material in this book. Instead I'll put all this customer research work in the larger framework of organization and personal service.

Latent/Unmet Needs, New Markets, and Experimentation. Two closely related chapters will cover these two closely related areas, which deal with innovation and creativity, important leadership issues that are often misunderstood and misapplied. Researching and focusing improvements on existing customers is only the management half of the long-term improvement equation (the half the service/quality movement has been heavily centered on). But it can bring short-term success and long-term disaster. We need to understand our existing customers at a level deep enough to see other products, services, or applications that meet their needs in new ways. We need to see our business broadly enough to discover or create new markets for extensions or adaptation of our technologies and expertise. Successful discovery processes rely on nurturing experiments, pilots, and "clumsy tries" to get an early jump on potential opportunities. If managed effectively, this experimental, "mucking around" approach is also a key part of building a learning organization or team.

Establish Goals and Priorities.   At this point, Focus and Context are clear. Existing customers' and partners' expectations and performance gaps are becoming apparent. New markets, services, and products are evolving from experiments, pilots, and related learning activities. Now it's time to set improvement goals and priorities. You can't do it all. *All improvement activities aren't equal.* A small percentage of improvement projects and processes will give you big payoffs. How you use the limited and precious time, energy, and focus of your team, organization, and yourself calls for difficult and critically important choices. It takes courage and discipline. And some of the very hardest work is organizing and managing your own time.

Improvement Planning.   Many organizations, teams, and some people have plans for working *in* their business or career. Only the more successful also have plans for working *on* their organizations, teams, or selves. How can you continually improve without an improvement plan, habit, system, or process? You can't. Too many people go on crash improvement programs as if they expected to turn a 240-pound chain smoker into an Olympic athlete within a few weeks. A crash improvement program can produce dramatic changes quite quickly. And it lulls many people into thinking they've really changed. But without ongoing improvement planning, habits, systems, or processes, the original culture or personal characteristics return.

After establishing the importance of growth, development, and improvement planning (Chapter 14), the next eight chapters (15 to 22) summarize the central improvement areas that need to be continually and systematically addressed. Many of these are management systems and processes. But they also contain a healthy mix of leadership issues. The improvement planning areas include:

- Infrastructure, process, and discipline
- Process management (balancing reengineering and process improvement)
- Teams
- Skill development
- Measurement and feedback

- Structure and systems
- Education and communication
- Reward and recognition

Change Champions and Local Initiatives. This servant-leadership component of team and organization improvement is the counterbalance to centralized planning and senior-management-directed improvement initiatives. Encouraging, supporting, and focusing change and improvement champions calls for a delicate balance. On the one hand, you want to harness and amplify their energy and ideas. On the other hand, their efforts often need gentle guidance to ensure that everyone is pointed in the same direction and focusing precious time and resources on things that will really make a difference to the team or organization.

Review, Assess, Celebrate, and Refocus. It's a big mistake to skip or quickly gloss over this step. Without periodic "time outs" (12–18 months is ideal) to assess our progress, we often don't have a sense of how far we've come and whether we're on track or slipping into the swamp. It also means we miss opportunities to reenergize ourselves and everyone else involved in the improvement effort. That can be fatal. An exercise as simple as listing all of your (big and little) accomplishments of the past year can produce a satisfying sense of accomplishment and an incredible amount of energy to renew your improvement efforts. As the improvement map shows, this review, assessment, and pause that refreshes is the jumping-off point for returning to the beginning of the next cycle back through the endless improvement process.

Taking Charge

The speed of the leader is the speed of the pack.
—Yukon proverb

The central improvement map used throughout this book is not a precise "follow every step in exact order" blueprint to your organization, team, and improvement effort. Rather it's a broad sketch of the key pathways and passages traversed by the very highest performers. But I know of no person or organization who's got all of this together perfectly. Some do well in some management areas, while others excel in particular leadership components. There is no one best or right way to put all this together. You need to look at the array of options, alternatives, traps, and pointers I'll be passing along as an outline of the many improvement routes available to you, your team, and your organization. Pick the tracks and trails that best fit your own personality, your team and organization's culture, and where you want to go. But remember that pearls come from irritation. Where you feel the most stretch, pain, or irritation may just be your area of biggest payback. *Highly successful leaders are willing to push themselves to do what most other people won't do.*

The Essence of Improvement

Success isn't purchased at any one time, but on the installment plan.

The key elements of organizational, team, and personal success could be boiled down to:

1. Get focused on who you are, what you believe in, and where you're going.
2. Learn how you can put your own and your team or organization's strengths and competence to the greatest service for the greatest number.
3. Explore, learn, and evolve your markets and offerings.
4. Set priorities and concentrate your limited time and resources.
5. Establish an improvement plan and process.
6. Develop the discipline, persistence, and follow-through to make it happen.

CHAPTER **6**

Who Are You and What Do You Want?

> *What our deepest self craves is not mere enjoyment, but some supreme purpose that will enlist all our powers and will give unity and direction to our life. We can never know the profoundest joy without a conviction that our life is significant—not a meaningless episode.*
>
> —Henry J. Golding

Two workers were digging a trench and laying cable. A neighborhood boy came by on his bike to inspect the work. He asked one of the workers what he was doing. The worker replied, "I'm laying a new combination phone and TV cable for this neighborhood." Another boy wandered up later and asked the other worker what she was doing. She paused, then said proudly, "I am helping to build our country's information highway to the twenty-first century."

A major movement in the Western world today is the search for meaning. We want more than just a job or an existence. We want to make a difference. We want to know that our short time on this earth counted for something. We want more than to just exist or get by, we want to live. We want to be energized. We want passion, excitement, and a sense of deeper purpose.

Focus and Context refer to what's at the very center of our organizations and our lives. It's whatever provides the ultimate focal point and meaning for us. What are our core values and beliefs? Where are we trying to go? What does success look like? What kind of team or organization are we trying to build? What kind of person are we becoming? How does our work align with our life's mission or purpose? These are some of the fundamental people issues that will ultimately determine the effectiveness of our technology, systems, and processes. These basic Focus and Context issues are the foundation of leadership. They define the heart, soul, and spirit of our teams and organizations. This is the heart that drives the head of rational systems and processes to direct the hands of technology.

PASSION: A RENEWABLE ENERGY SOURCE

> *If I were a heathen, I would rear a statue to energy, and fall down and worship it.*
>
> —Mark Twain

Too many people are indifferent about what they do and detached from their work. They drift through life, reflecting the attitude on a bumper sticker: "I am neither for nor against apathy." Working with them, or trying to follow their lead, is about as invigorating as sitting in cold drizzle watching your kid's team lose a baseball game.

As a fiery author and speaker on the topic, Tom Peters has done a great job of passionately making the case for leadership passion. It is vital. *Passionate leaders have the energy and drive needed to push and pull their teams and organizations forward.* This rousing passion is the energy source that powers the technology, systems, and processes that boost personal, team, and organization performance to ever higher levels. In his study of hundreds of "peak performers" that now spans three decades Charles Garfield found, "Preference with a passion—intense commitment to what they do—is one of the single most dramatic differences between peak performers and their less productive colleagues. . . . Many told me they can trace their performance more clearly to preference than to aptitude, more to how they feel about what they are doing than what they know."

Passion, energy, enthusiasm, commitment, intensity, fervor, and zeal have always been the driving force of effective leaders:

- "Failure is more frequently from want of energy than want of capital." —Daniel Webster, nineteenth-century American statesman and orator
- "Every great and commanding moment in the annals of the world is the triumph of some enthusiasm." —Ralph Waldo

Emerson, *Nature, Addresses, and Lectures: Man the Reformer*
- "Years wrinkle the skin, but to give up enthusiasm wrinkles the soul." —Samuel Ullman, author and poet
- "Genius is mainly an affair of energy." —Matthew Arnold, nineteenth-century English poet and critic

Leaders with a Cause

This the true joy in life, the being used for a purpose recognized by yourself as a mighty one.

—George Bernard Shaw

People rally around passionate leaders with a compelling vision and purpose. We're drawn, like insects to the back porch light, by those who are so passionate about their work that they have turned it into a cause. Norman Vincent Peale considered a burning conviction and contagious enthusiasm to be the most critical factor in successful living and leadership (listening to him speak was an inspiring and invigorating experience). He once said, "Your enthusiasm will be infectious, stimulating, and attractive to others. They will love you for it. They will go for you and with you." Whether you've loved him, hated him, or just wanted to ignore him, strong convictions are the reason Rush Limbaugh has been so popular. It's also why some of the greatest creations or transformations of our time were led by passionate leaders such as Lee Iacocca at Chrysler, Jack Welch at GE, David Kearns at Xerox, Sam Walton at Wal-Mart, and Bill Gates at Microsoft.

Effective leaders generate action. Leadership is action, not a position. One of the activities of leadership is creating energy through excitement (the pull or gain of what could be), urgency (the push to avoid the pain of poor performance), or some combination of both. This creates focus and harnesses the deep urge we all have to be part of something meaningful—to make a difference. We want to know that we are doing something worthwhile, that we are striving for a worthy goal (which may be to avert disaster). Effective leaders rally people throughout their organizations or teams as well as customers, suppliers, strategic partners, shareholders, and anyone else who can help around a cause. They transform jobs into crusades, exciting adventures, or deeper missions.

ORGANIZATION CULTURE AND CONTEXT: PEOPLE LEADERSHIP

When we are dealing with people, let us remember we are not dealing with creatures of logic. We are dealing with creatures of emotion, creatures bustling with prejudices and motivated by pride and vanity.
—Dale Carnegie

In most organizations, management has created a sterile and passionless culture. Strategies, budgets, and business plans are cold and lifeless. So teams and frontline performers go through the motions, put in their time, and go home. Technomanagers try to energize their people by using "leader speak" and imitating some of the things leaders do. They develop statements of vision, mission, values, "strategic purpose," and the like. However, improvement programs, such as reengineering, service/quality, empowerment, teams, or new technology, have no spirit. These programs may build up some speed and even get off the ground. But they never soar.

Morale and satisfaction levels in such technomanaged organizations have been on a long slide. I hear an increasing number of managers express their frustration with this growing energy crisis. The problem stems from the expanding gulf between rising expectations and the reality of the organization's traditional culture. *People want meaningful work in an organization with an exciting purpose.* What they get is a job. People hear senior management talk about empowerment, teamwork, and service. What they get are paternalistic pats on the head, motivation programs, and blame for not using the systems, processes, and technology dropped on them and their customers.

Too many managers are dispassionately trying to "do leadership" as if it were just another set of tools to be deployed ("I've done my vision thing"). But a team or organization's Focus and Context aren't techniques, statements, or approaches. They're much deeper than that. Focus and Context refer to feelings, causes, and convictions. They go to the very DNA of our being. You can't be dispassionate about passionate issues. Otherwise, while you do your "leadership thing," people on your team and in your organization will do their "commitment thing." So nothing is energized.

Caring for the Context

Organizations exist to enable ordinary people to do extraordinary things.
                                    —Ted Levitt, *Thinking About Management*

During a session reviewing and refining his organization's vision and values, a hospital CEO regretfully reflected on how he had been asked by the chairman why he was always out of his office and no longer available to take calls. The CEO was feeling guilty about that. He had been off giving another vision and values "stump speech" to a group going through a training program. He was getting increasingly frustrated that all those speeches and meetings with hospital staff weren't allowing him "to get his job done." As we talked about culture change, people leadership, and vision and values, he had an "Aha!" He came to realize that "caring for the context" was his job. Since then, the board has been educated on what the senior team is trying to do and he's talked to the chairman about how much more frequently he would now be out of his office. The CEO's redefinition of his role from operational manager to context leader has been one of the key factors in the strong success this hospital continues to have with its continuous quality improvement effort.

The more senior you are and the larger your organization, the more time you need to spend "caring for the context." One of the time-consuming aspects of Focus and Context leadership is developing *shared* vision, values, and purpose. Senior management can (and often should) start the process by taking a rough cut at establishing these. Decisions such as what business you're in belong to senior management. But if your organization's Focus and Context is to be widely owned by everyone who will draw from and give it meaning, then everyone needs to be involved in its development. That takes a lot of time and effort. It also redefines senior management's role. Senior managers spend less time managing the day-to-day business (isn't that what all their "empowered" people should be doing?) and more time caring for their organization's context.

Leadership Lost

Some people can think no deeper than a fact.
—Voltaire

Many successful companies are started by passionate zealots who have or develop a strong technical expertise matched only by their powerful vision and intense drive to succeed. This energy and excitement attracts like-minded people (team members, customers, partners, etc.) and fuels early growth. But because these companies aren't well balanced, their management systems and processes are often weak. So at some point in their development, either the financial struggle or the desire of the original owners to "cash out" triggers a sale, merger, or hiring of new senior managers.

Then the "professional managers" take over. Slowly, the spirit and vitality is squeezed out of the company. The sense of making a difference and being part of a cause is replaced with goals, objectives, and "the bottom line." Communications that once reported new customers, fledgling products developed on a shoestring, new market frontiers, and outstanding service delivered in extraordinarily tough circumstances are now filled with dry reports on progress in sales and profit goals, committee activities, strategies, budgeting, and business planning. It's uninspiring and lifeless. It turns people into their roles, systems, and processes. They become number crunchers, order processors, product producers, sales pushers, researchers, technical problem solvers, managers, and budgeters. Heart and soul is lost. Instead of being part of a cause that provides a paycheck, they're collecting a paycheck without a cause.

But many people aren't taking it any more. I've run into dozens of people in the last few years who have taken early retirement, gone back to school, started their own business, or turned down a bigger job assignment. They took a financial loss in order to make a deeper gain. Their personal net worth has been dramatically boosted by how they feel about the person staring out of the bathroom mirror each morning.

Many of these once exciting companies start as living, breathing (sometimes close to uncontrolled) organisms that, like a mysterious life form in a *Star Trek* episode, feed and grow on human energy (which they multiply and return). Much of that entrepreneurial energy comes from market and financial successes. Just the belief in that eventual success may be enough. But once the technomanagers take over, that once-living organism becomes a lifeless machine that feeds strictly on money. There is a vague sense that people and energy somehow help to create the money. But everybody is too busy looking for more money to pour into the increasingly demanding machine to bother checking out that fuzzy notion.

The intangible sense of spirit is even more critical in people-dependent service businesses. Having been in or close to the training and consulting field for more than 20 years, I've seen it mature and grow. Within this fast-evolving industry, many high-performing start-up firms have been acquired by or merged into larger technomanaged companies. As those spirited, organic firms become company machines, their founding spirit and best people slowly disappear. Because the training and consulting field has been in a high-growth mode since the early 1980s, these problems have been papered over with prosperity. Once the growth slows down and/or competition increases, many of these technomanaged companies with their hollowed-out souls will become mere shells of their former selves.

PERSONAL CONTEXT: SELF-LEADERSHIP

Without passion we're a mere latent force and possibility, like the flint which awaits the shock of the iron before it can give forth its spark.
—Henri-Frederic Amiel, nineteenth-century Swiss philosopher, famous for his journal *Intime*, "a masterpiece of self-analysis"

You can't impassion others about their work unless and until you're impassioned about yours. Creating leadership energy is an inside job. The spark that ignites the leadership energy you bring to your team or organization comes from within you. But you can't give energy if you don't have it. And it's hard to fake what you don't feel. That will cause you to resent your job and eventually the people associated with it. It also sends everyone's increasingly sensitive phoniness meter over the red line. All of this drains even more of your energy and makes your work truly work.

Have You Got Work, or Has Your Work Got You?

You are not here merely to make a living. You are here in order to enable the world to live more amply, with greater vision, with a finer spirit of hope and achievement. You are here to enrich the world, and you impoverish yourself if you forget the errand.

—Woodrow Wilson

If you're going to be an effective energy leader, then your work can't be work. You need a job that's not a job, but a joy. When you love what you're doing, you never have to go to work again. If I didn't love the personal and organization improvement field, I wouldn't study, note, and file hundreds of books and magazines each year. I wouldn't produce the dozens of columns and articles I've written. If it were truly work, you couldn't pay me enough to disrupt my family life and spend huge amounts of time on the fussy detail work involved in writing books. If I didn't love designing and delivering improvement workshops or speaking at meetings and conventions, traveling to and standing in front of yet another group would be true drudgery.

I am often asked how I develop the discipline to research, prepare, write, etc. What discipline? That's assuming I have to force myself to do this work. On the contrary, my problem is disciplining myself so that my work doesn't completely take over my life. That's because my work is highly aligned with my life purpose, vision, and values. So I am not working today; I am using this day to move one step closer to achieving a major part of my life's purpose.

You need to either find the work you love, or learn to love the work you have. Get passionate or get out. This is where many "wanna-be" leaders succumb to the victimitis virus. "How can I do my life's work when I am working flat out just to pay the bills now?" they sniffle. Well, if your current job isn't energizing you so that you can energize and lead others, you have four choices: (1) do nothing but wish for your fairy job mother to magically appear and straighten out your life, (2) get out of management so you stop dragging others down to your low energy level, (3) figure out what your personal vision, values, and purpose are and transform your current job into your life's work, (4) figure out what your ideal job is and go find or create it.

The good news is that you can find or create your ideal job. Career counselor Dick Bolles' multimillion-copy bestseller *What Color Is Your Parachute?* has been edited and updated numerous times since it was first published in 1970. I have found it very helpful in clarifying my life's work and identifying my ideal job. In another of his excellent career management books, *The Three Boxes of Life,* Bolles reports on his ongoing and extensive career research: "In the National Career Development Project, we have amassed a lot of evidence that . . . people of every imaginable background, age, sex, race, education, and skills can deliberately set about to find a job that gives them a sense of meaning and mission in life." The bad news is, if you haven't already done much thinking in this area, it takes a lot of hard, agonizing work to figure out where you want to go and why. Then the real time-consuming and most difficult effort is transforming yourself into that person you want to be, developing the skills you need, capitalizing on and creating your opportunities to move forward. I decided in 1976 that I wanted to be a professional speaker. I gave my first paid presentation (after hundreds of unpaid ones) in 1985 (I felt I had to earn the right to give advice to others and learn how to deliver it effectively first). With my first book, it took four years and about 1,400 hours of evening and weekend work to go from forming the concept to holding the completed book in my hands.

What's Your Career Path and Life Work?

The person who starts out going nowhere generally gets there.

Early in my management career I found that one of the keys to creating a high-energy culture was to align the vision, values, and purpose of each person on my team with the vision, values, and purpose of the team or the company. I then worked very hard (and lost more than a few nights' sleep) finding ways to match jobs that needed to be done or unexpected opportunities that arose to these well-grounded "people on the grow." This approach led to high-energy and performance along with very low turnover rates. People don't want to leave an organization that they're aligned with and attuned to while both are stretching, growing, and performing at ever higher levels.

This approach also meant I invested an extremely heavy amount of time in the hiring process. Candidates would go through repeat interviews, multiple meetings, and presentations to their potential teammates. Once it was clear that their skills and experiences were appropriate to the job (the résumé and first interview established that), the rest of this intense screening work was geared to understanding the candidate's personal vision, values, and life purpose. I was looking for career patterns and themes. In the last 20 years, I've interviewed or screened the résumés of well over 1,000 job candidates. Most of these people had no career theme or pattern. None. They answered career ads hoping that an ideal job would jump up and grab them. Questions about personal vision, values, and life purpose were answered with empty platitudes and vague generalities. They had spent more time planning their vacations than their lives.

BASIC FOCUS AND CONTEXT QUESTIONS

I respect those who know their own wishes. The greatest part of all the mischief in the world arises from the fact that many do not sufficiently understand their own aims. They have undertaken to build a tower, and spend no more labor on the foundation than would be necessary to erect a hut.

—Johann Wolfgang von Goethe

I've been involved in too many "vernacular engineering" debates where management teams argue about whether the statement they've been crafting is a vision or a mission, a statement of values and goals, or something else. Often these philosophical labeling debates are like trying to pick the fly specks out of the pepper. Unless you're a lexicographer and your company is in the dictionary business, don't worry about the precise definition of *vision, mission, values,* or whatever you may be calling the words you're using to define who you are and where you're trying to go.

What does matter is that you and your team have discussed, debated, and decided on the answers to these three questions (in no particular order): Where are you going (your vision or *picture* of your preferred future)? What do you believe in (your *principles* or values)? Why do you exist (your *purpose* or niche)? I call these the Three Ps—picture of preferred future, principles, and purpose. They are critically important questions. They're fundamental to leading yourself and others. This is the beginning point of effective leadership. These basic issues are the fabric with which you weave your Focus and Context. If you're attempting to change your team or organization culture, your answers to these basic questions define the culture you're trying to create.

If you're going to further improve your leadership effectiveness, you need to have thought through and answered these questions on your own. If you have a spouse or life partner, you need to work on these questions together.

What you and your team call your answers to these questions doesn't matter. They can be termed *vision, mission, values, strategic niche, aspirations, purpose,* and so on. And how snazzy, different, or original your words are doesn't matter much either. What does matter is whether you can give a unified answer to the three P questions. Is whatever you've developed clear and compelling? If you're a management team—and especially if you're a senior management team—does everyone on your team passionately own what you've developed? Do you give these critical leadership issues a sharp focus and meaningful context for everyone? That can be done only through skilled, live communications and consistent management behavior.

The next three chapters will deal with the what, why, and how of each one of these questions. I will guide you through the personal and team/organization applications of these fundamental leadership issues. There are no right answers to these questions. No consultant, expert, or anyone else can answer them for you. And there is no one way to answer them. Each of us has an individual, personal style and approach. However, I'll provide as many options, ideas, alternatives, and pathways and pitfalls as I can cram into a limited space.

I was in Washington, D.C., speaking at a quality improvement conference a few years ago. Following my presentation, I had the pleasure of hearing Bill Pollard, chairman of the hugely successful ServiceMaster Company, speak about the management principles and practices that took his organization to more than $3 billion in sales in a few decades. In his address he stressed the importance of clarifying and living the issues that were introduced in this chapter. He began by describing a message he'd encountered on someone's answering machine: "This is not an answering machine; it's a questioning machine. There are really only two questions in life: Who are you? and What do you want? Please leave your answer at the tone."

CHAPTER 7

Picturing Your Preferred Future

Soon after the completion of Disney World someone said, "Isn't it too bad Walt Disney didn't live to see this?" I replied, "He did see it—that's why it's here."
—Mike Vance, creative director, Walt Disney Studios

This is where my personal effectiveness quest began—in 1974 when I was just starting my straight commission Culligan sales job. Someone recommended I read Claude Bristol's book *TNT: The Power Within You.* The book sparked such an intensity of energy, excitement, and profound new awareness that I couldn't get a good night's sleep for almost a week. Even now, as I thumb through the book and recall that turning point in my life, a shiver runs up my spine.

Published in 1954, *TNT* was Claude Bristol's second book (his first—which I read later—was *The Magic of Believing*). Both books were based on his decades of searching for a deeper understanding of, and applying, what he called "mind stuff." This work came from his experience as a journalist studying and reporting on the full spectrum of spiritual and religious movements (especially fringe groups), building his own wealth and career as an investment banker, and studying thousands of books on "the science of thought."

Here are just a few of the key ideas from TNT that started my self-leadership juices flowing:

Picture the force! It is the explosive force of a mental picture of what you want in life, given by you to your subconscious, touched off by faith in yourself and faith in God. Whatever you picture, within reason, can come true in your life *if* you have sufficient faith in the power within! That's your TNT—a mental picture of what you want and the faith that you can and will get it! . . . we do not think in words. We think in pictures! The universal language is *feeling* . . . this creative

71

power operates like a magnet. Give it a strong, clear picture of what you want and this creative power starts to work magnetizing conditions about you—attracting to you the things, resources, opportunities, circumstances and even the people you need, to help bring to pass in your outer life what you have pictured! . . . what you picture in your mind, if you picture it clearly and confidently and persistently enough, will eventually come to pass in your life! . . . there is a universal law in the mental realm, "like attracts like."

TNT awakened me to the enormous power between my ears that I wasn't using. I began reading many books, and *Success Unlimited* (now called *Success*) magazine articles on these topics, and I attended presentations and workshops given by many of the leading authors, trainers, and speakers. I bought dozens of audiotapes on this and related "mental attitude" topics. Among the strongest early influences were Zig Ziglar's audiotapes and book *See You at the Top.* In his book he wrote about the importance of "seeing the reaching." He went on to state, "The world has a way, not only of stepping aside for men or women who know where they are going, but it often joins and helps them reach their objective." Over the next few years I used these approaches to build a highly successful sales and management career, quit smoking and biting my fingernails, lose weight and get into better physical shape, develop my writing and speaking skills, and help build Achieve into a very successful training and consulting firm. I even changed from being a "sickly kid" (I would miss weeks of school each year) to not missing a single work day because of sickness for a period of 19 years (I blew my record with a number of ailments, unprecedented depression, and "sick days" in 1993 when the picture of my career future was the foggiest it had ever been).

THE POWER OF OUR PICTURES

You merely picture in your mind having already accomplished or attained your goal, whatever it may be. Hold it firmly in your thoughts, picture it as already being yours, and amazing things will happen.
—Og Mandino, *The Choice*

I've been studying and trying to apply the power of positive pictures for over two decades now. These skills, habits, and techniques are often called visioning, imagery, and visualization. And they have a power for change, improvement, and energy creation that we're only beginning to understand. Here's a small sample of the research and examples I've collected over the years:

- A railroad worker was repairing a refrigerated boxcar when he was accidentally locked inside it. Once he discovered that, he called frantically for help. No one heard him. He finally lay down on the boxcar floor to freeze to death. Five hours later the man's dead body was discovered. But the refrigeration unit was broken and there was plenty of air to breathe.

- I have files and books full of examples of the sickly, deadly, or healthful relationship between our thoughts and pictures of our health and our bodies. Edward Shorter's book *From Paralysis to Fatigue: A History of Psychosomatic Illness in the Modern Era* is full of examples of past and current "fashionable" diseases and sicknesses that are caused by the unconscious mind. In the last few years a new medical field has developed with the tongue-twisting name of psychoneuroimmunology. This is the study of the dynamic links among the mind, brain, and endocrine and immune systems. Surgeon Bernie Siegel has practiced, taught, and written about many of these principles since he began a specialized therapy in 1978 called Exceptional Cancer Patients. In his book *Love, Medicine, and Miracles,* he writes, "Exceptional patients refuse to be victims. . . . One of the best ways to make things happen is to predict it. Pooh-poohed for some twenty years by the medical establishment, the placebo effect—the fact that about one-fourth to one-third of patients will show improvement if they merely *believe* that they are taking an effective medicine even if the pill they are taking has no active ingredient—has now been accepted as genuine by most of the profession. . . . I therefore use two major tools to change the body—emotions and imagery. . . . Our emotions and words let the body know what we expect of it, and by visualizing certain changes we can help the body bring them about. . . . There are no incurable diseases, only incurable people."

- Charles Garfield's two books (*Peak Performance* and *Peak Performers*) reporting on his long-term study of peak performers are full of studies and examples of what he often calls "mental rehearsal." He concludes, "Peak performers, particularly in business, sports, and the arts, report a highly developed ability to imprint images of successful actions in the mind."
- A study on the effects of visualization headed by Robert Jarn of the Princeton Engineering Anomalies Research (PEAR) group (and dean emeritus of the university's engineering school) found that people could measurably influence and increase the number of heads thrown by a coin-tossing device.

Powerful Pictures Produce Passion and Persistence

Imagery may be the highest form of mental energy we have. Reason can analyze and organize, but only the imagination can create. It is through our imagination that we create the future—ours and the world's.

—Emile Coue, early-twentieth-century
French chemist and psychotherapist

Visioning creates passion. The clearer and more compelling the vision, the stronger the passion. And the clearer the vision, the more likely we are to hang in there during the inevitable downs, discouragements, and defeats encountered as we reach for our dreams. Visioning or picturing my preferred future has been my greatest source of energy and focus. I've used this approach for specific situations, long-term projects, and making vital life choices and decisions. Here are some examples:

- Early in my sales career, I would pull myself together for a sales call by sitting in my car outside the house of the prospective customer I was calling on that evening and taking a few minutes to visualize a successful outcome. With the prospective customer's name at the top of an order form, I would see a hand signing the contract. Later I guided other salespeople I was accompanying and training through the same exercise as we prepared for the sales call together.

- When I began to give paid keynote speeches and presentations, I would review a list I kept of past speeches and presentations where I especially connected and was "in flow with the audience." I would relive and recapture the feeling of mastery and emotional electricity I felt in those rooms. I would then carry these feelings into meditation on my goals for this group and see myself delivering a highly successful "in flow" presentation to them.

- After a few unsuccessful tries, I used visualization to give up smoking for good in 1979. I stopped drinking coffee because it stimulated my urge for nicotine. I made up a list of every benefit I could possibly think of for not smoking. I developed a few short scenes in my head of situations where I was offered a cigarette or friends asked me about my smoking. Rather than saying "I am *trying* to quit," I practiced out loud and then drilled into each scene the words "No, thanks. I am a nonsmoker" or "I don't smoke." Whenever the urge for a cigarette would strike, I took deep breaths, repeated my list of nonsmoking benefits, and ran through those scenes in my mind. Because I was an internal sales and management trainer at the time, I used what I was doing as an example of visualization and self-discipline for every group and person I worked with in the company. Had I gone back to smoking, I would have had to find a new job, because my credibility would have been shot.

- Some days writing is a breeze. Other days it's about as much fun as having my head squeezed in a vise. But writing schedules hang overhead, and deadlines loom. What sustains me through those hard and long (often 14-hour) days and sunny summer weekends spent in my office is my vision of reviewing that completed chapter. Or I see the pride I can take in a successful section. Other times I picture that special day when the manuscript is sent off to the publisher. Or I see that magic moment when I hold the finished book in my hands, smell the fresh paper and ink, and see my hard-crafted work in print. Sometimes I have imaginary conversations with readers who tell me how much this book has helped them.

Or I reflect on the impact of past books and then project forward to the organizations and leaders who'll buy hundreds of copies of the book and successfully use it as a blueprint for their transformation and improvement. Other times, when writing seems like a painful punishment, I daydream about the fun of being an author on a media tour talking about the book.

- During my personal visioning sessions in 1989, I wrote a series of notes (titled "The Universe Is Unfolding as It Should") describing my ideal future in speaking, writing, and leading executive retreats. Half a page was devoted to describing a column I would write for Canada's national newspaper, *The Globe & Mail.* (Three years earlier I had begun a file of column ideas, wrote a few sample columns, and sent them along with a proposal to ten of Canada's major newspapers and business magazines. No one responded and my follow-up phone calls went unanswered.) In 1992, Gord Pitts, the editor of the *Globe*'s new weekly "Change Page," called me "out of the blue" to arrange lunch and convince me to become a columnist.

- My old dog-eared personal visioning file is full of all my career dreaming, periodic assessments of strengths and accomplishments, personal affirmations, personal mission/purpose statements, inspirational quotes on note cards, and numerous visioning notes of the past two decades. It also contains the notes from the yearly (around New Year's Day) visioning and progress reviews Heather and I began to undertake in 1985 when we were drifting apart and seemed to be heading down separate paths. Using a five-year time horizon, these notes describe our ideal life in seven areas: family, home (house), careers, financial assets and income, community involvement, spiritual life, and social life.

It's eerie (and now inspiring) to look back at all these notes. Their accuracy in "foretelling the future" is about 90 percent. Never mind all the research, studies, and expert opinion on imagery, visualization, and visioning. Here's all the proof I need that regularly and continually picturing your preferred future works.

What We Are Is What We See

> *See yourself and what you see you will become.*
> —Aristotle

It's hard to picture a positive, hopeful future if we're not positive and confident about ourselves. It's hard to see ourselves taking control of our destiny, developing an effective team, or leading a highly successful organization if we don't feel good about our own development, success, and skills.

Our self-vision or picture of ourselves is a major factor in our self-image. Years ago I heard Earl Nightingale, the radio commentator and personal effectiveness speaker, say "We become what we think about most." (Luckily I didn't hear this earlier in my life or I would have been a girl by the time I was seventeen!) What we think about and how we picture ourselves shows up in what we say about ourselves. Too often we excuse our performance or don't even bother trying because "I am not a speaker," "I am not a morning person," "I am disorganized," "I am not creative," "I am always late," "I am no good at paperwork," "I am not athletic," I am _____, _____ (add your own). These statements are the first step in a self-defeating cycle. The belief statement leads to a feeble attempt. That feeble attempt leads to poor results or failure. That in turn reinforces the original belief statement ("See! I told you I was no good at _____").

It would be more accurate to say "I've chosen to be disorganized," "I don't want to be creative," or "I don't think effective speaking is worth the effort." *If we want to change our personal output, we need to change the input.* Much of the rest of this book is devoted to the many steps and options of personal (as well as team and organization) improvement. An important element in making these personal effectiveness efforts work is changing your personal pictures and self-talk. You aren't destined to have or be stuck with any personal habits or characteristics. The ones you have, you've chosen to have. Until you see your choices and change your self-vision, you will never become the high-performance leader you want to or could be.

BALANCING GOALS AND VISION

We all live under the same sky, but we don't all have the same horizon.
—Konrad Adenauer, first chancellor of postwar West Germany

Like mission and vision statements and values, goal setting and visioning labels often get confused and used interchangeably. Generally that doesn't matter. As long as you and the people on your team and in your organization are clear and consistent with their meanings and approaches, don't get hung up on definitions and jargon.

But many people really are confused about the conflicting and complementary aspects of visions and goals. *Goals are management issues.* They deal with rational analysis, planning, measurement, and discipline. *Visions are leadership issues.* They deal with feelings, energy, ideas, and fantasy. These are not either/or choices—both are needed. These are and/also paradoxes to be balanced.

The chart summarizes the key differences between goals and visions. We'll take a deeper look at goal setting in Chapter 13. Goals follow out of the Focus and Context of visions. They are shorter term steps toward your longer term vision. Especially in today's fast-changing world, most detailed strategies or sets of plans aren't effective beyond 12 to 18 months. Effective visions define what you want you, your team, or your organization to

Differences Between Goals and Visions

Goals	Visions
Rational—use your head	Emotional—engage your heart
Mind	Spirit
What is wanted	What could be
Measurable objectives	Sense of direction
Detailed strategies and plans	Picture of preferred future—opportunistic
Focus	Purpose
Set priorities	Create energy

look like in about 5 years or more. To set goals is to be reasonable. To hold a vision is to be bold.

TEAM AND ORGANIZATION VISIONING

> *All of the leaders to whom we spoke seemed to have been masters at selecting, synthesizing, and articulating an appropriate vision of the future. Later we were to learn that this was a common quality of leaders down through the ages.*
>
> —Warren Bennis and Burt Nanus,
> *Leaders: The Strategies for Taking Charge*

Your ability to develop an energizing Focus and Context for your team or organization will determine whether you'll be a true (and effective) leader or just a technomanager, technician or technical expert, supervisor, project manager, administrator, or bureaucrat. *At the heart of caring for context and focusing yourself and others is your ability to develop and communicate a clear and compelling picture of your preferred future.*

Within two months of joining forces in 1981, Art McNeil and I developed the first of many visions for Achieve. It became a yearly ritual for us and, later, our team of Achievers to review and revise our vision (and values) and then set that year's strategies, goals, plans, and budgets. Starting with Tom Peters' Toward Excellence program in 1983, we went on to help hundreds of management teams (some much more successfully than others) in many countries establish their Focus and Context and then put together implementation strategies and build the leadership skills that brought it all to life. A powerful organization vision will:

- Create organizational energy and enthusiasm for change and improvement
- Provide an overarching "big picture" direction, focus, and passion to strategies, budgets, plans, systems, processes, and technological change
- Focus and build teams much more effectively than wilderness experiences, simulations, or group exercises (most "team building" activities are done in a vacuum and don't work)

- Counterbalance the pain, suffering, and helplessness that downsizing, disaster, or other such depressing activities usually bring
- Vaccinate people against the victimitis virus and pessimism plague by giving them a sense of hopefulness and self-determination
- Set up a "magnetic force" that will attract the people and "lucky breaks" needed to move toward the vision
- Repel those people who don't want to be any part of anything so "unrealistic," "fanciful," "stupid," etc.
- Boost "psychic pay" so that everyone feels like a winner who is part of an organization that's going somewhere exciting

Visioning and Strategic Planning

> Cynic, n., a blackguard whose faulty vision sees things as they are, not as they ought to be.
>
> —Ambrose Bierce, nineteenth-century American journalist and satirist

Strategic planning can be deadly. When taken too seriously, it leads to rigidity, obsessiveness with controls, and bureaucracy. Effective leaders manage the discipline of narrower, short-term goals and also the possibilities of opportunistic, longer term visions of their preferred future. Harvard Business School's Daniel Isenberg outlined this difficult balance extremely well in his article "The Tactics of Strategic Opportunism." He defines strategic opportunism as "the ability to remain focused on long-term objectives (or vision) while staying flexible enough to solve day-to-day problems and recognize new opportunities." It's an important paradox to manage. Most technomanagers miss new market, product, or other business opportunities because many can't be predicted or planned for. These usually evolve from accumulated experiences, informal feedback, "Band-Aid solutions," experimentation, "clumsy tries," and incremental learning. But if it's not in the strategic plan and hasn't been budgeted for, technomanagers let the opportunities slip by.

Henry Mintzberg of McGill University has written a number of outstanding articles and books on "crafting strategy" and management effectiveness. Although it's academic and not an easy read, his book *The Rise and Fall of Strategic Planning* is a must-read for anyone responsible for strategy formulation and planning. In it, he cites the growing body of research showing that strategic planning doesn't help most organizations become more effective, especially in today's fast-moving world. In a section titled "Strategic Vision and Strategic Learning," he writes, "the visionary approach is a more flexible way to deal with an uncertain world. Vision sets the broad outlines of strategy, while leaving the specific deals to be worked out . . . so when the unexpected happens, assuming the vision is sufficiently robust, the organization can adapt—it learns . . . thus, changes that appear turbulent to organizations that rely heavily on planning may appear normal to, even welcomed by, those who prefer more of a visionary or learning approach . . . *if you have no vision but only formal plans, then every unpredicted change in the environment makes you feel like your sky is falling*" [my emphasis].

Strategic opportunism, experimentation, stumbling into new markets and products, and organizational learning is a critical element of organization effectiveness that's overlooked in most improvement processes. That's why I've devoted Chapters 11 and 12 to this important leadership topic.

PATHWAYS AND PITFALLS

Imagination is the beginning of creation. You imagine what you desire, you will what you imagine, and at last you create what you will.

—George Bernard Shaw

Visioning is sometimes an innate natural skill just as leadership sometimes is. And the moon sometimes blocks out the sun—but not very often. Most people have had to consciously and with great effort continually work to strengthen their visioning. *Visionary leaders are seldom born that way.* Nor are they necessarily charismatic. They have had to work at making visioning habitual.

Organizational

> *The only way to lead people is to show them a future. A leader is a dealer in hope.*
>
> —Napoleon Bonaparte

- Here's a process I've used many times to develop a team vision: (1) The group hears a presenter, watches a video, and/or reads inspiring material defining a vision and differentiating it from goal setting. (2) A facilitator guides each person through a visioning exercise imagining the ideal team or organization in five years or more. (3) Group members describe their vision to the rest of the group (if the group is larger than eight people, break into subgroups of six to eight). No agreement or disagreement discussions are allowed. (4) After each person has been heard, the group discusses and summarizes the common themes or images. (5) The group sets action plans for further refining of the vision and communicating to or involving the rest of the organization in a visioning process.

- You and your team need to picture and describe your preferred future as vividly as possible. One approach is to imagine that it's five years from today and you're being interviewed by a leading journalist on the phenomenal success your company or team has had. Describe the results you've achieved and perhaps the approach you've used. Speak in the present tense as if it's all happening around you right now. Another approach is to pretend you have a time machine and you've traveled ahead about five years from now to look and listen in on the incredible success your improvement initiative has had. You will then travel back to today and report to your team what you saw, heard, touched, tasted, smelled, and felt. What were your highly loyal customers saying about your team or organization? How were the passionate people throughout your organization talking and acting? How about suppliers? Shareholders? Other external or internal partners?

- Too many managers try to delegate "the vision thing" to a committee. It doesn't work. If you're a senior manager, caring for the context and providing organization focus isn't just part of your job, it is your job.

- Unless you're an exceptionally clear and inspiring writer, be very careful about drafting a "vision statement" and using that as your communications centerpiece. Visions are about feelings, beliefs, emotions, and pictures. It's very hard to bring those across on paper (especially if the statement is developed by a committee). Vision ideas or summaries can, and should be, committed to paper and widely circulated—but as a "leave behind," follow-up, or reminder. Visions are most compelling when they are delivered in person by a leader who's an effective communicator. *Powerful personal communication skills and energizing leadership are inseparable.* Learn how to use "impassioned logic" by adding metaphors, stories, models, or examples to help everyone "see the big picture" and rouse their emotions to make it happen.

- Your team or organization needs a shared vision, not something that only a few people own. You need to make everyone a "spiritual stakeholder." That's usually a cascading process, but it can start in any part of an organization. Ideally, the senior management team defines the broad parameters of what business you're in and which direction you're heading. They can prepare a rough vision for input and refinement or leave things wide open for the rest of the organization to fill in. I prefer the first approach; senior management's role is to make those broad decisions and provide directional leadership. In what can be a long series of meetings in a large organization, everyone is brought together to hear a (passionate) presentation by a senior manager on the organization's current threats and opportunities and a positive, hopeful picture of how the organization or team will deal with those. Each group is then led through a series of exercises to give feedback or input to the vision. But generally the main focus is on developing the individual team's vision so that it links into the larger one. Each group then moves on to identify boosters and barriers to realizing the vision, determine improvements and changes needed, and set action plans.

- Vision is the critical focal point and beginning to high performance. But a vision alone won't make it happen. Unless the hard work of striving, building, and improving follows, even the most vibrant vision will remain only a dream.
- Invoke pride, stretch everyone's thinking, and stir the will-to-win emotions. Shoot to shake up the industry or change the rules of the game. Become the fastest, strongest, highest-quality, most innovative—the best—at something.

Personal

> *If one advances confidently in the direction of his dreams, and endeavors to live the life which he has imagined, he will meet with a success unexpected in common hours.*
>
> —Henry David Thoreau

- Stay away from people infected with the victimitis virus or the pessimism plague. Both are highly contagious and deadly to your future.
- At least once a year, spend a quiet evening of uninterrupted time "daydreaming" with your spouse or life partner. Take turns fantasizing, seeing, and describing an ideal life together while the other person takes notes. Look at family, house or home, your careers, your physical health, your financial health, community involvement, spiritual growth, and social life. Now you'll need to start setting goals and improvement plans to turn your fantasies into reality. We'll cover these important next steps directly in Chapters 13 and 14 (and indirectly in chapters following those two).
- To find the core of your deepest and truest inner desires and vision, you may need to keep a running "dream list" for a while. Record every dream, desire, or goal that pops into your mind. Once the list is complete and exhaustive, start sifting through it to look for patterns or clusters. Begin to group and assign priorities to your dreams until they're narrowed down to a manageable number. You've now uncovered your personal source of energy and passion. The next

step is unleashing that incredible power through visualization or imagery.

- Imagery is what "emotionalizes" and energizes a vision. It's
  a vitally important leadership skill. We seem to have a natural ability to imagine what we don't want and then bring it
  into being. Reversing years of negative conditioning and bad
  habits so we can learn to vividly see what we do want isn't
  easy. You'll have to work very hard at it. Since we're all different, there is no universal "one approach fits all" way to
  increase your picturing power. Here are a few ideas or keys
  that may help you develop this critical skill:

  - Do your imagery in a quiet relaxed place at your peak time
    of day (for me, that's early morning just after vigorous ex-
    ercise and a shower). Focus on your breathing, close your
    eyes, and watch your thoughts on a big movie screen at the
    front of your head.

  - Try this practice exercise—count the windows in your
    home by mentally walking through all the rooms. Now try
    it in the house you grew up in. Recall the distinct smells of
    each room. Feel the carpet or floor on your bare feet. Hear
    the happy sounds of others in the house. Taste your fa-
    vorite meal awaiting you in the kitchen.

  - Focus on an aspect or area of your preferred future.
    You've been wildly successful. Explore your success. Hear
    those ideal conversations. See the perfect setting or physi-
    cal elements. Smell the air. Taste the food or champagne.
    Feel the presence or touch of others or the material mani-
    festation of your dream. Savor the scene. Wallow in it.
    Enjoy it.

  - Try tape recording your descriptions of your vision. Play it
    back and use it to make notes. Continue taping your vi-
    sioning sessions until you've intensified the emotions and
    sharpened the clarity of the scenes you're describing to
    such a degree that listening to them sends shivers of ex-
    citement up and down your spine.

  - See the Appendix of Bernie Siegel's book *Love, Medicine,
    and Miracles* for his suggestions and other reference
    sources on relaxation, imagery, and visualization.

- Develop a number of personal affirmations. Napoleon Hill's best-selling classic *Think and Grow Rich* is based on 20 years of research on hundreds of highly successful business and political leaders. He found that "auto suggestion" or "self-suggestion" was a key to the success of the giants he studied. Today they're often called "affirmations." Whatever you call them, they are the messages you give yourself every day about you and your abilities. If your personal (and team or organization) visioning is going to be successful, you need to be reinforcing the qualities or characteristics you'll need to make it happen.

  Affirmations are very personal and specific to the visions they support. Here are a few of the ones I've used over the years: "I am a confident, compelling, and convincing speaker," "I love jogging and staying fit" (I hated it at the time), "We (Achieve) are flush with cash" (during a dark financial time), "I am a patient and loving father," and "Success is rolling in." Effective affirmations involve "lying" to your subconscious mind and convincing your deeper inner self that what you desire or want to be has already happened. Affirmations keep you focused and true to your aim. They help "magnetize" you and your vision.

  Put key affirmations tied to your vision in your day planner, on your desk, in your car, on your bathroom mirror—wherever you'll notice and repeat them. Move them around so you don't get used to seeing them and look past them. Supplement them with inspirational quotations on the theme or picture you're projecting.
- Develop the habit of picturing your preferred future and using your supporting affirmations every day. In *TNT*, Claude Bristol writes, "Whatever you need to fit into the pattern of achievement that you have pictured will be attracted to you by the power within if you persist in your visualizing, day after day, and put forth every effort in support of your heartfelt desire."
- Build your confidence and reinforce your vision by keeping a private "blessings and brag list." It should contain every accomplishment, strength, or success you've ever had along with all the blessings you've enjoyed—no matter how small.

Keep adding to it. Review it frequently, but especially when you're doubting or down on yourself. In *Living With Joy,* Sanaya Roman writes, "Whatever you appreciate and give thanks for will increase in your life."

- If your job drains energy and you can't get passionate about it, you'll never be an energizing leader. Invest the time and effort in visualizing your ideal job. You may even find that making changes in your current job will give you a dramatic energy boost. Richard Bolles's book *What Color Is Your Parachute?* has an exceptionally useful Appendix called "How to Create a Picture of Your Ideal Job or Next Career." It's an extensive step-by-step workbook exercise that I, and others I've recommended it to, have found extremely useful.

- Be very careful about whom you share your personal visions with. These are tender young ideas and fantasies. Many of your friends, family, or associates carry the pessimism plague. They can put together lots of convincing reasons that you've "lost it" or "you're dreaming in Technicolor" (it's always much easier to argue against, rather than for, a big stretch vision). *Share your vision only with people who truly want to see you succeed and will encourage you or help you get there.* However, share, broadcast, brag on, take bets toward, or otherwise publicly declare your improvement goals. That paints you into a corner. Your pride will push you to keep going toward that goal when you've got to pull yourself out of bed early, pass on the dessert, or practice those new skills.

Picturing your destination is a key source of energy as you blaze your pathway to higher performance. That picture is colored, framed, and supported by your principles.

CHAPTER **8**

Principles

Principles are to people what roots are to trees. Without roots, trees fall when they are thrashed with the winds of the pampas. Without principles, people fall when they are shaken by the gales of existence.
—Carlos Reyles, nineteenth-century Spanish author

When he spotted his grandpa asleep on the family room couch, the rambunctious 10-year-old saw his chance. With catlike stealth, Jason quietly crept up on Grandpa and gently smeared a small bit of smelly old cheese into his moustache. As Grandpa mumbled and stirred, Jason bolted from the room. Peeking around the corner, Jason fought hard to contain himself as he watched Grandpa open his eyes and take a sniff of the air. "Whew! This room stinks," Grandpa exclaimed. Rising from the couch, he went into the front hall. "Why, the whole house stinks," Grandpa declared, as he went out the front door into the yard. Watching Grandpa take a few deep whiffs of the air, Jason lost it. He burst out laughing as Grandpa bellowed, "Everything stinks."

Our principles, values, or beliefs are the lenses through which we see the world. We then find the evidence and examples to prove our point of view. If your behavior sometimes smells a little—you cheat, cut ethical corners, or "stretch the truth"—you assume (and often justify your behavior with) "everybody else is doing it." Then you notice just how many other people are doing the same—their behavior stinks. When you become a manager, you build on your assumptions and experiences by putting rules and practices in place to catch the "stinkers." As psychologist and personal effectiveness coach Peter Jensen puts it, "Most of what we see in others is what we project from ourselves."

PRINCIPLES SHAPE OUR CHARACTER AND CULTURE

Visions are values projected into the future.
—Leland Kaiser, futurist

Each one of us, as well as every organization and team, has a set of principles, beliefs, or values, which, whether optimistic or pessimistic or filled with hopefulness or helplessness, "magnetizes" and pulls toward us people and circumstances that share the same principles, beliefs, and values. What we get is what we are.

Visions and values are an inseparable matched set. One grows from and in turn spawns the other. Both provide the basis for the skills we choose to develop, time we choose to invest, and the improvement systems, processes, and habits we choose to use. Yesterday's vision and values have formed our personal character and—when taken collectively—the team or organization culture we have today. The vision and values we choose to fix in our minds today determine tomorrow's character and culture. We start to change who we're becoming and where we're headed when we change what we value and picture in our future.

Our Values Hierarchy

Don't part with your illusions. When they are gone, you may still exist, but you have ceased to live.
—Mark Twain

Our values are what we value. Each of us has a hierarchy of values, our sense of what's most important to what's least important. Our values hierarchy is a lengthy one. It includes things like health, family, security, wealth, cooperation, competitiveness, meaningful work, peace of mind, making a difference, friendships, innovation, status, happiness, freedom, adventure, spirituality, power, accomplishment, wisdom, love, creativity, integrity, participation, service, loyalty, pride, progress, teamwork, growth and development, helping others, physical or sensory pleasures, quality, order, control, respect, self-image, and the like.

Our values hierarchy sets our priorities. It determines where we spend our time. For example, do we choose to watch TV or invest that time in personal improvement? Do we sleep longer or go jogging? Do we spend time with our family or take on that extra project with heavy out-of-town travel? Do we take personal glory or share the recognition with our team? Do we trade up to that larger house now or invest that extra money to reap compounded financial rewards later? Who gets invited to important meetings? Which items get highest priority on the agenda? How much time is spent with customers and those doing the serving? These are important questions because we invest our time in those areas we value most.

Our values can conflict with one another. They create many and/also paradoxes to be balanced and managed. For example, business success and family time are both high on my values hierarchy. One evening when our son Chris was about two and a half years old, I was heading out the door on another trip. Chris turned in his high chair, focused his big blue eyes up at me, and asked, "Are you going home now, Daddy?" (About six months later I called Heather from my hotel room. Chris answered the phone and asked, "Are you my real daddy?" If Heather and I didn't have such a close and trusting relationship, I might begin to wonder. . . .)

The conflict between my business and family has been my biggest values conflict. Both are important to me. But I was drifting toward becoming a business success and a family failure. Unless I changed, I would become "Uncle Dad" and Heather would be a single mother with a part-time husband dropping in occasionally. To change that, I put a "personal travel policy" in place that said I wouldn't be away from home on Friday, Saturday, or Sunday night. I would also keep trips to no more than three nights away at one time. Over the years I have missed out on speaking, workshop, and consulting business using this approach. At times I haven't looked very responsive or accommodating to important customers (another key value). But that travel policy change and moving my office into our house improved our family time. And my business has prospered.

THE POWER OF CLEAR PRINCIPLES

If the "Know Thyself" of the oracle were an easy thing, it would not be held to be a divine injunction.

—Plutarch

Effectively using values to care for the context and provide focus to organization, team, or personal improvement has two major steps: (1) clarifying and assigning priorities to your personal and team or organization's shared values and (2) living and behaving according to your aspirations. Both can be very difficult leadership acts.

Clarifying Your Personal Principles

The way to gain a reputation is to endeavor to be what you desire to appear.

—Socrates

A key element of "knowing thyself" is sorting out what's really important to you. Without a clear sense of your personal principles and priorities, it's almost impossible to bring the picture of your preferred future sharply into focus. Through study, meditation, contemplation, talking with close and trusted friends, consulting with your spouse, keeping a journal, taking a personal development workshop, or whatever works for you, *develop a written list of your four to five top principles.* I've also found it's well worth it to agonize over writing a paragraph to a page for each value. That will force you to further sharpen and clarify your thinking.

Investing the time and effort to uncover and articulate your personal principles has many important benefits.

- You'll have a strong foundation to build your leadership upon. James Kouzes' and Barry Posner's study of credible and effective leaders led them to conclude, "Values are directly relevant to credibility. To do what we say we will do (our respondents' behavioral definition of credibility) we must know what we want to do and how we wish to behave. That's what our values help us to define."

- Clear personal principles give you a much stronger sense of your personal "bottom line." Knowing where you stand clarifies what you won't sit still for. As former CEO and chairman of J. C. Penney Company Donald Seibert explains in *The Ethical Executive,* this is another key characteristic of an effective leader: "Among the people I know at the top of the nation's major corporations, the personal quality that is regarded most highly is integrity."
- It's easier (but not always easy) to make choices involving conflicting opportunities, where to invest your time, what behavior is most appropriate, and where you need to concentrate your personal improvement efforts.
- You'll be much closer to finding your personal energy source and developing that critical leadership passion.
- Your self-identity, self-confidence, and sense of security will be strengthened.
- Along with your picture and purpose (discussed in the next chapter), your principles will provide the stable and solid core you need if you're going to transform rapid changes descending on all of us into exciting opportunities, rather than a terrifying threat.
- You can more clearly see to what extent your personal values are aligned with your team and organization values.

Clarifying Core Team or Organizational Values

> *Baldwin occasionally stumbles over the truth, but he always hastily picks himself up and hurries on as if nothing had happened.*
> —Winston Churchill

A number of studies have shown over the years that companies with "high standards of ethical behavior," "shared values," or "social conscience" have much higher than average performance.

That's because when a team or organization identifies and lives its core values:

- There's a sharp focal point and context for culture change or renewal.
- Values shape organization structure, define the use of power, and determine the degree of participation, shared leadership, or autonomy of teams.
- Teams are strengthened and collaboration is improved. James Kouzes and Barry Posner found that "leaders who establish cooperative relationships inspire commitment and are considered competent. Their credibility is enhanced by building community through common purpose and by championing shared values. In contrast, competitive and independent leaders are seen as both obstructive and ineffective."
- Managers are less likely to contradict one other and confuse people in their organizations. Management teams can "sing from the same sheet of music" in caring for the organization's context and focusing everyone on the improvements that really matter.
- Everyone makes more consistent choices according to a shared hierarchy of values.
- There's a deeper source of spirit and passion to draw from during continual change and constant improvement.
- People feel less helpless and more hopeful, even if the organization has been having performance problems. They feel they can better predict and influence what happens to them, their teams, and the organization.
- People spend less time playing political games and guessing what the "real reasons" are for management's actions. Everyone knows what to expect from one another and what behavior is and isn't acceptable.
- Trust, toleration, and forgiveness levels increase.
- Morale, pride, and team identity are enhanced.
- People in the organization are either excited or repelled by the alignment with their own principles and beliefs. They reinforce the values by supporting them, or else they leave.
- Hiring, promotion, reward and recognition, performance management, measurement and feedback, and skill development decisions and priorities are much clearer and more consistent.

- Customers, suppliers, and other external partners know what to expect.
- Rules and policies can be reduced and changed to treat people as responsible adults.

LIVING YOUR VALUES:
THE RHETORIC-REALITY GAP

The values gap is the largest single source of cynicism and skepticism in the workplace today.

—Andrall Pearson, former president of PepsiCo

Well-grounded, shared values that are alive and thriving in teams and organizations can do all that I've listed and more. Now here's the big BUT. Most organizations, management teams, and managers never bridge the major gulf between what they say and what they do. Because they confuse their intended behavior with their actual behavior, they don't recognize their own rhetoric-reality gulf. Sometimes they point to the declining work ethic as a reason for the inconsistent behavior on their team or in their organization. But that's a cop-out. The desire for doing meaningful work, being part of a winning team, and making a difference in our jobs has been on a steady increase throughout the Western world. If you feel that "people don't want to work any more," take a deep look in your management mirror. Maybe they just don't want to work with you.

Recognizing the need to become more "values-driven," many managers have developed statements of "core values," "management philosophies," "guiding principles," or "aspirations." Although this is a start in the right direction, many of these statements produce a high "snicker factor" throughout their organizations. Team and organization members dutifully humor their managers by placing their left hand over their heart, raising their right hand, pledging commitment to the pretty words—and then going back to work.

During more than a decade of work with hundreds of organizations struggling to redefine the desired values at the center of the new culture, I've found two common causes for the values rhetoric-reality gap. First is the failure to get to a few core statements or words. Too often, values statements are a laundry list pledging to be everything to everybody. Motherhood, apple pie, kitchen sink—managers throw it all in there. They declare a belief in all that's good. In one extreme case a utility company handed out pocket-sized folders to its thousands of employees listing the organization's thirty-six values!

More than three to four values aren't values, they're a wish list. As with so many issues of strategy and culture, executives need to set priorities about what's really important to the organization. Core values are those few single words or short statements that act as central "hooks" on which to hang the key behavioral guidelines that shape everyone's actions.

But, as with any idealistic target, an even bigger problem with values is instilling them in the organization once they have been articulated. Many managers make a mockery of a potentially powerful exercise like values clarification because their audio and isn't connected with their video. What managers do and who they are speaks so loudly team and organizational members can't hear what's being said.

Peanuts creator Charles M. Schulz once observed, "There's a big difference between a bumper sticker and a philosophy." Some managers have created "bumper sticker values" through their contradictory actions:

- During complaint-handling training sessions, a vice president at one financial institution often told frontline servers to maintain a smile in their voice "even if the customer is a mooch."
- Many managers talk about the importance of customer service and doing what's best for the customer. Then at month, quarter, or year end, they push their sales force to load up customers or the distribution chain with product so they can pump up their sales figures. So much for "the customer always comes first."
- The president of a major retail chain kept talking about integrity and trust. At the same time, he expressed frustration that store managers weren't "entrepreneurial enough" to keep extra merchandise that was shipped in error by external suppliers. "After all," he explained, "these companies are always jerking us around."
- Many people are fed up with management rhetoric about empowerment, involvement, trust, and teamwork. They're really not that gullible. They can easily look at the bureaucratic

rules and policies, time clocks, call reports, executive perks and huge salary differences, second guessing of decisions, internal politics, slash-and-burn cost cutting, traditional product or service development processes, whose ideas are listened to, how little time and energy is devoted to customers, light and casual training programs, stifling approval levels, rigid budgets and financial controls, and the overuse of waffling committees. These actions show loudly and clearly what management's true values are.

- Many senior management groups who declare teamwork to be a core value don't recognize how their own failure to work as a team raises the teamwork snicker factor. One management group discovered that the "sniping" they did to each other often turned into departments sniping at each other, pointing accusing fingers when something went wrong, and erecting walls around their turf. Little wonder that cross-functional teams floundered in this hostile culture.

Effective cultural change has at its core a simple, basic definition of the beliefs that are to shape the organization's character. Then comes the hardest leadership test of all: consistently showing, rather than just telling, what the organization stands for.

Numerous managers have "done their values thing" and produced pretty parchment papers filled with inspiring words. However, many are frustrated because they feel that people throughout their organization or team "aren't getting the message." But people do get management's message. They see it loud and clear.

THE FISHTANK FACTOR:
WHAT YOU SEE IS WHAT THEY ARE

Our conduct is influenced not by our experience but by our expectations.
—George Bernard Shaw

"Tell me about the people at the organization you just left," said the senior manager who was screening candidates to fill a key leadership role. "They were uneducated and lazy," the candidate responded. "You always had to keep an eye on them because they were constantly trying to goof off or rip off the company. They were lousy communicators, resisted change, and only cared about themselves." "That's too bad," replied the senior manager. "I'm sorry to say that's same type of people you'll find here. This doesn't sound like a job you would enjoy."

Once the next candidate was seated, she was asked the same question. "Oh, they were great," she said. "Although many of them couldn't read and we had some trouble communicating with each other, they were very driven to succeed. Once we all got to know each other, they were constantly helping one another and working together." "Great," the senior manager responded. "That's the same type of people you'll find here."

Everyone who becomes, or aspires to be, a leader of others (whether that's as a manager, project leader, teacher, coach, or parent) should be required to read the 1969 *Harvard Business Review* classic, "Pygmalion in Management," by J. Sterling Livingston. Pygmalion was a sculptor in Greek mythology whose statue of a beautiful woman was later brought to life. George Bernard Shaw's play *Pygmalion* (the basis for *My Fair Lady*) used a similar theme. In the play, Eliza Doolittle explains "the difference between a flower girl and a lady is not how she behaves, but how she is treated." Livingston goes on to present a number of his own studies and cites other research proving "if a manager's expectations are high, productivity is likely to be excellent. If his expectations are low, productivity is likely to be poor."

Years ago, Zenger-Miller cofounder Jack Zenger used a metaphor to describe the "Pygmalion effect" that's always been very powerful for me. He explained that goldfish will grow larger or stay smaller according to the size of the fishtank or pond they're in (someone later told me whitefish do the same). I've since come to think of the influence and expectations of leaders as the Fishtank Factor. If leaders expect mature and responsible adult behavior, that's what they generally get. If managers expect "their people" to behave like immature, irresponsible kids, that's what they generally get. Whether you think they're eagles or turkeys, they'll prove you're right. Many people don't believe in or understand the power of self-determination. So especially in their formative years, they grow large or remain small according to the environment their managers, coaches, teachers, or parents have put them in. But it's never too late to help them grow by expanding their environment and teaching them self-leadership.

The research on the Fishtank Factor is powerful and compelling. Doctors can affect the success of medical treatment by their expectations of their patients: Positive or negative conversations overhead, suggestions made, or attitudes conveyed while patients are asleep, in a coma, or under anesthesia have been proven to influence treatment outcomes. Teachers' expectations of students have a dramatic impact not only on their grades, but on their IQ scores as well. (The title of Livingston's article was inspired by Robert Rosenthal and Lenore Jackson's book *Pygmalion in the Classroom,* describing "the effect of expectations on the intellectual development of children.") Parents' expectations and reinforcement of their kids (especially before age eight) strongly influence their character and behavior. A more recent study by David Upton of Harvard Business School on the billions of dollars invested to increase manufacturing flexibility concluded, "Plants that managers think are flexible tend to get a lot of practice and get better at it. It's a self-fulfilling belief. We've found that flexibility is determined much more by the people in the plants, their industry experience and the practice they get than by the use of a certain type of technology."

It's a values issue that's very closely related to visioning or imaging— the behavior we get in those who look to us for leadership is often shaped by the picture we have of them. They become what we expect.

PATHWAYS AND PITFALLS
Organizational

In almost all cases, the leaders became living embodiments of the cultures they desired. The values and practices they wanted infused into their firms were usually in display in their daily behavior: in the questions they asked at meetings, in how they spent their time, in the decisions they made.

—John Kotter and James L. Heskett, *Corporate Culture and Performance*

- If your management team hasn't developed an explicit set of core values, this is the place to start. Here's what you're after:
  - Three to four words or short phrases (five words or less) that you can use as "verbal pegs" to cluster or summarize

many of the related values at the top of your values hierarchy
- Words or short phrases that are easy to understand and meaningful to your team and organization
- Broad understanding and ownership of the core values by everyone on your team or in your organization

Your team's shared values should represent a blend of those principles from your past that you want to preserve and the beliefs that your team will need to share as you look to your preferred future. Looking at the past shows respect for and builds on your organization's heritage, successes, and strengths. It helps to turn resistance to change into confidence and energy for facing the future. When you look at future values, you're examining the underside of your team or organization vision. Forming the picture of your preferred future calls for a different set of priorities about what's really important.

Debating and developing your core values should follow the development of your shared vision (discussed in the last chapter). Values clarification can be a painful process. But it doesn't have to be long and drawn out. If you have a skilled facilitator lead you, it's common to have a rough version of your team's shared value words or short phrases within a few hours. That's because shared values aren't created, but articulated.

- Once your team has developed your core values, I've found the following exercise is a useful way to further debate, try them on for size, and start you into the most important part of values—living them. You can break into three groups or do this as a brainstorming and discussion exercise in a large group. Here's the exercise using three groups (for the large group discussion, do these in the same way and order): (1) One group brainstorms a list of ways to visibly signal each value to the rest of the organization. These must be specific, such as "meet with our distributors to get their ideas and feedback," not motherhood generalities like "communicate better." (2) Another group discusses ways that the team and/or individuals on the team often inadvertently violate each value. (3) The last group looks at ways the team and individuals on it can get feedback from others in your organization on how well they are living the values. Now everyone gets back together to hear and discuss each group's perspectives. Action plans and next steps conclude the process.

- Unless you're trying to build an old-fashioned command-and-control organization culture, you need wide debate, discussion, and ownership of a set of *shared* core values. This consensus-building process can take a fair bit of time and energy. It's usually best combined with discussions of the organization's vision and an outline of, or invitation to contribute to, the organization improvement plans and process. Some organizations have started with blank sheets of paper and invited the dozens, hundreds, or thousands of people throughout their organization to articulate the organization's core values. I've found that to be a slow and inefficient process. It's not worth all the extra work of gathering, consolidating, reviewing, summarizing, debating, and finally deciding on core values. I prefer the cascading process that I described in the last chapter (page 83) for developing a shared vision. The values are presented as being rough or in a draft form. If they need further refinement or clarification, that's a useful function of the participative process. But don't just tack new values or ideas on at the end. If you get beyond four words or short phrases, you no longer have critical, core values. You now have a list.

- As you try to articulate your espoused values, don't allow yourself to fall into the trap of "we're not living this way now so it can't be a value." Like visioning, you're trying to describe where you want to be. Once you know what you want to become, then you can work on making these lived values.

- Revisit and revise your values every few years to keep them alive and relevant. They can too easily become stale, stifling, or just ignored. In Achieve's early years, I wrote a three-page statement of Achieve's core values that were later named ACT—Attention to Service, Commitment to Quality, and Trust through Value. The values were used to hire dozens of Achievers in the following few years. As we went through a major change and redefinition of our business, everyone in the company participated in a series of "getting into the

ACT" discussions that spanned almost a year of our regular national meetings. Ultimately the three ACT values remained, but each line of the accompanying explanation was edited and revised. The document went from three pages to two. The most significant outcome was not the final two pages of painfully debated words. The biggest benefit came from the participation of every Achiever in internalizing the revised values. They provided a stable and reassuring beacon for navigating the stormy seas of major change and adverse financial conditions we were going through at the time.

- Use a series of fine "values fit screens" once new job candidates have made it through the technical qualifications and work experience screens. If your values say anything about empowerment, teamwork, participation, or involvement, get those people who will be the teammates of the new candidate actively involved in the hiring and selection process.
- If you're not using your values as key criteria in performance appraisal/management and especially promotions, they're just bumper stickers. For example, far too many managers talk eloquently about teamwork or partnerships, customers, and innovation. Then they promote the meanest, toughest technomanagers who haven't seen a customer in weeks (or even longer), are lone wolves, and have left a bunch of dead bodies in their wake. "But," argue some senior managers, "they get the job done." Fair enough. So stop being hypocritical. Declare "the bottom line" or "getting the job done at any cost" or "making your numbers" as your values. Because that's really what they are. Who gets promoted for what kind of behavior is the single clearest indication of an organization's true values.
- What gets measured gets managed. If you're not measuring and providing feedback to everyone on each of your core values, you're not really serious about them. For example, if innovation is a value—measure it.
- If you have a set of values and you want to assess how well you're living them, here are a few ways to do that:
  - Look at your key organization systems, processes, and structure. Whom do they serve? Do they help or hinder people trying to live your values?

- Ask a random group of customers, external partners, and people throughout your organization to jot down the three things that your organization or team seems to care most about.
- Have those people whom your team is leading give you anonymous ratings on how well you're living your values. Do this at least annually.
- Ask people in your organization to describe what gets somebody fired or promoted.
- Look at your last (or current) crisis. What values were really tested? How did you do? Who says so besides you?
- Assess where you spend your time. What's on the agenda for your team meetings? Are you planning, directing, and controlling? Or are you caring for the cultural context, focusing your organization on key priorities, and improving everyone's effectiveness?
- What are people rewarded and recognized for?
- Get out and get active with customers, external partners, and people in your organization. You loudly signal your values through visible and active leadership. "Your people more attention pay, to what you do than what you say."
- Make sure your values are deeply imbedded in, and drive, your training and organization improvement efforts.
- If you're trying to bring about a big values shift, look for dramatic, visible ways to demonstrate the new values.
- Never make a promise you can't keep and keep every promise you make.
- Post your values on the wall at all your team meetings. Begin the meeting with everyone reflecting on how he or she has lived the values personally. Or each person might give recognition to someone else on the team for a strong example of signaling the values. End the meeting with a team assessment of whether your values were alive and actively used in the meeting.
- Weave references to your values in all the speeches, presentations, and discussions you have with people you're leading.

Remember, we lead people and manage things. Core values are critical to effectively leading people. Peter Drucker is on the mark when he says "making the right people decisions is the ultimate means of controlling an organization. . . . your people decisions are your key decisions, because they tell your organization what you value."

Personal

We stand at the crossroads, each minute, each hour, each day, making choices. We choose the thoughts we allow ourselves to think, the passions we allow ourselves to feel, and the actions we allow ourselves to perform. Each choice is made in the context of whatever value system we've selected to govern our lives. In selecting that value system, we are, in a very real way, making the most important choice we will ever make.

—Benjamin Franklin, *The Art of Virtue*
(compiled and edited by George Rogers)

This section is built on the underlying theme found throughout this book—you can't build a team or organization that's different from you.

- Go back to the "values hierarchy" in this chapter (pages 89–90). On a sheet of paper, start your own hierarchy by adding to or modifying the ones I've mentioned here. You might review your blessings and brag list and personal journal to see what they reveal about what you value. Develop a comprehensive list of all your possible values. Now rank each one as "A" (high importance), "B" (medium importance), "C" (low importance). Review your A and B values. Are there any that you feel are essentially the same value or is one an obvious subset of the other? If so, bring them together and rename if necessary. Rank-order the remaining list from highest through to lowest priority. You should now have your top five core values.
  Focusing on your core values:
- Ask yourself whether these are your true, internal "bone deep" beliefs or an external "should" value. These are very tough questions to answer. We often don't recognize a lifetime of conditioning that has left us with other people's belief systems. Replace any "should" values with your own.

- Examine each core value to ensure that it is your end value and not a means to some other end. For example, wealth is seldom a value in itself. It's usually the means to status, power, security, recognition, freedom, accomplishment, pleasure, helping others, or some other end value.
- Write out a "statement of philosophy" that outlines and explains each of your core values. This is for your own private use, so be as honest and candid as you can.

These exercises are rarely done quickly. It could take you dozens or even hundreds of hours to sort through the "shouldas," "oughtas," and "couldas" and get to your basic, core principles. The more meditation, contemplation, and writing time you put into this, the truer and more energizing your core values will eventually become.

- Along with your joint visioning exercise, you could also go through this values clarification exercise with your spouse or partner.
- Have a few close friends, associates, your manager, or your spouse give you their A, B, C ranking of what they think your priorities are on your values hierarchy. Instruct them to rate your values according to what they think you value, not their own values. Discussing the reasons for their choices with each of them can be a very rich source of feedback. It also provides a great external perception of what your behavior says about what you value most.
- Are core values consistent with your vision (last chapter) and purpose (next chapter)?
- Check your values against your current job. How well are they aligned? There's a direct relationship between your level of job energy or satisfaction and your personal values. If there's a big misalignment you probably hate your work and resent all the demands people put on you. If that's the case, you need to make changes to your work (such as developing new skills or taking on new assignments) or change your work.
- When you're faced with major personal decisions or tough choices, pull out your core values for help in deciding what to do.

- Put yourself to your own values test. Look back at decisions and choices you've made. Were they consistent with your core values? If you had to make those choices again, would you make them differently now that you've clarified your core values?
- Use a priority and goal-setting system and a disciplined time management process to allocate your time according to your values (more about that in Chapter 13).
- Your values and priorities will change as you move through different stages of your life. It's one of the reasons that setting aside regular vision, values, and personal development time is so important (more about that in Chapter 14).

The picture of your preferred future and your principles are clearest and the most energizing when they reflect your purpose, which is the next essential element in developing your Focus and Context.

CHAPTER **9**

Purpose

The secret of success is constancy of purpose.
Benjamin Disraeli,
nineteenth-century English statesman,
prime minister, and novelist

Why do you get out of bed in the morning? Why do you go to work? What do you want to be remembered for when you're gone? Why do you exist? What about your team or organization? Why does it exist? What's its value-add? What's its function? How do you want to be positioned in the market and minds of your customers? What business are you in?

These are all questions of purpose. They deal with the deeper motivations and assumptions underlying and intertwined with your visions, values, goals, and improvement intensity. Purpose is the third Focus and Context component we'll look at. It could easily be the first. But arguing whether the picture of your preferred future, principles, or purpose comes first is about as productive as arguing whether air, water, or food is most important to life. They're all vital.

Purpose is also called mission, meaning, reason for being, calling, life theme, niche, strategic intent, value-add, business definition, and the like. As with vision and values, which labels you use don't matter. As long as you, your team, and your organization have clear answers to the questions that open this chapter, use whatever terms make sense. Just be sure the label you use is clear to everybody and is used consistently.

A PERVASIVE PURPOSE

There is no higher religion than human service. To work for the common good is the greatest creed.

—Albert Schweitzer

There's a recurring, consistent pattern in the mission or purpose of most effective leaders, teams, and organizations. That pervasive, underlying theme is *success comes through serving others*. In the front of Zig Ziglar's book *See You at the Top*, he singles out and highlights this declaration: "You can get everything in life you want if you help enough other people get what they want." That philosophy (which he weaves throughout the rest of book and his presentations) left a very deep impression on me early in my career. It has profound and powerful implications for defining a personal, team, and organizational purpose.

In *Principle-Centered Leadership*, consultant and author Stephen Covey presents a convincing case for a leaders' universal mission statement. This, he writes, "is intended to serve leaders of organizations as an expression of their vision and sense of stewardship." The leaders' mission statement he proposes is "To improve the economic well-being and quality of life of all stake-holders." This universal statement is a starting point, or general philosophy; it shouldn't be adapted as is. We all need to develop our own. Part of the reason for "growing our own" mission is to have one that's in our own words and relevant to us. But the biggest benefit comes from the process of thinking and verbal wrestling that goes into formulating the statement.

Developing a personal, team, and organization purpose that's aimed at serving others adds a richer sense of meaning to any improvement Focus and Context. It taps into the deep craving we all have to make a difference. We need to feel that that the world was in some way a little bit better off for the brief time we passed through it.

PERSONAL PURPOSE

To give life meaning one must have a purpose larger than one's self.
—Will Durant

Thinking about death can produce a passion for life. Early in my career I was introduced to the idea of clarifying my life's purpose through contemplating my death by Charlie Jones, an author and speaker on personal effectiveness and leadership development. He said, "You're not ready to live your life until you know what you want written on your tombstone." That's a powerful thought. It forces you to crystallize all your goals, plans, and activities so that you can recognize the core reason you exist.

What kind of account would you like to be able to give for your life? What would you want your family, friends, community, or church members to say about you at your death? How about the team members, business associates, people in the organizations you've led, customers you've served, or other external partners you've worked with? In the end, were you a contributor to, or a taker from, society?

Stephen Covey calls this "beginning with the end in mind." It's the second of the habits he outlines in his very popular book *The Seven Habits of Highly Effective People.* Around the time Charlie Jones got me thinking about what I would like to look back on in my life, I heard someone repeat Oliver Wendell Holmes's comment that "most of us die with our music still in us." What a tragedy. How many people go to their graves with the songs or poems they were going to compose still in them? How many people die with the book they were always going to write buried in their head? Or the love they always meant to express still in their hearts? How many innovations and businesses that might have made a real difference went to a grave without coming to life? Just how many unrealized dreams have died with their dreamers?

The determination to live out my purpose and dreams has been a strong personal motivator. When I need a push to counteract my lazy, sloppy, or "that's good enough" tendencies, the picture of my preferred future and my purpose have been a powerful energy source. My biggest struggle has been in articulating my purpose.

Reducing deeply felt inner convictions and thoughts to mere words has been a difficult and somewhat frustrating experience. But the struggle of wordsmithing is well worth the effort. It has clarified and intensified the emotions and convictions of my purpose. I now express it in two parts. First is what I call my "life theme." That's "loving, laughing, learning, and leading" (you've probably guessed by now that I like alliteration). The second part of my purpose is my "reason for being." This basic thought and focus has remained the same for more than fifteen years. But the way I've tried to express it has evolved from a full page of points and statements to this phrase—"building a better world by helping others grow and develop." It doesn't do justice to what I feel, but it's getting close.

Just a Job or Building a Business?

> *From my eleventh year I have been launched upon a single enterprise which is my main business! My life has been permeated and held together by one idea and one goal: namely, to penetrate into the secret of the personality. Everything can be explained from this central point, and all my work relates to this one theme.*
>
> —Carl Jung

The owner of a car wash and gas station was at a conference where he bumped into an old employee.

"Hi, George. I enjoyed your presentation. You had some great ideas and insights for the group."

"Thanks, Charlie. It's great to see you again. It's sure been a long time. Is this little Joey?"

"Yep. Joe's grown a bit since you last saw him. He's going to be taking over for me next year. If there's any business left for him to run."

"Great."

"Boy, you've done well in the past eight years. How many locations do you have now?"

"Fifty-one."

"Wow! And you're going national soon?"

"Yeah, in a few more months.

They chatted a bit longer. Once they had parted, Joe asked, "Dad, why is George doing so well while we work our butts off just to pay the bills?" In a flash of rare insight and candor, his dad slowly replied, "Well, you know, years ago I set out to run a car wash. When George left me to go on his own, he set out to build a business."

Are you just marking time, or is your job part of your bigger purpose and life theme? Is your job just a means to getting a paycheck so that you can get on with real living, or are you doing your life's work? These are critically important leadership issues. If your job is just a job, you won't have the energy to energize others. You can't build a team or organization that's different from you. If you're not impassioned by what you do, how can you possibly excite anybody else? If you don't clarify and become passionate about your purpose, you may be a good manager, but you'll never become a strong leader.

But before you go looking for that exciting new job or organization to become passionate about, make sure you have thoroughly explored your current one. You may be overlooking acres of diamonds in your own backyard.

By 1910, Russell Conwell had delivered his speech "Acres of Diamonds" more than five thousand times to eight million listeners. The fees from his talks raised millions of dollars to found Temple University in Philadelphia and two important hospitals. The speech centered on Ali Hafed, an ancient Persian farmer. When an old Buddhist priest told him about the fabulous wealth diamonds could bring, Ali sold his farm to look for them. Ali spent years wandering through most of the known world searching for those elusive diamonds. After endless disappointments and futile searching, he became completely discouraged. On the shore of the bay in Barcelona he threw himself into the tide and drowned.

Meanwhile back at the farm, the man who bought the farm from Ali had found a large, glittering stone and put it on his mantel as a curio. One day, the Buddhist priest returned to the farm, saw the flash of light from the stone, and exclaimed, "Here is a diamond! Has Ali Hafed returned?" "No," the farmer replied. "This is just a stone I found down by the river." They went down and found many more like it. And so the diamond mine of Golconda, "the most magnificent diamond mine in history of mankind," was first discovered.

We are all surrounded by acres of diamonds. We have only to look around us for them. But like that curious stone on the mantel, they may not look like anything valuable at first glance. Research consistently shows that successful leaders got their starts in just about every job, function, position, and company imaginable. There is no particular job, industry, or organization that magically transforms "just a job" into passionate life work. However, to spot an opportunity you need to know what you're looking for.

ORGANIZATION PURPOSE

Prosperity is only an instrument to be used, not a deity to be worshipped.

—Calvin Coolidge

If the reason for your company's existence is profit, you won't be very profitable. Eventually your company probably won't even exist. The dollar sign isn't a cause. It doesn't stir the soul. Operating margins and return on investment don't excite and inspire. As an ultimate objective on its own, the pursuit of profits is hollow and unsatisfying. Such naked greed is one-dimensional. It comes from, and leads to, the naked selfishness of "what's in it for me?" Profit seekers are out to serve only themselves. In *The Intelligent Enterprise,* James Brian Quinn writes, "An overemphasis on profits rather than on those things that achieve profits, with rare exception forces an internal and short-term orientation that is actively destructive to service delivery."

Few people today want to buy from, work for, or join forces with a company that's out only for itself. That's like taking a set of elaborate architectual drawings for a huge, luxurious dream home into your team or organization and saying, "If you all work real hard, someday this will be mine." About ten years ago I came across a mixed-up manufacturer that had produced a slick little logo and published this mission statement—"In Pursuit of Profits." I haven't heard of that company for a few years now. I don't think it's in business any more.

But if your company isn't profitable and financially strong, it won't exist long enough to serve any other purpose. You need clear financial objectives, goals, and priorities. You can't afford waste and inefficiency. You need strong feedback and measurement systems to eliminate the "nice to do" activities and focus everyone on doing only the "need to do" work that produces profitable results.

That's the paradox to be managed; companies that exist only to produce a profit don't last long. And companies that don't pay attention to profits can't exist to fulfill their long-term purpose. *Pursuing profits without a higher purpose or pursuing a purpose without profit are equally fatal strategies.* These aren't either/or positions to choose between. They're and/also issues to be balanced. But get them in the right order. As the values studies I referred to in the last chapter have repeatedly shown, profits follow from worthy and useful purposes. Fulfilling the purpose comes first; then the profits follow. Profits are a reward. The size of our reward depends on the value of the service we've given others.

What Business Are You In?

The leader's job is to help people see beyond what the organization is now to what it could become.

Many companies define their business too narrowly. As a result, they often miss new market opportunities. Or they don't provide a broader level of service support to their basic products or services. So customers start looking elsewhere. At the other extreme, some companies define their business too broadly. As a result, they often expand beyond their core competencies into businesses they don't understand. The results are often expensive (and sometimes fatal) learning experiences.

In Achieve's early years we were clearly in the training business. Distributing Zenger-Miller's training programs, we provided a well-designed "hardware" package of videotapes and participant workbooks. The "software" was the training of our client's own internal support staff and/or managers to train others in their organization, following Zenger-Miller's well-scripted leader's guide. The training was orginally aimed at improving supervisory and management skills in many of the interpersonal and coaching skill areas. Later team leadership, nonmanagement personal work-effectiveness skills, problem-solving processes, and related training programs were added in "pick and choose" modules.

The Zenger-Miller program was award-winning, highly effective training. It had a solid research base proving that, when used as directed, it could produce dramatic individual behavior change. But many clients weren't getting the full benefit of this powerful training. That's because they weren't using it within a larger organization context and improvement process. So Achieve began years of difficult learning, experimenting, and searching for ways to reposition and support the core training programs within a larger organization improvement effort. We redefined our business. Our reason-for-being statement became "Improving Personal and Organizational Performance." We saw ourselves as needing to provide consulting services that helped clients put together broad, organization-wide improvement strategies. But that took us far from our core competencies and into the consulting field. We soon found ourselves being drawn into a business we didn't know or understand—generating revenue through billable hours rather than packaged materials.

Eventually an "Implementation Architecture" and supporting services emerged. This allowed us to use customer service and quality improvement as a focal point for building a series of executive retreats and internal coordinator training sessions to support the use of our core training. So we put a broader, strategic implementation framework around our core tactical training. This highly successful process built on Achieve and Zenger-Miller's experience and expertise in packaging complex, dynamic, interactions and human processes and developing internal delivery resources (this whole process is detailed in my book *Firing on All Cylinders: The Service/Quality System for High-Powered Corporate Performance*).

PATHWAYS AND PITFALLS

There is no medicine like hope, no incentive so great, and no tonic so
powerful as expectation of something better tomorrow.
                              —Orison Swett Marden, founder of *Success* magazine

---

Your personal, team, or organization purpose is interconnected
with your principles and picture of your preferred future. It's almost impossible to tell where one stops and the other begins. But
it doesn't matter; all three are needed. They are the air, water, and
food of your Focus and Context. Together they provide the
changeless inner core that allows you and everyone else to confidently deal with constant external changes.

Organizational

To forget one's purposes is the commonest form of stupidity.
                              —Friedrich Wilhelm Nietzsche

- As you and your team work on your vision and values, spend
  some further time on defining just what business you're in.
  You might use one or two of these questions to stimulate
  your discussion:
  - Why do we exist?
  - What value do we add to society?
  - What business are we in?
  - Is our business definition too narrow? Is it too broad?
  - Does our business definition match our organization
    strengths and capabilities?
  - What does (or should) set us apart from others in our type
    of business?
- Once you have a general agreement on what your organiza-
  tion's purpose is, try to boil it all down to a phrase or state-
  ment that captures who you are or what you're trying to do.
  Sometimes these become slogans like Panasonic's "Just
  Slightly Ahead of Our Time," Ford's "Quality Is Job 1," or
  Bata's "Shoemaker to the World." This can be a powerful
  way to encapsule and "emotionalize" your mission.

- An effective way to get everyone in your organization involved in internalizing your mission is to have a contest to develop your slogan or purpose statement. You'll be pleasantly surprised by the energy and creativity that people will put into this if you've captured their imagination and heart. Introducing the contest or getting their input to your organization's or team's purpose should go along with the vision and values work you're doing with them.
- Too many mission statements are written by committees of technomanagers who clearly wish they were lawyers. They have a high "Say What? Factor." They're often full of rambling prose, platitudes, and bland statements that don't mean much. This problem illustrates the importance of communicating Focus and Context through people-driven, not paper-driven, channels. A leader standing in front of a group talking passionately from the heart about the higher purpose that team or organization exists to fulfill has many times more value than any written mission statement.
- If you're going to provide effective leadership to others, you need to coach them to uncover their own reason for being. You can then work to find or create a better alignment between their personal purpose and that of the team or organization they're working in.

Personal

Someone who knows his desires and works with purpose to achieve them is a person whose feelings, thoughts, and actions are congruent with one another, and is therefore a person who has achieved inner harmony.

—Mihaly Csikszenthmihalyi,
Flow: The Psychology of Optimal Experience

- Developing a personal mission statement is a discovery and learning process, not a problem to be solved. It takes a lot of time and thoughtful reflection to sort out what's most important to you. Your purpose is intertwined with your vision and values. Defining it is part of that same process. Here are some questions to ask yourself or ways to approach developing your personal purpose:

- Who are the key people in all aspects (work, family, community, church, friends, etc.) of my life? If they were all giving a eulogy at my funeral about how I had affected their lives, what would I want them to say?
- What does my "dream list" reveal about my inner desires and purpose? Is there some "music" in me that might be buried with me, never to be played?
- If I had only two more years to live, what are all the things I would make sure I did?
- What sort of work or activities really excite and energize me? When do I feel the most vibrant and alive?
- What special talents or strengths do I have?
- Review your blessings and brag list for insights to some of these questions.

- Once you have defined your personal purpose, use affirmations to "magnetize" it and focus you on fulfilling your reason for being. You might also use inspiring quotations to illustrate and energize your affirmations.
- How well is your personal purpose aligned with your team or organization's? If it's not close, look for ways to live out your purpose within your current work. You need to search within your own organization or team for diamonds before you go out looking for them elsewhere. You might start by having a mission alignment discussion with your manager. You could begin a list of all the positive, energizing points about your work. Review it frequently. You might also keep a running list of all the mission alignment opportunities that exist in your job, team, or organization. You'll be surprised at how many glittering stones you'll start to notice.
- Work with your family members to write a statement of family values and mission. Have all members describe their individual pictures of the ideal family future. Use this to develop common themes and a composite vision of what your family life together could be.
- Don't confuse goal setting with picturing your preferred future, clarifying your principles, and identifying your purpose. Your Focus and Context is the road you've chosen; goals are

the mileposts along the way. Setting and reaching stretch goals is a critical part of fulfilling your purpose and moving toward your vision. But goals are means, not ends. Goals have a beginning and completion. Your Focus and Context is an unending, continuous process.

- Make sure your purpose is yours, not a role you feel others want you to play.
- Don't write your purpose statement to inspire or impress anyone else. It's designed only to inspire and impress you. To avoid the problem, don't show it to anyone else.
- Keep working at clarifying and articulating your vision, values, and reason for being. This is an ongoing, continuous process. Just like milking the cows on the farm I was raised on—it never stays done.
- Cultivate the habit of setting aside some quiet, contemplative time for inner reflection, meditation, and spiritual renewal. This is time to do your vision, values, and mission clarification work. It's a time to discover and listen to your inner music. Over the years, I've found that investing about 30–45 minutes per day (some days an early morning start or busy schedule prevents it) has paid huge dividends in energy and focus. It's a tiny price to pay to ensure that the other 16 hours of your day don't compound into a life of regrets. As the nineteenth-century American poet John Greenleaf Whittier put it so well, "Of all sad words of tongue or pen, The saddest are these: 'It might have been!'"

CHAPTER **10**

Pinpointing Your Customer/Partner Performance Gaps

Customer demands are getting harder and harder to meet. That's great because it's getting tougher for our competition to survive.
—The CEO of a very successful manufacturing firm

Effective teams, organizations, and leaders exist to serve others. And those who provide the highest levels of service/quality enjoy the richest rewards. That's not just some platitude or warm and fuzzy theory; it has become a well-proven fact. In *Firing on All Cylinders* (especially Chapter 1) I reviewed much of this evidence. I showed that those organizations with the highest service/quality levels have the highest levels of growth in revenue, customer satisfaction and retention, market share, productivity, safety, and employee morale while also reducing costs. So it's not surprising that the best service/quality leaders are also profitable leaders. Since I wrote *Firing on All Cylinders,* the research has continued to pour in. My files are bulging with study after study showing that outstanding service/quality performance is one of the key contributors to outstanding financial performance.

It's nothing new. Peter Drucker has been reminding us for decades now that the only reason for the existence of any business is to get and keep customers. Winston Churchill once said, "If you aim to profit, learn to please." A century ago, Russell Conwell would conclude his famous "Acres of Diamonds" speeches by urging his listeners to start their search for riches by "first knowing the demand." He continued, "You must first know what people need, and then invest yourself where you are most needed."

Understanding and managing toward existing customer expectations means having both the will and the way. You and your team must first decide that your customers' expectations and perceptions of the value they receive from you is a key driving force in your business. Then you need to systematically turn soft customer expectations and perceptions into hard, manageable data. That calls for the discipline of a rigorous management system and process. The improvement map on page 53 breaks this into three major steps: (1) identify current customers/partners, (2) prioritize expectations, and (3) gap analysis. The map shows that these sequential activities are in the rectangular, left-side boxes of management. That's because this track links to the rigorous goals, measurements, and standards you need to continually improve the products and services you now provide to existing customers. In the next two chapters we'll balance this chapter's management steps with the leadership actions of exploring, searching, and creating tomorrow's markets and customers; innovation; and organizational learning.

LOTS OF CUSTOMER TALK, LITTLE ACTION

> *Ninety-five percent of managers today say the right thing. Five percent actually do it.*
>
> —James O'Toole, leadership professor, quoted in *Fortune*

I've spoken to, or worked with, hundreds of management teams interested in becoming more "customer-driven." Many aspire, some understand, but only a few truly do. Despite all the proclamations, catchy advertising slogans, and customer service publicity, service levels have improved only marginally in the last few years. As Harvard Business School professor Rosabeth Moss Kanter puts it: "Despite the recent media coronation of King Customer, many customers will remain commoners. . . . Most businesses today say that they serve customers. In reality, they serve themselves."

Over the next few years, a massive computer industry shakeout will give us plenty of examples of what happens when customers aren't clearly identified and their expectations aren't uncovered—let alone met. I've had my fill of dealing with companies who provide a reasonable piece of hardware or a good software program and then can't even answer the phone. Trying to get service support from one of these companies is about as much fun as having an ingrown toenail removed. At a software conference, a leading computer market researcher told me that his biggest challenge is getting usable customer lists. In other words, many of his computer industry clients have no idea who their customers are. That's because they're focused too much on product. Many are one-product wonders who developed a specialized product or found a narrow niche and have never really had to compete for business. They haven't had to worry about service because there were always more customers to replace those lost through careless neglect. Many are destined to become roadkill on the "information superhighway."

How Intense Is Your Customer Focus?

> *"What's Mr. Smith's condition?" asked the raspy voice on the phone.*
>
> *"He's recovering so well he'll be going home in a few days," answered the nurse. "Whom shall I say called?"*
>
> *"This is Smith calling. My doctor won't tell me anything!"*

One reason so many organizations aren't really customer-focused is that their innocently ignorant managers don't understand what intense customer focus really looks like. And they don't fully appreciate the why and how of balancing their focus on the final or ultimate customers with their focus on external partners, such as distributors, retailers, dealers, agents, suppliers, and physicians.

The chart illustrates the vast differences in customer and partner focus. To make your team or organization a high performer, get your focus and activities into the "Intense" column.

Levels of Customer/Partner Focus

Casual	Moderate	Intense
The needs and expectations of markets, customers and external partners (like distributors or suppliers) are lumped together.	A few segments and partnerships have been highlighted.	The needs and expectations of key market/customer segments and partnerships have been assigned priorities.
Infrequent market, customer, and external partner data collection and analysis.	A trickle of data helps to focus improvement activities.	Major strategic and operating decisions are based on a heavy stream of continuous data.
Managers and internal production or support teams occasionally see customers or partners.	Visits from and visits to customers and partners are becoming more frequent.	The boundaries between customers, partners, and your organization have blurred.
Some customer and partner expectations are occasionally collected.	Expectations are assigned priorities and weighted along with effectiveness ratings to identify performance gaps.	Customer and market gap analysis provide competitive benchmarks and broad market comparisons.
Product/service development, improvements, and innovations are pushed out to the market.	Customer/partner input and pilot testing help identify and shape innovation and improvement.	Customers, partners, and people working in the field explore, experiment with, and guide improvements and innovations.
Budgets (primarily through sales and marketing) focus on customer acquisition.	Increased investments in service/quality research, development, and improvement.	Customer retention and partner improvement is a key investment focus.
Departmental organization structure follows internal logic and needs.	Process improvement and reengineering refocuses and restructures the organization.	A decentralized, team-based organization is built around key markets, customer/partner priorities, and strategic processes.
Training teaches everyone how to smile and "handle" customer and partner complaints.	Training teaches how to trace the root cause of errors and eliminate them.	Training provides the tools to identify internal and external customers and partners, set expectation priorities, analyze performance gaps, and make improvements.

A CUSTOMER CULTURE IS
BUILT ON A SERVICE ETHIC

Rank is an appointed position. Authority is an earned condition. Rank is decreed from above. Authority is conferred from below. Authority vanishes the moment those who bestow it stop believing, respecting, or trusting their appointed boss, though they may defer out of fear.

—Ted Levitt, *Thinking About Management*

There are many reasons that teams and organizations haven't developed a culture of intense focus on their customers and partners. Some are management issues—they don't have the right tools and techniques or they haven't established disciplined listening and response systems and processes. In these cases, managers don't know how to become more customer- and partner-focused. They don't have the way.

But the root cause of casual or moderate customer and partner focus goes deeper. It has to do with will. Most managers don't focus on their customers and partners because they're too busy managing. They've become technomanagers focused first on technology and management systems. Technomanagers don't want to serve, they want to control. They lord over and boss people. Although they may say something very different, technomanagers *act as if* people (customers, partners, and everyone in their organization) serve their technology and management systems. Srully Blotnick, a psychologist and *Forbes* columnist, spent 27 years following the lives of 6,981 men. In his book *Ambitious Men: Their Drives, Dreams, and Delusions,* he writes, "It's difficult to say to someone, 'I am your humble servant,' and in the next breath hit them with, 'but I am also your social superior.' . . . 45 percent of all the ambitious and talented men we studied who failed did so because of difficulties directly connected with the simultaneous pursuit of these two goals."

Effective leaders know that without disciplined management systems and leading edge technologies, outstanding service is nothing but a dream. But they act on a belief system that management systems and technology exist to serve people. This belief system is nourished by a personal purpose encompassing the key service principle that success comes through serving others.

Servant Leadership

> *I don't know what your destiny will be, but one thing I know, the only ones among you who will be really happy are those who will have sought and found how to serve.*
>
> —Albert Schweitzer

In 1977, retired AT&T Director of Management Research Robert Greenleaf published a philosophical leadership book that's enjoying a resurgence because the highly successful retailer Wal-Mart has used his concepts so effectively in building its service culture. His book is called *Servant Leadership: A Journey into Legitimate Power and Greatness*. It's an inspiring and insightful book that points the way toward the involvement and empowerment movements we've seen in the last few years. He writes, "A new morale principle is emerging which holds that the only authority deserving one's allegiance is that which is freely and knowingly granted by the led to the leader in response to, and in proportion to, the clearly evident servant stature of the leader . . . the servant-leader is servant first. It begins with the natural feeling that one wants to serve, to serve *first*. Then conscious choice brings one to aspire to lead."

It's another powerful paradox to be managed. On the one hand, leaders provide direction. They guide, influence, and persuade people on their team and throughout their organization. But once the Focus and Context is clear, leaders continuously ask customers, external partners, and their internal partners how they can harness and improve the organization's core technologies, processes, and systems to meet everyone's needs. Then they put themselves in the management harness to establish goals and priorities along with the transformation and improvement plans that work to close the gaps between what is wanted and what is delivered.

HOW TO FOCUS ON CUSTOMERS AND PARTNERS: BOILED DOWN TO THE BASICS

You achieve customer satisfaction when you sell merchandise that doesn't come back to a customer that does.
—Stanley Marcus, chairman emeritus of Nieman-Marcus Co.

If you have the will to serve, there are countless ways to understand and work toward meeting your customers' and partners' expectations. Thousands of new books, papers, and articles detail the many research and measurement tools and techniques you can use. The number of seminars, workshops, training programs, researchers, and consultants available to help you has exploded in the last decade. Advice on figuring out whom you need to serve and how you can best serve them has never been as easy to get as it is today.

If you have the will to serve, the next problem is choosing among the many ways. The models, methods, and approaches are overwhelming. These include personal conversations, market research, focus groups, advisory panels, surveys, hot lines (often using an 800 number), complaint systems, structured interviews, user or partner groups, conferences, team visits (both by you to your customers' and partners' sites and by them to your sites), trade shows, and the like. (For a brief overview and examples of these listening tools and techniques see Chapter 8 of *Firing on All Cylinders*.) There is no one best method to use. You need to use them all. The question is to what extent, in what combination, and how to best apply each of these listening methods.

As I've worked with management teams trying to improve their customer and partner focus, I've seen many get themselves tied up in highly technical and complex research and analysis. In other cases, management teams have used an approach that's too narrow or that's missing important elements. I've concluded that you can boil customer and partner focus down to three steps:

1. Identify your current customers and partners (both external and internal).
2. Uncover and prioritize customer and partner expectations.
3. Using their ratings of your current effectiveness, pinpoint your performance gaps.

To simplify even further, Whom have you chosen to serve? Whom do you need to work with to serve your ultimate customers? What does everyone want from you? How are you doing at meeting the needs of these people? The answers to these questions become the input for the improvement planning that sets you, your team, and your organization on your own pathways to performance.

Identifying Current Customers and Partners

Identification is clearly the starting point. But it takes a lot more thought and discussion than most management teams realize. You need to identify the various end users or customer segments you choose to serve. In today's fast-moving world, you can't be everything to everybody. Segmenting your markets and customers is critical. You might divide them by demographics, such as size, age groups, geography, income levels, buying patterns, frequency of doing business with you, and so on. Many companies with moderate and intense levels of customer focus are already well down this road.

However, few organizations have also looked at their customers from a psychographic perspective by examining the values and attitudes that define the customer's organization culture or personality type. This type of segmentation or analysis is especially useful in developing a composite profile of ideal customer segments. Not all customers are equal. Some are more profitable, easier to serve, better fit to your organization's unique strengths, or just more enjoyable to do business with. These are important considerations in deciding whom to target your customer acquisition and retention efforts toward.

Once you've identified your target customer segments, it's useful to draw a customer-partner chain. This is a decades-old approach to mapping out the key players, relationships, and processes involved in serving a customer segment. Put the name of a customer segment at the far right. Draw a line back to any external partners such as dealers, distributors, agents, retailers, professionals, consultants, representatives, and the like who aren't employed directly by your organization but are key to serving your ultimate customers. To the left of your external partner, chart the internal teams or individuals your partners and/or customers deal with or rely upon for delivering that product or service. To the left of them identify the internal teams or individuals they depend upon. Keeping moving back through the chain until you've included external suppliers. You now have a picture of everyone in your customer-partner chain (it's also the first rough diagram of a process map). However, you're likely missing staff support people and management. They either help or hinder everyone doing your organization's real work in the chain. When they don't understand their servant-leadership role or see this big picture, they usually get in the way. Your diagram will also be missing your shareholders, board of governors, owners, or funding partners. Everyone needs to understand who they are and just what they expect from the organization.

Prioritize Expectations

In *Top Performance,* Zig Ziglar tells of an elderly couple celebrating their fiftieth wedding anniversary. After a long day of celebration and honors, they prepared to retire for the night. As he had always done, the husband prepared their bedtime snack of buttered toast, jam, and milk. When his wife sat down to the snack in front of her, she burst into tears. Concerned, her husband went to her, embraced her, and asked what was wrong. She tearfully replied that after such a special day she had hoped that he would have finally stopped giving her the end piece of bread. Shocked and surprised, her husband replied, "But after all these years I thought you knew that I think that's the best piece of all."

What a perfect example of mistaken assumptions and misperceptions. So often the priorities we assume others have are projections of our own values and preferences. That assumption can be deadly. We need to go beyond the Golden Rule. Instead, we need to serve people the way they—not we—want to be served. There might be a big difference. Because we're seeing customer and partner expectations from inside our organization or management team, we can't possibly have the same perspective as they do.

So, how do you check the expectations and priorities of those you're serving? Ask them. Never assume anything. And when you think you understand what's important to your customers and partners, ask them again. And again. And once more. Never stop checking your assumptions and their preferences. Thanks to the service/quality revolution, there are many tools and techniques such as Quality Function Deployment, value matrices, and the like to help you.

However detailed or complex you ultimately make it, here are the basics for uncovering and prioritizing expectations:

- Getting customers or partners together in focus groups is generally the most productive method of uncovering expectations. But you can gather expectations through individual interviews as well.
- Gather perceptions and expectations from your competitors' customers, people who've stopped doing business with you, and those who could—but don't—use your products or services now.
- Always start with a blank sheet of paper, never a preconceived list. Ask your focus group to brainstorm the factors most important to them when using the products or services your team or company offers.
- Once you have a complete list, get your focus group to rank or weight all the factors on the list. You could do this by giving them each ten voting points to distribute according to how strongly they feel about the top factors.

Gap Analysis

The point of all your customer and partner research is to pinpoint and target areas for improvement. In step two, you learned what your current customers and partners, as well as the broader market, consider to be the most important product, service, and support factors. Now you want to analyze and assess the gaps between their expectations and your performance. With these targets, you can aim your improvement efforts much more accurately to close the performance gaps. They also provide the basis for benchmarking your performance against other highly effective teams or organizations.

Brad Gale's book *Managing Customer Value: Creating Quality and Service That Customers Can See* is one of the most helpful in understanding customer and partner expectations and pinpointing performance gaps. When he was with the Strategic Planning Institute, Gale was one of the key players in compiling the authoritative and widely quoted PIMS (Profit Impact of Market Strategies) database. In *Managing Customer Value,* Gale adds a couple of important elements to the research approaches summarized in this chapter: "*Market-perceived quality* is the customer's opinion of your products (or services) compared to those of your competitors. *Customer value* is market-perceived quality adjusted for the relative price of your product." These additional perspectives add important, and much broader, elements to customer and partner gap analysis. His book is filled with useful tools, techniques, and examples of "customer value analysis." These are aimed at "moving 'customer satisfaction' from a slogan to a science."

Performance gap analysis can be as narrow and as simple as the difference between the top priorities of a particular customer or partner and how well they perceive you're delivering on their preferences. Or the analysis can be broad enough to encompass an entire market, including your competitors' customers and people who don't use your type of products or services—yet.

PATHWAYS AND PITFALLS

A success is one who decided to succeed—and worked. A failure is one who decided to succeed—and wished. A decided failure is one who failed to decide—and waited.

—William Arthur Ward, *Ward's Words*

- Get everyone on your team to individually identify where your team or organization falls on each of the points in the chart on page 121. Compare and discuss your scores. Decide which areas need attention, and put improvement plans in place.
- Identify your organization's key external customer segments. If you need more information, decide how you can get it.
- Draw a customer-partner chain for your team or organization's key customer or market segments (as described on page 125). Using focus groups, interviews, and/or surveys, uncover and set priorities for the top expectations of each group in your chain. Have those same groups rate how well

your team or organization is doing at meeting their expectations. Have them rate your competitors as well. Using this data, identify your key performance gaps and improvement opportunities.

- Make all these data as visual and available to everyone in your organization as possible. Nobody can hit targets they can't see.

- Don't overlook your internal partners. The research clearly shows that dissatisfied people can't produce satisfied customers. Find out where the gaps are between expectations and performance for people throughout your organization. Close those, and you've gone a long way toward closing performance gaps with your external customers and partners.

- What does servant-leadership mean to you? How should you serve the people in your organization? Discuss this with your management team.

- Who's serving whom? Is your head office serving the servers in the field and those producing or supporting your products and services? Or is the reverse what's really happening? How do you know? How intensely are you identifying internal service gaps?

- Institute a "Golden Hours Rule" to protect the time of people dealing with your external customers or partners. For example, a leading retailer doesn't allow head-office staff to call any store between 11:00 A.M. and 2:00 P.M. because that's a peak customer traffic time. No internal issue is so important that it can't wait until external customers or partners are served.

- You can increase your sales, service, and customer-support staff by 30 to 50 percent without adding any additional overhead. Get them to stop serving the bureaucracy. Radically streamline all the reports, internal communications, and the other useless activities that take these key people away from time spent with external partners and customers. Start by asking them what's getting in the way of serving their customers.

- Every time you gain a customer, ask why you were chosen. When you lose a customer or one becomes inactive (which is how most customers are lost), ask why. Compile these data to see what they tell you about the market, your competition, and your organization's performance.

- One of the strongest ways you signal your personal service ethic and true servant-leadership values is how quickly you return phone calls, voice mail, or E-mail messages. Your standard should be one business day. There's no excuse for anything beyond two business days. People appreciate a terse "Got your message. I am tied up right now but I'll get back to you by _____" more than silence. Slow responsiveness loudly shouts, "You're not important enough to even acknowledge." Get a cellular phone, notebook computer, administrative assistant, better time management system, revamped set of priorities, more discipline . . . but promptly return those calls and messages.

- If you're not prepared to respond or try to close the performance gaps your customers and partners identify, don't ask. Asking for their input raises their expectations. Even if your performance stays the same, you've just widened the performance gap.

- Don't rely too heavily on just a few research tools and techniques. For example, many of us are suffering from survey fatigue. You need to find as many different ways of uncovering your customer and partner expectations and performance perceptions as possible.

- The customer is not always right. If he or she is abusing other partners or taking advantage of the organization, the customer is wrong. But your customers' opinions are always their reality. They "calls 'em as they sees 'em." Your job is to make sure you thoroughly understand how they see them and why.

- Double or triple your complaint levels in the next 12 months. Fewer than 5 percent of your unhappy customers bother to complain to you. But they tell lots of other people about your shortfalls. Get them to help you improve. Make it very easy for them to complain (and quickly resolve their problem) when your products or services don't meet their expectations. Analyze these data to identify trends and patterns that point to important opportunities.

- Too many organizations that do any kind of customer and partner research don't hear what the customers are saying because it doesn't fit with their own view of the world, products, services, or competencies. So those expectations are dismissed as unrealistic ("They expect us to solve all the interconnectivity and integration problems of the computer and telecommunications industries"). Like our son, Chris, when he was two, these managers clap their hands over their eyes and act as if not seeing "unrealistic" expectations will make them go away. Some try to change or modify those expectations. That's very dangerous. If you succeed in suppressing those expectations, you have at best achieved a short-term victory. As soon as someone else figures out how to meet your customers' or partners' expectations, you've lost them.

- Set up a system and process for getting the input of those internal partners who work most directly with your external partners and customers. Internal partners are a rich source of market, competitive, and customer intelligence that most companies don't use very well. But make your system as non-bureaucratic and easy to use as possible. For example, you might set up a voice mail box that internal partners can use to verbally dump their observations or field reports into. You should be running regular focus groups and input sessions with them. That's another easy way they can keep you abreast of what's really going on.
- Get out there yourself. Spend at least 40 percent (and ideally much more) of your time with external customers and partners.

Understanding your customer and partner expectations is a vital starting point. But it's all useless and wasted work if you don't have a process for aligning yourself, your team, and your organization to act on what you've heard. Starting at Chapter 13, most of the rest of this book is dedicated to closing those performance gaps.

But first we need to cross over to the leadership track. We need to look at how to see beyond today's customers and existing performance gaps.

CHAPTER 11

Tomorrow's Markets and Customers: Exploring, Searching, and Creating

---

Do not follow where the path may lead. Go instead where there is no path and leave a trail.

Success is one of the leading causes of failure. Market and customer research is a leading cause of tunnel vision.

- When trains were first developed, the King of Prussia confidently predicted, "No one will pay good money to get from Berlin to Potsdam in one hour when he can ride his horse there in one day for free."
- In 1903, the president of the Michigan Savings Bank gave this market advice to Horace Rackham, Henry Ford's lawyer: "The horse is here to stay. The automobile is only a fad, a novelty."
- A British Parliamentary Committee assessed whether Edison's lightbulb would ever be useful. They concluded it was "unworthy of the attention of practical or scientific men."
- Edison himself made these market assessments: "The phonograph is not of any commercial value" and "The radio craze will die out in time."
- In 1946, Darryl Zanuck, then head of 20th Century Fox, predicted, "Video (television) won't hold any market it cap-

tures after the first six months. People will soon get tired of staring at a plywood box every night."

- News item in an 1868 New York paper—"A man has been arrested in New York for attempting to extort funds from ignorant and superstitious people by exhibiting a device which he says will convey the human voice any distance over metallic wires so that it will be heard by the listener at the other end. He calls this instrument a telephone. Well-informed people know that it is impossible to transmit the human voice over wires."
- In 1980 a Wall Street auto analyst told a Senate committee: "General Motors, already the automotive king of the road, will become even more dominant by the mid-1980s and will be the only auto company capable of building a full range of cars and trucks."
- And from some early market research on steamships— "What, sir, would you make a ship sail against the wind and currents by lighting a bonfire under her deck? I pray you excuse me. I have no time to listen to such nonsense." —Napoleon Bonaparte to engineer and inventor Robert Fulton

Management is concerned with understanding and improving what is. Disciplined management calls for rigorous market and customer research to pinpoint the performance gaps seen by our current customers and partners. But as vital as that is, it's just the beginning. Far too many service and quality improvement professionals, customer-satisfaction specialists, and market researchers stop here. They become prisoners of the present. Like the old elephant who finally has the chain removed from his leg, they've become conditioned to never go beyond the radius of past experience.

Seizing the opportunities of tomorrow calls for leadership. It means taking off the blinders of what is in order to see what could be. To lead is to look beyond prevailing products, current services, today's competitors, and existing markets. Customer, partner, and market leadership means exploring, searching, and creating new and unique pathways that lead to your vision.

STRATEGIC PLANNING SMOTHERS
INNOVATION

How far would Moses have gone if he had taken a poll in Egypt?
—Harry Truman

From a standing start, a financial services company had two decades of very strong growth. The company was entrepreneurial and opportunistic. New products, services, and distribution channels evolved and developed as the leaders passionately pulled the organization toward their vision. But its growth wasn't always a pretty sight. Product and service ideas seemed to come from the wrong people, at the wrong time, in the wrong ways, and for all the wrong reasons. Often they had to be developed on a shoestring budget or using the philosophy of "make a little, sell a little, make a little more." However imperfectly, customers were well served, product leadership was established, and, in key markets, dominance was achieved.

Then senior management changed. The original, fairly well balanced, senior management team was eventually replaced with technomanagers. When they looked back at the twisting and turning paths left by product development and marketing, they were determined to "bring some order to this craziness." These were "processes out of control," management declared. "They need to be reengineered." So a Strategic Planning Committee was formed. It consisted of fifteen senior managers and support staff from quality improvement, customer service, accounting, marketing, human resources, and planning. Over the next few years, they surveyed, researched, collected data, discussed, analyzed, diagrammed, and planned marketing strategies and new products. They wrote a powerful vision, values, purpose, and strategic planning document that could have been a business school case study.

Each thoughtful new product and marketing campaign took off with a bang . . . and then slowly fizzled. None was an outright failure. But the company's history of ever rising sales success flattened out. Key people started leaving. Passion and energy levels slowly sank. Today the company is struggling to catch up with its changing markets and ever stronger competitors.

McGill University management professor Henry Mintzberg has been extensively studying, teaching, writing, and consulting on management effectiveness, strategy formulation, and planning since 1968. His book *The Rise and Fall of Strategic Planning* is a dense, lengthy report on the exhaustive research and thinking he's been doing on this popular management technique. He cites a mountain of evidence proving that the strategic planning practiced in most organizations doesn't improve their effectiveness. Sometimes it's used for centralized and political control. In other cases, it aims to take the unpredictability and uncertainty out of markets and organizations (a foolishly impossible goal). In a passage on neurotic and compulsive management he writes, "Above all, the machine organization [what I call technomanagement] . . . is obsessed with control, first of the workers but everyone else after that. . . . All this is done to ensure the stability of the operations and the smooth functioning of the bureaucratic machine." He concludes that the biggest reason strategic planning doesn't work stems from "the planning school's grand fallacy: *Because analysis is not synthesis, strategic planning is not strategy formulation. . . .* Ultimately the term strategic planning has proved to be an oxymoron."

The new senior managers at the—now mediocre—financial services company proved to be caretaker or maintenance managers. They fell into these all-too-common strategic planning traps:

- Strategy formulation was treated as a separate task. It isn't. No matter how much time and analysis you give it, no committee, staff support professional, consultant, or brilliant strategist can develop an effective strategic plan in isolation. Strategy is an interactive process. It might be separated from daily management, but can't it be separated from leadership. It is leadership.
- Management committed the classic blunder of applying logical hindsight when looking back at a series of opportunistic and serendipitous product and market innovations. In his book *Serious Creativity*, creativity guru Edward De Bono puts his finger on the problem, "If every valuable creative idea is logical in hindsight, then it is only natural to suppose, and to claim, that such ideas could have been reached by

logic in the first place and that creativity is unnecessary. That is the main reason why, culturally, we have never paid serious attention to creativity."

- Adding up all the time the fifteen Strategic Planning Committee members spent in the market either finding or serving customers produced a total of less than 10 percent for the whole group. Theirs was an artificial world of budgets, plans, analysis, strategies, concepts, theories, and numbers. The valuable experience of the sales, service, and field support people who lived in the real world (the market) was reduced to aggregate data points, opinion survey categories, and disembodied quotations on questionnaires.
- Senior managers lost the rich learning, opportunistic, and urgent nature of evolving their strategies "on the fly" in the market. Effective strategic opportunism, like effective servant-leadership, both leads and follows.

It probably sounds as if I don't believe in planning. That's not so. Effective planning is a critical success factor. But the focus and type of planning are what's critical. Two types are needed. First, personal, team, and organization planning should focus especially hard on improvement. This critical planning establishes systems and processes to continually build and improve understanding, skills, and competencies. So when those unexpected opportunities come along that fit your vision, values, and purpose, you're able to capitalize on them. The second type of planning is implementation or action planning. It's disciplined, short-term (today, any detailed action planning beyond a year or two is ludicrous) and centered on annual goals, monthly or weekly priorities. Chapters 13 to 15 are built around both of these types of planning.

LOOKING BEYOND WHAT IS TO WHAT COULD BE

I skate to where the puck is going to be, not to where it has been.
—Wayne Gretzky

Customer and market research, competitive benchmarking, and focusing on market share could be detrimental to your organization's future performance. These approaches are critical improvement tools. Top-performing organizations have turned them into a disciplined and useful science. But they can also lead to "me-too" followership or—even worse—commodity products and services that compete only on price.

Market share, for example, is meaningful only if you're in a stable, contained, and well-defined market. Fat chance of that today as markets merge, converge, and diverge. In our turbulent markets with such high levels of flux, market share measurements can easily distract you from creating whole new product or service categories, markets, or even industries. How good an indicator of future success was market share, customer satisfaction, and quality levels if you built horse-pulled carriages in 1912? Harvard Business School professor Clayton Christensen found that modern technology companies that lost their market leadership "had their competitive antennae out, saw the new next technology, invested aggressively, and still missed the next wave." He concluded that these basically good companies focused too heavily on current customers to the exclusion of future markets.

Today, the boundaries of markets in computers, telecommunications, entertainment, financial services, health care, consumer products, retailing, professional and consulting services, and just about every other field are melding and blurring. Traditional customer and market research will focus many of your improvement activities and keep you grounded in current reality. But that's not enough. You need to manage the paradox of paying close attention to closing today's customer and partner performance gaps while you explore, search, and create tomorrow's new markets, customers, and partners. Here's the three-stage process that leads to market leadership:

1. Pinpointing performance gaps with current customers and partners
2. Pinpointing performance gaps across your entire market(s) and against your key competitors
3. Searching for latent or unmet needs and exploring new markets, products, or services

Stage one is vital to high performance. Your customer and partner focus needs to be intense. As important as it is, it's just a beginning. Effective implementation of stage two brings the "voice of the market" into every nook and cranny of your organization. But that's not enough any more. If you're going to be a leader, you need to meld, combine, or create new markets and customers. You need to extend existing products, develop new ones, and spin off new services. The speed with which you do that will determine just how long and sharp your competitive edge will be.

Successfully executing stage three calls for a critical leadership skill that many managers lack. It means that managers need to learn how to balance their cost and quality control skills with growing the business. The management skills of analyzing, controlling, and containing will continue to be important. But you can't cost-cut your way to growth. Reengineering, quality improvement, and involvement will continue to be vital. But your current and future competitors are working just as hard as you are to drive overhead down and quality up. To grow your business, you must become a leader who can innovate, transform, and create. A study of 847 big public corporations by Mercer Management Consulting found that cost cutters who attained higher-than-average profit growth but lower revenue growth than their industry average saw a compound annual growth rate of 11.6 percent in the market value of their companies. But investors value companies on the basis of growth and future potential. Consequently, companies with higher-than-average profits from higher-than-average revenue growth realized twice as much growth in their market value with a 23.5 percent increase during the same three-year period.

Companies with poor customer service or low quality levels won't even get into the competitive game today. But while responsive customer service and high quality once made you stand out, they're fast becoming the minimum standard to stay in today's game. The leadership skills of searching, exploring, and creating new products, services, customers, partners, and markets has always been the key to success of high-growth entrepreneurial companies. As markets heave and service/quality gaps close, innovation is becoming the next competitive imperative. Searching for latent or unmet needs and exploring new markets, products, or services has never been more important to your future. This level of innovation is rooted in a deep understanding of your customers and markets.

INTIMACY, EMPATHY, AND INNOVATION

Above all, we know that an entrepreneurial strategy has more chance of success the more it starts with the users—their utilities, their values, their realities. . . . The test of an innovation is always what it does for the user. . . . It is by no means hunch or gamble. But it is also not precisely science. Rather, it is judgment.

—Peter Drucker, *Innovation and Entrepreneurship*

Just because you're spending money on research (such as markets, customers, or new technologies) and development doesn't mean you'll get innovation. Innovation, as with advertising, training, or many other organization investments, depends on the quality of the investment as much as the quantity of resources you put in it. A high proportion of innovative new products, services, and companies flop. That's often because managers build better mousetraps without first making sure there are any mice out there. Or that people still want to catch them.

Innovations often come from systematic and constant improvement to existing products and services for current customers and partners. But they also come from intuitive insights, creative leaps to whole different paths of thought. Creativity guru Edward De Bono calls this "lateral thinking." Innovations that come from continuous improvement flow naturally from knowing your customers' and partners' expectations and perceptions of performance gaps.

Many innovations come from a deeper level of customer and market understanding. They go beyond what current customers say they need. They solve problems that customers either don't realize they have or didn't know could be solved. These innovations create needs and performance gaps only once customers start using them and get turned on to the possibilities. For example, in the early 1980s, no focus group, survey, or customer satisfaction measure could have shown a big demand for fax machines. Yet how could you function today without one? In the mid-1980s, had a market researcher asked me, I would have put a cellular phone, voice mail, or notebook computer very low on my list of needs and expectations. But I would never have been able to move my office to my home and relocate our family back to our hometown without them (a lifestyle choice I didn't know I had until I started using the technology).

Every product and service we now take for granted was once silly, interesting, or just an odd curiosity. What would you have said to a market researcher asking about a video machine for your TV when there were few movies to rent? How about CD players when there were no CDs to buy? What about a bank card to withdraw cash from an ATM? How about a personal computer? In the 1950s, how highly would you have rated the need for jet planes when your business was conducted within a few-hundred-mile radius of your office? These are a few examples of the thousands of innovations that customer or market research and competitive benchmarking would never have identified a need for. The companies who pioneered these sorts of innovative breakthroughs had years of spectacular revenue growth and market leadership.

Walking in Your Customer's Shoes

> The need for innovation on an unprecedented scale is a given. The question is how. It seems that giving the market free rein, inside and outside the firm, is the best—perhaps the only—satisfactory answer.
>
> —Tom Peters, *Liberation Management:*
> *Necessary Disorganization for the Nanosecond Nineties*

Innovation is a hands-on issue. It calls for an intimate understanding of your current customers and markets, potential new customers or markets, team and organization competencies and improvement opportunities, vision, values, and mission. You can't develop that intimacy from a distance. Studies, reports, surveys, graphs, and measurements wouldn't give it to you. Effective innovation depends on disciplined management systems and processes. But it starts with people. People searching for creative ways to do things better, differently, or more effectively. People trying to understand how other people use, or could use, the products or services their organization could produce. That makes innovation a leadership issue.

Beyond the management tools of surveys, focus groups, and the like, innovation leaders find a multitude of ways to live in their customers' world. They're learning how to learn from the market, not just market research. Innovation leaders look for ways to align the organization's product and service development competencies with latent or unexpressed market and customer needs. Because customers don't know what's possible, they often can't identify innovations that break with familiar patterns. At the other extreme, leaders recognize that their organizations are constantly in danger of developing products and services with little or no market appeal. So many new (or extended) products and services come from *empathic innovation*. These are innovations that flow from a deep empathy and understanding of the intended customers' problems and aspirations.

Through living in and empathizing with their customers' world, innovation leaders focus their organization's development capabilities on solving problems or meeting needs that customers may not have been aware of. As Achieve was working with current and prospective clients to move beyond the training field to organization improvement, we stumbled across the need for senior management education, strategy formulation, and implementation planning sessions. Recognition of this need came from working closely with clients struggling to get people in their organization trained and using new approaches to customer service, quality improvement, and teams. It became clear that how the senior management group pulled everything together and led the effort was the key stumbling block or stepping-stone to the whole effort. After experiments, pilots, and a few failures, Achieve's highly successful executive retreat process evolved and developed to meet a need no one had anticipated.

PATHWAYS AND PITFALLS

Finding is reserved for the searchers. We don't find what we need, we find what we search for. Needing is not a prerequisite to getting value. You can't be a needer, you have to be a searcher.

—Jim Rohn, successful entrepreneur and personal effectiveness author and speaker

---

- Make sure the "voice of the market" pervades every part of your organization. Bring customers into your company offices and plants for visits, joint problem-solving and planning sessions, celebrations, focus groups, conferences, barbecues, presentations, and the like. Get everyone in your organization out to see customers or into the real world on a regular basis. Your management and support staff (accounting, human resources, purchasing, marketing, administrative assistants, and the like) should be working with visiting customers and should be out with customers at trade shows or on the service desk. They should be shopping competitors, accompanying salespeople on sales calls, resolving customer complaints, and the like. If you provide an improvement process and training, they'll make the time for all this customer and market contact by learning how to focus on the things that really matter. They can then cut out all the bureaucratic, non-value-added and useless work.

- Don't allow any manager, technical specialist, or support professional (such as accountants, marketers, or human resource staff) to participate in product, service, or market development decisions unless they're spending a minimum of 25 percent of their time with current or prospective customers and partners in the market.

- Use the approach followed by senior partners at large, successful accounting and consulting firms. Make your senior managers responsible for at least some business development and ongoing customer service. They should be spending 25–35 percent or more of their time with customers (the same amount of time should also be spent with external and internal partners). Ensure that some part of their compensation is linked to your team or organizations's new business or product development success. Don't allow senior managers only to cost-cut and quality-control their way to profitability and performance bonuses. Make sure innovation and growth are part of the balance.

- One of my favorite examples of servant-leader innovation is the architect who waited to put the sidewalks into his new residential complex until the buildings' customers had worn paths in the grass. Then he laid the sidewalks over those paths. The people selling in your target markets and serving your customers are innovating every day to meet unexpected needs, beat out a competitor, or capitalize on a new opportunity. Unless you have a user-friendly, easy process (not an administrative bureaucracy) for gathering all that experience and market intelligence, you're recklessly squandering one of your organization's richest sources of innovation. You might hire a business student to seek out and document all this innovation and entrepreneurship. You should also build an ongoing process to keep this experience base updated and widely available to everyone. This, rather than strategic planning, is the kind of planning a strategic improvement team should be working on. But you want to be sure that they keep the process easy to use and user-friendly.
- Darrel Rhea is president of Cheskin & Masten, a California-based design research consulting firm. Here's how that firm uses what he calls an "identity audit" for a deeper understanding of the teenage market:
  - Read what's being written for teens.
  - Tear out ads aimed at teens and put them on the wall to find patterns.
  - Interview 50 teen market experts a year.
  - Talk to the owners of Viacom and MTV.
  - Talk to the writers of the David Letterman show.
  - Talk to successful teen marketers like Nike and Reebok.
  - Bring in teens with their best friends (to improve honesty and openness) for interviews.
  - Give hundreds of teens a camera and four rolls of film to take pictures of their lives. They put tens of thousands of these images per year on CD-ROM and analyze them for patterns.

- By tuning into your organization's customers and markets you can spot opportunities for better aligning your career with your personal preferred future, principles, and purpose.
- Identify your leading-edge external customers and partners and bring them into your product and service development processes. Ideally, these are customers and partners who use your products and services extensively. But they keep pushing everything and everybody to the limit. They are always looking for new and better ways to use whatever you can provide. Find out what problems they're trying to solve that no one else in your market provides solutions for. But don't confuse leading-edge customers with those that scream the loudest, are the most loyal, or give you the most business. Many good or vocal customers don't push your thinking or teach you how to apply your product and services in new ways. Leading-edge customers are often "bleeding edge" customers as well. They're not always easy or fun to deal with.
- Establish active user and support networks. Provide regular face-to-face, electronic, print, or audio-video forums to help customers, external partners (like distributors and suppliers), and internal partners exchange experiences, ideas, and problems to be solved. Capture and disseminate all this learning throughout your organization.

Keep asking your customers and partners lots of "what if" questions. Take good notes and circulate them throughout your organization. Don't allow anybody to write all of this off as just wishful thinking. Remind them that somebody's wishful thinking brought us every service and product we use today, developed our modern economy, and gave us one of the richest lifestyles in the history of the world. Leaders find ways to translate wishful thinking into the "logical and obvious" products and services we eventually take for granted.

CHAPTER 12

Innovation and Organizational Learning

---

*We need a new way of thinking about our problems and our future.
My suggestion is the management of paradox, an idea which is itself a paradox, in that paradox can only be "managed" in the sense
of coping with. Manage always did mean "coping with" until we
purloined the word to mean planning and control.*

—Charles Handy, *The Age of Paradox*

Mark Twain once said, "Name the greatest of all inventors. Acci-
dent." He was right. Most innovations and breakthroughs come
from mistakes, serendipity, false starts, setbacks, and misapplica-
tions. Many innovations were unplanned and unexpected. At
their outset, many were unrecognized and unwanted. Innovations,
breakthroughs, and major changes often come from unpredictable, chaotic, and random events. That's why the accuracy
record of the confident, logical-sounding projections and predictions made by economists and planners is so abysmal. It's amazing how the same people who laugh at fortune-tellers often take
these elaborate plans and projections seriously—especially if
they're computer-generated.

Yet when innovative opportunities knock, many managers
are in their backyard looking for four-leaf clovers. But if someone who can't count finds a four-leaf clover, how lucky is he or
she? The editor and author Elbert Hubbard observed, "A failure is someone who has blundered, but is not able to cash in
the experience." Most managers fail to cash in on unexpected
opportunities. There seem to be two core reasons for that.
First, they don't recognize the failure, setback, chance event,
unexpected offer, or new wrinkle as a potential innovation

they could cash in on. That's often because they haven't progressed to the empathic level of customer and partner listening and understanding. They take the market or customers at face value. They're looking only at today's data or current performance gaps. These near-sighted managers can't see beyond what is to what could be.

A second reason many managers fail to cash in on unexpected opportunities is because there's no effective process for doing so. If it's not in the official development plans or budgets, the unhatched, potential innovation has no place to incubate, break out, and grow. That brings us to the innovation paradox: Random, chaotic, and unpredictable innovations need a stable management system and process to nurture the growth and development of "lucky breaks." As a long-time student and practitioner of innovation, I still find James Brian Quinn's 1985 *Harvard Business Review* article one of the most useful on the topic. The title of the article says it all: "Managing Innovation: Controlled Chaos." It's a perfect description of the management-leadership balance found in highly innovative teams and organizations. Controlled chaos aptly describes the unstable and stable, unplanned and planned process of successful innovation.

STRATEGIC OPPORTUNISM AND ORGANIZATIONAL LEARNING

The universe is full of magical things patiently waiting for our wits to grow sharper.

—Eden Phillpotts, early-twentieth-century English novelist

In his article "Crafting Strategy," Henry Mintzberg provides good insight to how strategies and innovative actions evolve and complement each other in top-performing organizations: "Out in the field, a salesman visits a customer. The product isn't quite right, and together they work out some modifications. The salesman returns to his company and puts the changes through; after two or three more rounds, they finally get it right. A new product emerges, which eventually opens up a new market. The company has changed strategic course." But in most organizations that salesman would be told to get back out and "do his job" by selling the customer the original product or some high-priced add-on or support service. If he did make modifications, he'd have his knuckles rapped for not following the standardized process. In other cases, he'd be told to submit a Product Modification Input Solicitation form, sending copies to product development, strategic planning, and three other committees to review. His regional manager would need a copy attached to his Call Report explaining where, when, who, why, and how he was spending each day of his time.

Successful strategies and innovations that evolve and cash in on unexpected problems or opportunities are part of a dynamic, organization learning process. Experiences, expertise, ideas, market and customer shifts, feedback, input, and the like shape the emerging strategies and point the way to innovation pathways.

A PROCESS FOR CONTINUOUS INNOVATION AND CONTROLLED CHAOS

Now, more than ever, management is a balancing act—the juggling of contradictions to try to get the best of attractive but opposing alternatives. Order is a temporary illusion, strategy a moving target. Leaders cannot impose authority on a world of constant motion; they can only hope to steer some of that action toward productive ends.

—Rosabeth Moss Kanter,
Harvard Business School professor

Today's leading organizations are knowledge-creating companies that thrive on continuous innovation. It's a big competitive edge. New products and services can be "knocked off" or copied. But it's much harder for competitors to duplicate a management system and corporate culture that produces a continuous stream of successful product and service improvements, innovations, adaptations, and extensions.

That continuous innovation stream comes from controlled chaos. It's a tricky process, as you can see from the diagram. This diagram consists of four main stages. The first two stages are dependent on leadership skills. Stages Three and Four lean heavily on disciplined management systems and processes.

1. Exploration is a broad, open search for strategic partnerships, unresolved problems, latent or unmet needs, new markets and customer segments that potentially fit your team or organization's Focus and Context as well as core competencies.
2. Experimentation consists of pilots, clumsy tries, and "mucking around" to test the potential opportunity for viability and to learn what would be needed to make a new product successful.

The Innovation Funnel

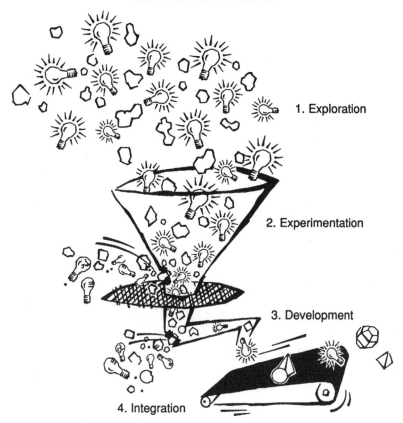

1. Exploration

2. Experimentation

3. Development

4. Integration

3. Development means that major resources are now committed to fully developing or refining the few new products, services, or businesses that are clearly ready to be capitalized on.
4. Integration occurs when the new product, service, or business enters your organization's mainstream.

These four innovation stages aren't as neat and orderly as described here. They run in parallel, overlap each other, and sometimes clash. For example, stage two often involves field and development people. That means that stage-three work may already be proceeding while the project is still in stage two. In a smaller company like Achieve, the close involvement of our field people in stages two and three meant that many of them were trained by the time we found ourselves in stage four.

Your organization's emphasis on the unstable, chaotic first two leadership stages or the last two stable and more controllable management stages tends to pulse. At some point, you may have many exploration and experimentation activities underway. That entrepreneurial environment is both exciting and unstable. Too much instability can be dangerous to the health of your ongoing business and the people who are trying to hold your core operating processes together. As all those experiments and pilots are developed, your organization may go through a "settling down" period. That can be comforting, but dangerously stable. Spend too much time here and you won't have enough exploring and experimenting going on to ensure future innovations. The key is to find a rough balance (you'll never get it exactly right, so why expect to?) between exploring and experimenting while you try to develop, integrate—and keep your core business operating every day. That's the unsolvable paradox of controlled chaos. It's about as easy as changing the tires on a moving car.

The first two innovation stages are broad and fairly inclusive. The wider your scope of focus and people, the higher your chances of "lucking out" on significant breakthroughs that will soar. But without some limits and controls, your organization could lose its way exploring every interesting path and side road you come across. That's where a strong and clear Focus and Context is very helpful. It will help everyone more easily assess whether a potential opportunity should be pursued further or dropped now. Strong vision, values, and purpose will also "mag-netize" and draw "lucky" opportunities, relationships, or people to your team or organization.

The cost and determination to never turn back rises steeply in stages three and four. That underscores the importance of intense learning from high levels of exploration and experimentation.

EXPERIMENTS, PILOTS, AND CLUMSY TRIES

If at first you don't succeed, you're running about average.

Early in my sales career I was introduced to the Law of Averages. It's been a key concept of direct sales for many decades. The Law of Averages basically teaches salespeople that if they want to dou-ble or triple their sales, they need to double or triple the cold calls and sales presentations they make. I found that if I made ten cold calls to interest people in home water-treatment equipment, I gen-erally got one appointment for a sales presentation. Three ap-pointments usually gave me one sale. So to get one sale, I needed to make about thirty cold calls. As I got better at prospecting, choosing prospects to call on (people who had just bought a home, for instance), and increased my sales presentation skills, I improved those averages.

A vital—and painful—lesson I learned was that I would always get more no's than yeses. To increase my yeses, I had to increase my no's. Of course, averages never play out in smooth and even increments. Some days I could get fifteen or twenty no's in a row before hitting a yes. The difficult discipline to develop was not quitting at the end of the fourteenth no. Some of my toughest sales involved convincing myself to get excited about a long string of cold no's because it meant I was getting closer to a clump of warm yeses. Later, at Achieve we developed a number of marketing approaches that eliminated the need for cold calls. But, thankfully, the Law of Averages was burned deep into my psyche. As I started studying innovation and trying to apply what I was learning to Achieve's product, service, and market develop-ment, the Law of Averages came back into play. It became a key part of the reason Achieve eventually discovered pathways to a strong leadership position in a few key training and consulting services and markets.

I first saw the Law of Averages applied to innovation in 1983 when Zenger-Miller and Achieve worked with Tom Peters to develop the Toward Excellence process based on the lessons of *In Search of Excellence*. It made so much sense. To double your innovation success rate, double your failure rate. Clearly, effective managers don't want to fail. The goal is not failure; it's success. But since innovation is so unpredictable, you have to "fail your way to success." Those—initially clumsy—tries are the only way to learn what does and doesn't work. Based on his extensive research on innovation, James Brian Quinn found, "No one can predict whether a particular solution will work, how well it will work if successful, whether customers will accept it if it works, or how customers will use it once they have it. The first use of major innovations is often in unexpected markets, and market research is often wildly wrong. . . . *the unexpected is what always happens. . . . (it's) predictable unpredictability*" [my emphasis]. If I looked at a street of thirty homes, I knew there was a sale to be made somewhere on that street. But unless I suddenly developed the psychic power to read minds, the only way I was going to find it was to talk to twenty-nine people who didn't want to see me.

Successful Failures

Failure is the discipline through which we advance.
—William Ellery Channing,
nineteenth-century American poet

One of the more dangerous myths about entrepreneurship is that you have to be a risk taker to be successful. Speculators, commodity traders, and "paper entrepreneurs" might thrive on the risks and rush of "doing deals." But entrepreneurs building long-term businesses aren't risky gamblers. Successful entrepreneurs and innovation leaders are obsessed with developing new products, services, management systems, leadership approaches, markets, and businesses that will give them a big competitive edge. But they refuse to bet their company on a few big all-or-nothing projects. Managers who take that approach are either innovation-ignorant (they don't understand the basics of successful innovation) or irresponsible. The business graveyard is full of managers who invested very heavily in "sure fire" innovations that flopped.

Opportunities for innovation leadership always look bigger going than coming. Using the Law of Averages, innovation leaders nurture many experiments, pilots, trials, tests, and the like at very early stages to screen out those few promising innovations they will eventually direct into their managerial mainstream. They cheat. By the time an innovation is ready for official investment approval to move into stage three, all the rich learning that came from stage two substantially reduces the risk (and some of the development work is already underway).

Successful experimentation means you need to kiss a lot of frogs to find that prince. As you do, you learn. So it helps to begin recognizing royal froggy behavior or see the faint marks on their heads left by little crowns. That should help reduce the number of frogs you have to kiss, but you still have to keep looking. In his article "Building a Learning Organization," Harvard Business School professor David Garvin writes, "Experimentation involves the systematic searching for and testing of new knowledge. . . . A study of more than 150 new products concluded that 'the knowledge gained from failures (is) often instrumental in achieving subsequent successes.' . . . *In the simplest terms, failure is the ultimate teacher*" [my emphasis]. When asked why he wasn't getting results with his countless tries to successfully develop the lightbulb, Thomas Edison replied, "Results? Why, man, I've gotten a lot of results. I know several thousand things that won't work."

Charles Kettering was one of the greatest inventors of the early twentieth century. At NCR, he developed the first electric cash register. In 1909, he founded Dayton Engineering Laboratories Company (Delco), where he invented the electric starter and other automotive electrical equipment and systems. He once said, "An inventor is simply a person who doesn't take his education too seriously. You see, from the time a person is six years old until he graduates from college, he has to take three or four examinations a year. If he flunks once, he's out. But an inventor is almost always failing. He tries and fails, maybe a thousand times. If he succeeds once, he's in. Those two things are diametrically opposite. We often say that the biggest job we have is to teach a newly hired employee how to fail intelligently. We have to train him to experiment over and over and to keep on trying and failing until he learns what will work."

PASSIONATE CHAMPIONS AND SKUNKWORKS: PATHFINDERS AND PIONEERS

Every new opinion, at its starting, is precisely in a minority of one.
—Thomas Carlyle

Advertising executive Charles Brower once said, "A new idea is delicate. It can be killed by a sneer or a yawn; it can be stabbed to death by a quip and worried to death by a frown on the right person's brow." When innovations are in stage one, they need a champion to take them through the rest of the stages. Otherwise, the bureaucracy, politics, and people who can see the fledgling and potential innovation only through today's glasses will smother it or let it quietly die from malnourishment. Peter Drucker defines a champion as "a monomaniac with a mission." It's a good way to describe the passionate, visionary leadership that an innovation needs if it's going to get someone to protect, nurture, and fight for the resources to give the new idea a chance to try to prove itself. The more radical the change, the stronger, more forceful, and persistent its champion must be. Studies going back to the early 1960s have repeatedly shown that most successful innovations were led by fanatical champions.

In today's interconnected and interdependent organizations, even the most passionate and effective champion needs support and resources. He or she can't possibly do it alone. But because most innovations upset the established order, "going through regular channels" will lead to almost-certain death. So champions often find, organize, or attract to them a sometimes motley crew of like-minded people. These groups are often called "skunkworks." In his "controlled chaos" article, James Brian Quinn writes, "Every highly innovative enterprise in my research sample emulated small company practices by using groups that functioned in a skunkworks style."

These ad hoc groups of turned-on innovators are what management consultant and author Bob Waterman also refers to in his book *Adhocracy.* He writes, "Adhocracy is any organization form that challenges the bureaucracy in order to embrace the new. It cuts through organizational charts, departments, functions, job descriptions, hierarchy, and tradition like a hot knife through butter. . . . Ad hoc organizational forms are *the* most powerful tools we have for effecting change." Don Frey has been vice president of product development at Ford, CEO of Bell & Howell, and a management professor; he was awarded the National Technology Medal by President George Bush. In his article "Learning the Ropes: My Life as a Product Champion," he writes about his experience as part of Lee Iacocca's hugely successful Mustang development team: "I learned the never-to-be-forgotten importance of how a few believers with no initial sanction, no committee, no formal market research, and no funds could change a company's fate."

ORGANIZATIONAL LEARNING: YOU CAN'T HAVE INNOVATION WITHOUT IT

It is no longer sufficient to have one person learning for the organization, a Ford or a Sloan or a Watson. It's just not possible any longer to "figure it out" from the top, and have everyone else following the orders of the "grand strategist." The organizations that will truly excel in the future will be the organizations that will truly tap people's commitment and capacity to learn at all levels in an organization.

—Peter Senge, The Fifth Discipline: The Art and Practice of The Learning Organization

---

I am as fervently in favor of "the learning organization" as I am of individual learning. You can't have innovation and higher performance without learning. And Peter Senge is right; organization improvement can no longer depend on a few key leaders. But like "change management," teams, empowerment, reengineering, quality improvement, and a host of other popular organization programs, "the learning organization" is a means, not an end in itself. It's not a destination; it's a main thoroughfare on the road to higher performance. Maybe that's why "the learning organization" seems to be as fuzzy a concept as the OD (organization development) field to me. It's all too theoretical. You can't argue with many of the models and paradigms (if you can understand them; many have a high "Huh?" factor). But most of this stuff is written for academics and philosophers, not practicing managers. I find that many of these books and articles don't pass the "so what?" test. So, other than games, exercises, and some vague platitudes, what could I do differently tomorrow morning?

When it comes to both organization and personal innovation and learning, the problem isn't a lack of failures and clumsy tries. It's that most individuals, teams, and organizations don't cash in on their experience. They're learning-impaired. It's not a question of ability or IQ points—some of the brightest people have crippling learning disabilities. It's an implementation problem. *Many managers, teams, and organizations haven't developed the disciplined habit or an effective process for systematically studying, reviewing, revising, and retrying in a continuous cycle.* As the revolutions of this learning cycle add up, continuous improvements and innovations—higher performance—result. Countless studies on highly successful individuals, teams, and organizations continue to show that ability and aptitude certainly help. But these factors pale in comparison to application power. What you know is less important than what you do.

The rest of this book will deal with the habits and processes involved in doing. We'll look at the key skills and steps for putting into practice the most crucial elements of organization improvement, leadership development, and personal effectiveness.

A CULTURE OF TRUST, OPENNESS, AND TOLERANCE OF MISTAKES

One who fears failure limits his activities. Failure is only the opportunity more intelligently to begin again.

—Henry Ford

The environment of most organizations is too poisonous for innovation and organizational learning to flourish. A mistake is generally a CLM—career-limiting move. Making a mistake in front of many managers is like cutting yourself in front of Dracula. People become defensive. They cover up problems, setbacks, and missed goals. When people in closed, mistake-averse organizations encounter problems, they immediately go to work on fixing the blame. Everyone becomes so busy denying mistakes that no one can possibly learn from them.

There's a direct and strong relationship between organization trust and experimentation. If I feel that management is just waiting for me to trip up so that a big black mark can be put beside my name, why would I risk trying something new? It's far safer to be a critic. I can speak up at meetings and write memos pointing out how imperfectly other people have done things that I am too afraid even to try. I can establish a wonderful batting average by going to the plate only when I'll face a very weak pitcher. Why would I give a new idea a clumsy try if I believe that anything less than total success would be frowned on?

If you want more experimentation and learning on your team or in your organization, establish an atmosphere that builds self-confidence and trust. Trust is extraordinarily fragile. Building it is a subtle, long-term process. It doesn't come from what you say—from telling people to trust you or talking about trust as a core value.

Trust is built or destroyed by what you do. How are mistakes treated? How much experimenting do you personally model and encourage in others? Who gets rewarded and recognized for what behavior? What management support systems and processes are in place? How much and what type of skills are developed and for whom? What information is shared, by whom, and with whom? Do you and your team keep your promises? Do you truly live according to your espoused values? Is Focus and Context something you're trying to do to everyone else, or is it a way of being? How clear and consistent are your goals and priorities? These are just some of the trust issues. But as you contemplate your answers to these questions, the most important question of all is, How do you know? Go ask those people whose trust you need to build how they would answer these questions. To get their truthful responses—and lay the foundation for trust building—let them answer anonymously.

A big cause of team and organization learning impairments is lack of openness. As mistakes are made, pilot tests run, and tries clumsily attempted, learning occurs. Unless those results are openly and widely shared, everyone is reduced to learning only from personal experience. That's an expensive waste of time and resources. You need active internal networks and processes for sharing all that rich learning experience. But these are useful only if you have a high level of trust within a culture that sees mistakes as opportunities to advance the team or organization's learning.

PATHWAYS AND PITFALLS

> *The way to avoid mistakes is to gain experience. The way to gain experience is to make mistakes.*
>
> —Laurence J. Peter, *Peter's Competence Principle*

If your team or organization doesn't have a disciplined management system and supportive leadership culture, innovation and organizational learning are just matters for wishful thinking.

- The only place you should try "doing it right the first time" is with established, repetitive processes. Beyond that, this quality improvement cliché is dangerous. A major study from the American Quality Foundation concluded, "We don't do things right the first time. Trial and error—making mistakes, experiencing failures, and learning from them—is how we improve. We need mistakes in order to learn; they are an integral part of how we get better. Urging Americans to 'do it right the first time' means asking them to omit a step in their improvement process. It won't work. . . . If Rocky had done it right the first time, there would have been no movie."
- Recently I received a seminar brochure advertising an "innovation lab" and a "change workshop." These were "designed for mid-level management and professional employees with responsibilities for change and innovation." *Everybody in the company is responsible for personal, team, and organization change and innovation.* You can't separate these responsibilities any more than you can separate quality improvement, customer service, or people leadership.

Developing a staff group of "innocrats" is a sure-fire way to kill innovation and increase resistance to change.

- How many experiments, pilots, and clumsy tries are currently underway in your organization? Depending on your Law of Averages, you will need three to four times as many projects and pilots in stage three than you hope to get out of stage four.

- Peter Drucker has been giving us some very sound advice for at least three decades now: "Every three years or so, the enterprise must put every single product, process, technology, market, distributive channel, not to mention every single staff activity on trial for its life. It must ask: Would we *now* go into this product, this market, this distributive channel, this technology *today?* If the answer is 'No,' one does not respond with 'Let's make another study.' One asks, 'What do we have to do to stop wasting resources on this product, this market, this distributive channel, this staff activity?'"

- You can't make your organization more innovative by acquiring an entrepreneurial company. Within two years the acquiree will be at the same level of innovation as your organization. You can make your organization more innovative only by changing its management systems, processes, and leadership culture.

- Establish a regular review process for yourself, your team, and your organization to reflect on the reasons for both your failures and successes. This is a fundamental and critical component of learning. Based on the input of everyone involved, some organizations produce substantial documents or booklets on "lessons learned" following a major new product, service, or business launch.

- Set up an innovation slush fund to provide seed money to champions and skunkworks. Couple that with allowing your key operations people 10–15 percent of their time to work on projects that they feel have some high innovation potential. The only condition of getting the money or time is a periodic report (preferably voice mail, E-mail, videotape, or group presentation rather than a bureaucratic memo) on the key lessons learned. Circulate these reports widely.

- Set up an internal "best practices and good tries" system, clearinghouse, or network to continuously spread the learning about what works and doesn't work across your organization. Many organizations are setting up electronic databases, learning and improvement coordination processes, active networks, and the like.
- Put on regular product and service fairs that allow all areas of your company to show off their results, explain what they're working on, and swap ideas. A giant 2-day fair at a large housewares manufacturer resulted in 2,000 ideas for new products.
- Make sure that you, your team, and teams throughout your organization spend lots of time in external benchmarking and "corporate tourism" mode looking for good ideas to swipe. Many of the opportunities or problems you're facing now are old hat to somebody somewhere. Learning from other people's experiences—both their successes and their failures—can take years and millions of dollars off your learning curve.
- Build strong personal, team, and organization measurements and feedback loops. If you don't know how you're doing, you can't improve. If you want more innovation, set up measurements to chart your progress. Lack of feedback is one of the biggest contributors to learning disorders.
- Develop strategic alliances and partnerships with organizations providing complementary products and services in your target market. If the fit is right, it can be a great way to extend your products and services, reduce your own development risk, and learn.
- Increase your rate of personal learning. You can't build a team or organization into something that's different from you. Your personal rate of change, innovation, and learning sets the pace for everyone else.
- Do you have an experimenting mind-set? What are some recent examples of personal routines or habits you changed?
- How do you deal with defeats, failures, and setbacks? In his work to understand why "the smartest people find it the hardest to learn," Professor Chris Argyris finds, "Because many professionals are almost always successful at what

they do, they rarely experience failure. And because they have rarely failed, they have never learned how to learn from failure. So whenever their single-loop learning strategies go wrong, they become defensive, screen out criticism, and put the 'blame' on anyone and everyone but themselves. In short, their ability to learn shuts down precisely at the moment they need it most."

- Ensure that your reward and recognition processes encourage cooperation, open learning, and innovation across boundaries and departmental lines. If you're not sure, ask.

- A mind-set that embraces experimenting, piloting, and clumsy tries must pervade all parts and areas of your organization. That includes human resource systems, training, administrative support services, management systems and processes, product and development, customer service, purchasing, supplier management, external partnerships, and so on.

- Consider setting targets for innovation. 3M has long measured management performance by the percentage of revenues that come from products and services that didn't exist 5 years ago.

- Put an intense focus on shortening your product and service development cycles, especially stages three and four. Radical improvement (aim for a ten times reduction) of these key processes will make your organization a leading innovator, leaving your competition choking on your dust. All your supporting management systems will have to be realigned to sustain this change.

- Develop prototypes and pilots in parallel. Avoid committing yourself to any one as long as you can without spreading your support so thin so that none can survive (a tricky paradox to manage). Once you've selected the approach or product you're going to develop further into stages three and four, you might keep your options open with a few quiet pilots still bubbling in the background.

- Appointed champions and assigned skunkworks don't work. They haven't got the passion and commitment to beat the odds against an innovation's surviving the bureaucracy, inertia, and threatened power bases. These people rise to the surface in environments that welcome and support them. The most successful venture capitalists invest in people, not promising companies, products, or markets. A key criterion in deciding whether to support an innovation is the passion of its champion.

- Use many small mistakes to avoid the deadly big one. Experiment early and often on a small scale. You want a series of ten $50,000 learning experiences that notch your learning forward rather than one big $5 million flop.

- If innovation is truly important to you, you'll hire and promote unconventional thinkers, "boat rockers," and passionate people who have a history of successfully bucking the system. How many do you have now?

- The flatter, more decentralized, and team-based your organization is, the higher your levels of innovation will be. Head office and management need to serve the operational and improvement teams working to find better ways to produce products and enhance service. The more that people feel they're running their own show, the more they'll act like entrepreneurial partners.

Exploring, searching, creating, learning, and innovating are critical ongoing activities in finding your best routes to higher performance. But these scouting activities must lead to decisive action. You've got to plot a course and follow through. You need to establish goals and priorities.

CHAPTER **13**

Establishing Goals and Priorities, Getting Organized, and Managing Time

He that is everywhere is nowhere.
—Thomas Fuller, seventeenth-century
historian, scholar, and author

A frantic manager burst into a travel agency and exclaimed, "I need an airplane ticket immediately!" "Where would you like to go?" the travel agent asked. "I don't care, just get me on a plane. I've got business everywhere," was the desperate reply. Time management specialist R. Alec Mackenzie once observed, "Urgency engulfs the manager; yet the most urgent task is not always the most important. The tyranny of the urgent lies in its distortion of priorities. One of the measures of a manager is the ability to distinguish the important from the urgent, to refuse to be tyrannized by the urgent, to refuse to manage by crisis."

Unsuccessful organizations are often beehives of activity and hard work. Reflecting on the performance of his struggling company, a departmental manager observed, "We have lots of projects, goals, and priorities. We're constantly making lists and setting action plans. But we seldom see anything through to completion before some urgent new priority is pushed at us. Our division manager's thinking seems to be 'random brain impulse.' He's like a nervous water bug that flits from one half-baked strategy to another."

In the midst of tumultuous change, many managers are confusing "busy-work" activity with results. Missing what's really important to long-term growth and development, they allow themselves to be tyrannized by short-term urgencies. But you just can't do it all.

The list of dreams you could pursue to realize your Focus and Context is a lengthy one. The improvements you could make to close your customer and partner performance gaps are countless. Searching and exploring to create tomorrow's markets and customers can uncover endless innovation possibilities.

So you've got to choose. From all your long-range options, alternatives, and possibilities you've got to establish short-term goals and priorities. There are as many things you've got to stop doing as there are actions you've got to start taking. Some actions will drive you forward, many will hold you back, and some won't matter much either way. But without clear targets and a strong sense of what's most important, you—and everyone on your team or in your organization—won't be able to tell the difference.

As the improvement map shows (page 53), Focus and Context is the starting point. Pinpointing customer and partner performance gaps comes next. At the same time, you must be exploring, searching, and creating new markets and customers. This leads to experimentation, pilots, and ultimately innovation. The next step is action planning—deciding what needs to be done in the short term to take you toward your long-term destiny.

Effectively establishing goals and priorities has both strategic and tactical components. The strategic decisions are *what* goals and priorities you choose to pursue. Tactics are *how* you get organized and manage your time to reach those goals.

STRATEGIC IMPERATIVES: URGENT AND IMPORTANT

Effective executives know that they have to get many things done—and done effectively. Therefore, they concentrate—their own time and energy as well as that of their organization—on doing one thing at a time, and on doing first things first.

Peter Drucker, in a chapter titled "First Things First,"
The Effective Executive (published in 1966)

It was a story with a plot line that's becoming all too familiar. I was meeting with the executive vice president of a large service organization and his quality improvement support staff. They were frustrated. After a few years of educating thousands of people in their organization, forming and training teams, mapping, analyzing, and "reengineering" a multitude of processes, and "empowering" everyone to improve quality and customer service, little was happening. For the first 18 months, they explained their lack of results by telling everyone this was long-term culture change that would take years. So they assured their CEO and board that, if they would be patient, results would follow. Now, a year later, the only results were higher costs.

Cynicism was growing throughout the organization. After the initial excitement of the big changes everyone could expect had died down, people waited. And waited. And waited. A few teams did see some exciting results. Their process cycle times, costs, and effectiveness improved, sometimes dramatically. Some of them went off to conferences to talk about their success. But the organization's total results weren't improving. Costs continued to inch up, productivity lagged, sales dragged, and profits were flat.

There were many problems with how this organization was trying to transform itself and improve performance. One of the biggest was confusing activity with results and motion with direction. Not all improvements are equally important. Many of the teams were making changes that didn't really matter. They were focusing on trivial issues that had very little impact on organization performance. Because teams were working on issues that weren't important, they made changes that consumed time, energy, and resources—but weren't important. Management had failed to guide the organization's improvement activities and establish clear improvement priorities. So there were many and varied local improvement goals and an overwhelming list of top priorities. That led to a desperate "do something—anything" flurry of unfocused activity that sent the organization scurrying off in all directions at once.

Many organizations, in their frantic rush to install the latest improvement program, have essentially said to their teams, "Don't just sit there, improve something." Often that means teams hurriedly make improvements that hurt another part of the organization. Not only are these cause-and-effect relationships often unrecognized, but the team may also be rewarded because, at the local level, their improvement project produced "results."

As is the case with so many "activity-frenzied" improvement efforts, that service company's attempt lacked a disciplined, intense fix on its most important goals and priorities. Successful team and organization improvement efforts zero in on the key organizational issues and goals with laser-sharp clarity. It's the management of attention. There is only so much you and people on your team or in your organization can give your attention to. So make sure you're aiming at high improvement targets that really matter. The faster your pace of change and improvement, the clearer your goals and priorities must be. Otherwise, you'll overwhelm and confuse your organization with the volume of activities and changes to be made.

A key component of providing focus to an organization calls for leaders to identify what my writing and consulting colleague, Barry Sheehy, calls "strategic imperatives" or "must-do's." These are the team or organization's critical leverage points. Strategic imperatives are those vital few 12- to 18-month goals, priorities, and improvement targets that—when reached—hurl the team or organization toward its vision, values, and purpose.

It Better Be Urgent

Things are little different than when God told Noah to build an ark so that he, his family, and all the species of the earth could survive the flood he'd let loose in two weeks. Shocked, Noah said, "Two weeks? God, do you know how long it takes to build an ark?" And God replied, "Noah, how long can you tread water?" It got done in two weeks.

—Ted Levitt, *Thinking About Management*

There's a direct correlation between the sense of urgency for improvement and the intensity of any improvement effort. The stronger the urgency, the more intense the improvement effort. The illustration shows what the relationship looks like.

The intensity-urgency relationship is the reason some organizations don't achieve breakthrough levels of improvement until they're standing on the brink of oblivion looking at the long leap to safety on the other side. In those cases, strategic imperatives are often painfully clear. In the words of Henry Kissinger, "the absence of alternatives clears the mind marvelously."

Effective leaders don't wait for, nor rely on, disaster to urge people into action. They will often turn up the heat and build a sense of urgency for change well before desperation sets in. These far-sighted leaders, their teams, and managers are constantly scanning the horizons for new competitors, market shifts, changing customer and partner expectations, new technologies, and other changes that could threaten the organization's performance. Proactive organizations will often pull the fire alarm when they spot those changing conditions and fan problems into a looming crisis. Everyone is urged into immediate action.

Although some people and organizations live in a constant state of crisis and high anxiety, it's not healthy over the long term. A crisis atmosphere eventually leads to burnout. When a crisis is real, it can be a rallying point—if people haven't lost all hope and self-

Intensity-Urgency Relationship

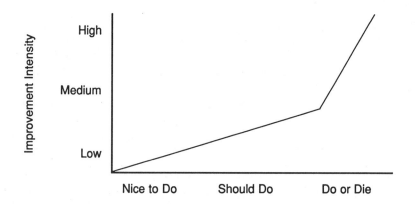

Urgency From Perceptions of Pain/Gain

confidence. But when potential and emerging problems are constantly turned into a crisis, everyone starts catching on to—and ignoring—the Chicken-Little managers who are constantly rushing around shouting that the sky is falling. So effective, long-term leaders use a combination of pain and gain to keep the urgency for change and improvement high. They fan the flames of passion with an exciting Focus and Context that provides high-improvement intensity.

I am often asked the question, "How do we get our executives, managers, or employees leading or supporting the improvement effort?" From my study and experiences with this critical issue, my reply is "connect the improvement process to their critical issues." In other words, don't make the effort a nice-to-do or even should-do issue. Find the combinations of pain and gain that will raise the urgency to an intense do-or-die level. If you're not sure what those issues are, ask.

TAKING IT PERSONALLY

Let him that would move the world first move himself.
—Socrates

Many managers are trying to establish goals and priorities for their team and organization. Most organizations use some form of annual budgeting or operations planning. Some managers use variations of Management by Objectives (MBO) to then direct the effort of people who report to them. A few organizations are using rigorous planning techniques such as "Hoshin Planning," or "policy deployment" that were imported from Japan as part of the quality movement.

These effective systems and techniques for setting team and organization goals and priorities often don't work very well. Goals get fuzzy, priorities proliferate, and people become confused by their rapidly multiplying targets. Reasons for this problem vary. In many cases the root cause is a lack of discipline. Managers don't maintain the aim. They waver, they get distracted, or they succumb to the "tyranny of the urgent" and pursue unimportant improvement opportunities.

But I find that these are symptoms of an even deeper underlying problem. Too many managers are trying to make their teams or organizations into something different from them. Their personal goals are unclear, but they try to set clear ones for everybody else. Their own priorities are constantly shifting, but they try to establish priorities for everyone else. They are disorganized, but they try to organize everyone else. The don't manage their own time well, but they try to manage everybody else's time. It can't be done. Setting goals and priorities doesn't start with "them." It starts with "me." Manage, control, and organize yourself before you try to help others set goals and priorities.

Personal Goals and Priorities

> *People seldom hit what they do not aim at.*
> —Henry David Thoreau

Goals are precise and measurable objectives with exact time frames and targets. Goals are set within the arena of Focus and Context. They are short-term steps toward your long-term vision. Goals are specific points along your journey to higher performance. They can be organization or team improvement objectives such as targets for cycle time, customer satisfaction, error or defect rates, new products or services, costs, or revenues. Personal goals can include targets such as income level or financial position; a new home, car, or other item; an academic or technical qualification; a business you want to start; or a position you want to reach. One study on the power of goals found that only 3 percent of graduates from a Yale class in the 1950s had written down their goals. A follow-up of these graduates 25 years later showed that the 3 percent with written goals had accumulated over 90 percent of the entire group's wealth.

Clear and powerful goals set priorities. They narrow the wide field of options and choices to those few activities that leverage your limited time and attention. They keep you focused on finding the shortest, most direct route to your destination. That means goals point out where not to go and what not to do as much as where to go and what to do. So clear goals lead to faster, clearer decisions that move you more quickly toward your goals.

Long-term goal setting has always been vaguely unsatisfying for me. I lean more naturally toward visioning. Part of the reason I am uncomfortable with long-term goal setting is because goals are shallow. *Goals define what you want to have, not what you want to become.* They are a means, not an end. Another reason goal setting has been less satisfying is because I've never been very good at it. Most of the time frames on my projections, forecasts, and predictions are wrong. I suppose I should ask for a refund on my cloudy crystal ball. But through persistence and staying true to my course, I've eventually reached and then reset my visions. I've generally got to where I wanted to go and became the person I wanted to become. But it was always through a route different from that I first expected to take. I guess that's called learning?

So there's the paradox of goals. I believe in personal, team, and organization goal setting. I continue to set goals. And I continue to help leaders set goals and objectives for themselves, their teams, and their organization. Goals are targets that help us immensely in moving from a general vision to a specific set of priorities and actions. We need to take them seriously—but not too seriously. There are many reasons that we may not reach our short-term goals. Some of them are good—a better, unforeseen route came into view, we learned that a narrow focus on that goal would mean losing someone or something else we care about, or we realized we had to take time out to strengthen our capability before stretching for that particular goal. Other reasons for missing our goals are bad—we didn't follow through and persist, we failed to change our habits or develop new skills, we lost control of our time and priorities, or we became distracted and wandered off track.

Set goals. Establish priorities. Get as specific and measurable as you can. But within a larger, looming Focus and Context, treat goals as vital learning points. Disciplined and effective goal setting means that at the end of the time frame you've set with every goal, you pause long enough to understand why you've hit or missed that goal. Was it your action or some larger wave you happened to catch that carried you there? Could you repeat the success if you faced the same set of circumstances again? If you missed a goal, why was that? Was it unrealistic? Did conditions change en route that pushed the goal away from you? Could you have done something better to reach the goal? Because your goal is part of a larger Focus and Context, you now reset it and establish new priorities. With a new goal in sight, you now set out for this next learning point toward fulfilling your bigger vision, values, and purpose.

Personal Time Management and Organization

Lost, yesterday, somewhere between sunrise and sunset, two golden hours, each set with sixty diamond minutes. No reward is offered, for they are gone forever.

—Horace Mann

The most valuable and perishable personal, team, or organization asset is time. You can always find a way to get more money. You can borrow it, save it, sell something for it, inherit it, beg it, or even steal it. But you never get more time. The 24 hours you and I get every day is all we'll ever get from a day. Once an hour, day, week, month, or year is gone, it's gone. But like money, time can be well invested today for bigger payoffs tomorrow. Or it can be squandered and dribbled away. Because most people and organizations don't have the same disciplined accounting system for time as they do for money, the huge waste of those precious "golden hours" and "diamond minutes" goes unnoticed.

Time frittering is as deadly and contagious as the victimitis virus and pessimism plague. With leaders as the main carriers, whole cultures become infected. Here are some far-too-common examples:

- Phone calls, voice mail, or E-mail messages not returned promptly (one business day or less)
- Meetings that start late and run overtime
- Phones that ring more than twice before they're answered
- Letters or notes not returned within four to five business days
- Cluttered desks, credenzas, and file cabinets
- Double-booked, missed, or late appointments

- Misplaced notes or files
- Missed deadlines and commitments
- Poorly maintained discussion or contact records

There's no excuse for this carelessness. There are explanations and root causes. These start with the team or organization's leaders. They are either undisciplined, unskilled, unfocused, or all three. They may be trying to do too much at once. Whenever I run into these problems in an organization, I always find the same behavior in its leaders. I have yet to find a leadership team whose members are highly disciplined, clearly focused on its key goals and priorities, and skilled in managing their time with an organization culture that manifests the sloppy habits just listed.

How you manage your personal time shouts your goals and priorities very loudly to everyone on your team and in your organization. Establishing team and organization goals and priorities is an inside job. It all starts with you. Unless you're well organized, you can't effectively organize others. Unless you manage your time well, you'll never become a good custodian of your team's and organization's precious time.

Self-management, like self-improvement, is highly personal. What works for one person may be ridiculous to another. Over the years I've evolved a personal management system that's worked extremely well for me. I think of it as PODS:

- *Priority setting.* This is where goal setting has become the most meaningful for me—at the daily, weekly, or monthly level. Starting with a paper time management system (in a leather binder I took *everywhere*—work or play) and now on my notebook computer, I make a note of *everything* I want to do on a particular day, week, or month. These are recorded whenever I get an idea, make a commitment, or set plans. At the beginning of the week, I prioritize all the ideas, commitments, and plans that have accumulated for that week. With my Personal Information Manager (PIM) program on my notebook computer it's a breeze. Detailed notes can be shuffled to tomorrow, next week, next month, or next year. I begin each day by arranging the phone calls and tasks for that day in descending order of importance. At the end of the day I shuffle what's left into tomorrow or some other date.

- *Organization.* Very few people can concentrate on two things at once or flit back and forth from one piece of paper or project to another. I certainly can't. So I've found the clean desk approach to be the most effective. The only things on my desk and credenza are ornaments, family photos, computer, telephone, and an out-basket. My in-basket is the top drawer of my desk. All incoming mail, faxes, and paper go in there. That way, when I am working on something, I am not distracted or overwhelmed by other papers fluttering and waving to get my attention. Nothing is allowed to stay in my in-drawer overnight (unless I am out of town). When I go through the paper in this drawer, it immediately goes to one of four places: the wastebasket or recycling bin, my filing system, my out-basket, or my "pending" file folder for reading or responding to on an airplane. There are no other places for paper to pile up.

- *Discipline.* Thomas Henry Huxley, the nineteenth-century English biologist, teacher, and writer, once observed, "Perhaps the most valuable result of all education is the ability to make yourself do the thing you have to do, when it ought to be done, whether you like it or not; it is the first lesson that ought to be learned." Discipline is the engine that drives the whole PODS approach. It would grind to a halt without it. Lack of good habits (discipline) is at the heart of most performance problems. I've invested decades now in constantly fighting "hardening of the oughteries."

- *Systems.* I've become one of those people who's too lazy to look for things. I like to know where everything is and find it the first time I look. Personal systems take time—and especially discipline—to set up, consistently use, and maintain. But like investments in training or quality improvement, investments of time in personal systems pay back many times their costs by saving huge amounts of time later. Keys go on the same key rack by the garage door as soon as we come in the house. Files go right back in their file drawers. Articles are coded and filed in my library system for book, column, or presentation research later. Books go into their respective sections in my library. Presentations or workshop designs are filed for later reference so I don't have to start from scratch on something similar months or years from now (many of the ideas, illustrations, or sections of this book were drawn from notes in files as much as 15 years old). About once a year I go through my filing system and toss things out, consolidate files, or move files to my attic archives.

Since 1989, all correspondence, articles, columns, books, workshop or retreat designs, and anything else I "word processed" are filed in my notebook computer. In the last few years I've added databases for thousands of my personal contact records (the conversations of everyone I talk to are recorded here). I've added a quotations database filed according to the same filing system I use for articles (most of the quotes sprinkled throughout this book came from that database). I have also created and filed hundreds of overheads and slides in my presentation software program. All of these are compatible software programs in my notebook computer. So whether I am in an airport, on a plane, or in my office, I can search files, presentations, quotations, and databases. I can then easily retrieve, cut, paste, and create something new (to be filed for later reference).

My PODS approach won't fit you. I am continuing to customize and evolve it to fit me. There is no one right or preferred time management and organization system. How effective is yours? Unless you're well-organized, you can't effectively organize others. Unless you manage your time well, you'll never become a good custodian of your team and organization's precious time.

PATHWAYS AND PITFALLS

Concentration—that is, the courage to impose on time and events his own decision as to what really matters and comes first—is the executive's only hope of becoming the master of time and events.

—Peter Drucker, *The Effective Executive*

Organizational

- Your management team must identify its three or four strategic imperatives for the next 12 months. A laundry list of urgent goals diffuses focus, spawns unproductive "busy work," and provides enough bureaucratic cover to justify any pet project or protect turf. There are many roads to determining strategic imperatives. Doing this as a group activity isn't necessary, but it helps build broad consensus and commitment. Here's a possible process:

1. Post on the wall and review your vision, values, and purpose.
2. Brainstorm a list of the key goals or objectives (call them one or the other, but don't get hung up on definitions) that must be reached in the next 12 months to propel you toward your vision.
3. Consolidate and combine closely related goals or objectives.
4. If you have more than four left, draw the relationships between all the goals or objectives, determining which ones are subsets of larger goals until you have four strategic imperatives remaining.
5. If needed, have the group distribute voting points among the list to force a ranking of the top four.

- Establish a few specific measures for each of your strategic imperatives (we'll be looking at this further in Chapter 19).
- Set specific improvement targets for each strategic imperative. The clearer the target, the surer the aim. "Improving customer satisfaction," "reengineering key processes," or "changing the culture" show up on every organization's wish list today. Setting concrete, measurable goals for improvement turns the rhetoric into reality.

  Improvement goals should be absolute targets (for example, actual number of dissatisfied customers), never percentages. Percentages allow you to turn problems into impersonal statistics. They also relieve the constant improvement pressure since anything over 90–95 percent sounds pretty good ("after all, perfection is impossible"). Real numbers force you to think about the actual number of dissatisfied customers, defects, etc., and their costs to the organization.

- Each member of your team then sets three or four personal or team goals or objectives that flow directly out of your strategic imperatives for their area of responsibility. They also establish measurements for each of their goals or objectives along with the level of improvement they are shooting for in the next 12 months.

- Every member of your team now meets with individuals or teams reporting to them to repeat the process based on your team members' goals or objectives. This continues throughout the organization until everyone is included.

- This process can be driven in a traditional top-down way or can be participative and interactive. In a top-down approach, each level of management essentially decides and commits to (with perhaps some discussion) the targets for everyone they're leading. A participative approach is much more difficult to manage and takes a few years to getting rolling smoothly. Using this method, goals, objectives, measurements, and improvement goals are set by the team that will make them happen. Team members do this in negotiation with the manager or director they report to. The manager or director then takes these commitments to peer meetings, to pull everything together and coordinate whether the commitments and planned activities will be enough to reach overall goals and objectives. This "rolls up" the organization until everything is consolidated and reviewed by the senior team responsible for the original strategic imperatives. I prefer this much messier, clumsy, and participative process.

- A key part of this cascading goals and objectives process is the learning, coordination, and communication that happens in quarterly reviews. Each team meets with the teams or individuals reporting to it to review progress on the goals and objectives. This should not become a "snoopervision" exercise. The purpose of the meetings is early, joint problem solving and learning. After the review with the people and teams reporting to them, teams and individuals then meet with the team they report to for a similar problem-solving and learning session.

- Focus all organizational systems and key processes on your strategic imperatives. Training, measurements, information systems, improvement teams, human resource systems, and other resource-intensive activities must pass the value-added test; does this work help or hinder movement toward our strategic imperatives?

- Ensure that all your improvement and project teams' activities are ultimately linked to strategic imperatives. Intensify and concentrate your improvement process by connecting it to the important and urgent organization issues that are keeping you and your management teams awake at night. Far too many department and process improvement teams are wasting valuable time and resources making improvements that don't really matter. Concentrate precious resources on key leverage points.
- Push yourself and others to set breakthrough objectives and stretch goals. An increase of 10 or 20 percent doesn't excite imaginations. We can keep doing things the same old way. Targets of ten times improvement force people to break out of their old patterns, habits, and ways of thinking. Big stretch goals inflame creativity and innovation. Help people fulfill their deep craving to be on a winning team. Help them become "the best" at whatever you're aiming for.

Personal

The chains of habit are too weak to be felt until they are too strong to be broken.

—Samuel Johnson

- What are you so busy doing? Are you working on high-leverage activities that will catapult you, your team, and your organization toward your vision? Or are you just busy? In *First Things First,* Stephen Covey, Roger Merrill, and Rebecca Merrill write, "People expect us to be busy, overworked. It's become a status symbol in our society—if we're busy, we're important; if we're not busy, we're almost embarrassed to admit it. Busyness is where we get our security. It's validating, popular, and pleasing. It's also a good excuse for not dealing with the first things in our lives."
- Know thy time. Figuring out how effective your busyness is starts with a time log. This takes some real discipline, but the

learning and personal effectiveness you'll gain is immeasurable. For a few weeks (ideally a month), keep a log of how you spend each 15-minute block of your day from the time you get up until the time you go to bed. Before you start, develop categories such as reading, learning, meetings, family time, relaxation, travel, telephone calls, visiting, preparing, planning, etc. Estimate how much time you spend in each activity before you start your log. Once your log is complete, compare your estimates to the way you actually use your time. Then compare that to your vision, values, and context. Identify the key areas for improvement.

- Plan your time. Use a time organizer system or notebook computer. Take it with you everywhere you go. Develop weekly or monthly activity lists that link to your Focus and Context (so you're always doing the most important things). Over the weekend or first thing Monday morning, sketch out your week. Each morning reset priorities to your day's activities and plans.
- Practice servant-leadership: Put returning calls and messages at the very top of your daily priority list.
- If you have activities of equal priority, start with those you hate to do most first. That will remove the dread and procrastination factor from your day's work. It also guarantees that you won't keep putting the task off and having it eat at you. Once the unpleasant work is done, everything else is easier.
- Don't be a "time doodler." Use your travel and waiting times effectively. I am constantly amazed at the number of managers who use their quiet, uninterrupted airplane time to watch movies, sleep, read casual material, or have idle conversations. I've read dozens of books and articles; opened and answered mail; written columns, articles, and book chapters; or prepared presentations on airplanes. If you consider this relaxation time, check your time log. I'll bet the work you don't get done during this highly productive time cuts into weekend or evening family time or other things you've said are important to you.
- Put a cellular phone in your car. Use it to check and answer voice mail or make calls. If you deal across time zones, you

can connect with a lot of people on your way to and from work. Schedule calls when you're in your car. Portable cellular phones allow you to do the same thing in cabs to and from the airport.

- Always have a book, magazine, mail, or other reading material with you when you travel to a meeting or appointment. Leave lots of extra travel time to compensate for traffic or not being able to find your destination right away. If you're early or kept waiting, catch up on your reading (or make a few phone calls).
- Build an audiotape library. Listen to these tapes in your car. In the last few decades I've "attended" dozens of conferences (many record and sell audiotapes of conference presentations), "read" numerous books, and listened to many experts while stuck in traffic. Carry a portable tape player along to record ideas for later review and filing.
- With today's technology (notebook computers, cellular phones, E-mail, and the like), there's no reason you can't be productive anywhere. If you travel at all, invest in your future, invest in this technology.
- Invest the time and take the courses to learn how to use the time-saving features on all the technology you use.
- Start every project or activity by asking, "What's my objective?" or "What outcome am I looking for?" I find that investing the time to clarify chapter or presentation goals and to prepare a detailed outline is time extremely well spent. I keep pushing at and coming back to "What am I trying to say here?" or "What are my main points?" I sometimes spend as much time on this focusing work as I do on the writing. But I always feel the final work is clearer and of higher quality because of this investment.
- Learn how to lead effective meetings. Poorly run meetings cost you and everyone else an enormous amount of precious time. Effective leaders start and finish on time, have clear meeting outcomes and agendas, keep discussions on track, minimize disruptions, or handle conflict effectively. It's a skill issue. Improve yours, and you'll free up time for everybody.

- Spend one or two hours of uninterrupted time in your home office or study each morning before going to your office. When I worked in an office 30 minutes from home, I would work at home until 9:30 A.M. and then head in. That way I could avoid traffic and reach people in my time zone in their offices from my cellular phone.

- Do your most demanding creative mental work during your peak performance time. If you're a morning person, do it then. If you're a night owl, save it for that time.

- Learn how to say no.

- Don't allow people on your team to "delegate up" to you. Develop them, guide them, empower and energize them. But don't do work their work for them.

- Break big jobs into little pieces and set small, incremental goals. Terry Fox was an inspiring young Canadian who lost his leg (and eventually his life) to cancer. To raise money for cancer research, he ran more than three thousand miles on an artificial leg. He ran a marathon (about 26 miles) a day. When he was running, his short-term goal was "to run to the next telephone pole."

- Develop, use, and continue improving your own customized PODS approach.

- Don't overdo planning and prioritizing your time. Use strategic opportunism in your daily work. Chance encounters, unexpected visits, or unplanned phone calls often present small, but significant opportunities to move a few steps closer to your vision. Most of those events can't be planned. If they're related to important issues, pursue them. If not, move on. But don't let a rigid schedule or plan bind you too tightly. It's all the more reason to set priorities for your day. If you get only two things done on today's "To Do" list, make sure they're the two most important.

- Setting personal breakthrough goals that are well beyond your current character, ability, or habits is to set yourself up for failure. That's why crash diets and so many New Year's resolutions fail. Build a series of small wins and new habits that gather momentum and confidence to keep you moving forward.

Establishing goals and priorities, getting organized, and managing time is about balance. In *A Better Way to Live,* personal effectiveness author Og Mandino puts it all in perspective: "Any goal that forces you to labor, day after day and year after year, so long and hard that you never have any time for yourself and those you love is not a goal but a sentence . . . a sentence to a lifetime of misery, no matter how much wealth and success you attain."

CHAPTER **14**

Sketching Your Pathway to Performance

A foolish cabin owner eventually lost his cabin to the rot that set in through the leaky roof. When it was raining, he couldn't fix the roof. When the sun was shining, he was too busy outside doing other things—and the roof didn't need fixing then anyway.

As Yogi Berra would say, "It was déja vu all over again." Five years earlier I had conducted a few introductory service/quality improvement workshops for the senior management group and head office support people of a large wholesale distribution company. Performance and feedback surveys were conducted and reviewed during these and follow-up workshops. The company clearly had problems with sagging morale and customer service, rising costs from inefficient processes and quality problems, and low innovation levels. I recommended they begin a multiyear service/quality improvement process. Basing my recommendations on the Implementation Architecture described in *Firing on All Cylinders,* I showed them how they could significantly boost the performance capability of the organization. The senior management team wouldn't buy it. They felt the time and money needed to plan, coordinate, train, and support such an extensive improvement process was far too high. Instead they threw a few "home-baked" service, quality, and motivation training programs at everyone. Then they hired expensive consultants to design and install millions of dollars worth of new computer systems. This decision was based on an extensive strategic plan that took months of senior management time, market studies, financial analysis, and more expensive consultants.

Now, here I was five years later, watching the CEO deliver a presentation to his company's managers and head-office support people. He outlined the company's stalled results for the past few years and talked about the changes needed. He said everyone needed to work together better. They had to get costs down. He said they all needed to work harder and smarter. Service and quality levels had to rise. Managers needed to take more responsibilities and empower people.

But there were no plans for doing all this. He was merely exhorting them to improve. He was clearly operating on the assumption that if they knew better they'd do better. He urged them to help change the culture to "full participation, full communication, and full disclosure." He argued for "not thinking in traditional ways" and "finding innovative ways to get the job done." He suggested they "look for ways to add value through totally accurate shipments, timely delivery, quick turnarounds, a positive attitude, eliminating unnecessary paperwork and tasks, cooperative teamwork, an open-door policy, improving efficiency, sharing ideas, reducing shrinkage, and initiating change." He went on to outline "a suggestion program" (which was a form to fill out and send to him) and stressed the company's open-door policy. He then suggested that managers should be "kind enough to have meetings with your staff" and have them fill out a suggestion form and send these to him. "I will take a hard look at it and if there are any worthwhile suggestions there, I will act on them very quickly."

That was it. No skill development, no systems alignment, no systematic approach to process reengineering or improvement, no measurement and feedback systems, no education and communication, and no changes to the company's reward and recognition systems and practices. In short, there was no improvement plan. There was nothing but good intentions and exhortations to improve. He was trying to get different results while continuing to do the same things!

CHANGES TO, RATHER THAN JUST IN, YOUR ORGANIZATION

What you are going to be tomorrow you are becoming today.

Unfortunately, this company's senior management team has lots of company. Many managers confuse making changes within their organization with making changes to their organization. Both are needed. But they have to be balanced. Changing your organization or team's composition or reporting structure, introducing new technology, pulling people and money from one area, or pumping money and people into another area isn't enough on its own. Unless organization and team skills, systems, processes, or habits are changed, other changes won't improve performance in any lasting way.

In a dingy, unused warehouse down by the waterfront, a real estate agent found a curious old machine covered in cobwebs, grime, and decades of dust. As he was wiping the dust away and inspecting the old contraption, he found a few pieces of yellowed paper in a cracked leather pouch. He chuckled softly to himself when he pulled them out and found they were titled "Operating Instructions for The Perpetual Money Machine." "What's the harm in following them?" he thought, as he turned rusty dials and pulled creaky old levers according to the directions. Suddenly the machine whirred, clanked, and clamored to life. It coughed and wheezed a few times, a bell rang, and out dropped a bundle of crisp new $20 bills with a red elastic around them. The agent was stunned. As he was inspecting the stack of bills, the bell rang again and another bundle dropped out. Then it happened again. And again. By nightfall, the agent estimated he had about $50,000. In the gathering darkness, he found the instructions to shut the machine off and went home.

Within days the agent had bought and secured the warehouse. He now spent every day operating the incredible money machine. He carefully followed all the instructions. But the "Care and Maintenance" section was becoming especially irksome. It clearly spelled out that the machine could operate no more than 10 hours per day. It must have an hour of greasing and oiling each day. And the machine needed at least one day of complete rest per week. Within a few weeks, the agent began to find that this care and maintenance schedule was a big bother. The down time was costing him a lot of money. So he started trimming back on maintenance. The machine kept producing money. Encouraged, he operated it for 11, then 12, hours a day and continued to reduce maintenance time. Those magical $20 bundles started to slow down, but they still kept coming. Soon he was operating it 7 days a week for 18 hours a day.

But then the stream of bundles slowed to a trickle. Frantically, the agent went back to the maintenance schedule. But it was too late. The bundles of $20 bills all but stopped. One day, the agent became frustrated with waiting for the next bundle of bills to finally drop. He picked up a big wrench that he once used for maintenance and angrily smashed the side of the machine. With a loud, long hiss, the machine gradually shrank, shriveled, and faded into a mound of rusty iron filings on the black, greasy floor.

THE LAW OF IMPROVEMENT DISPLACEMENT

The thorns which I have reap'd are of the tree I planted, they have torn me, and I bleed. I should have known what fruit would spring from such a seed.

—Lord Byron

Both the true example and fictional story are variations of a very old performance principle. I call it The Law of Improvement Displacement—short-term performance pressures drive out long-term improvement activities. The growth, development, and performance of many organizations, teams, and people is severely stunted by their failure to recognize and overcome this natural law. Too many managers fail to balance cash flow and wealth. They allow today's cash-flow needs to crowd out tomorrow's wealth-producing activities. These short-sighted managers forget that today's cash is the result of yesterday's wealth investments (some of which go back decades).

Few managers would ever allow physical assets like buildings, technology, production equipment, or vehicles, to crash or burn out from lack of care and maintenance. Repair schedules are followed, insurance coverage is purchased, computer and telecommunication systems are regularly backed up, upgraded, and tested, parts are greased, and oil is changed. Yet many managers fail to make the same investments in themselves, their teams, and their organization. They're so busy trying to produce today's cash that they neglect to build tomorrow's wealth. So when tomorrow finally comes, there's little wealth to produce cash.

In a knowledge-based economy, an individual, team, or organization's wealth is its capabilities. That's the source of tomorrow's cash. An organization's future revenues, for example, will come from finding and exploiting new markets, customers, and unmet needs better and faster than anybody else. Customer loyalty (and continuing revenues) will be earned by closing product or service performance gaps better than anybody else. Those "prime directives" depend on capable internal and external partners: creative partners who know how to innovate and have the hard management systems and cultural support to do so; passionate partners who are enthusiastic about and energized by being part of a winning team with an exciting future, rock-solid principles, and soul-stirring purpose; caring partners who provide the same high levels of service they're getting from their servant leaders. These are capability issues. They determine the organization's future wealth, from which future cash will flow or trickle. If you want to expand tomorrow's wealth, expand today's capabilities.

SUCCESSFUL CHANGE FLOWS FROM LEARNING, GROWTH, AND DEVELOPMENT

Leaders in learning organizations are responsible for building organizations where people are continually expanding their capabilities to shape their future—that is—leaders are responsible for learning.

—Peter Senge, "The Leader's New Work:
Building Learning Organizations"

Change can't be managed. Change can be ignored, resisted, responded to, capitalized on, and created. But it can't be managed and made to march to some orderly step-by-step process. However, *whether change is a threat or an opportunity depends on how prepared we are.* Whether we become change victims or victors depends on our readiness for change. One of the inspiring quotations I've used for my ongoing personal improvement quest came from Abraham Lincoln (whose decades-long string of failures in business and politics before becoming one of the United States' greatest presidents is inspiring itself). He once said, "I will prepare myself and my time must come." That's how change is managed.

We can't cram in few days or weeks for a critical meeting or presentation that our key program, project, or even career depends upon. We can't quickly win back customers who've quietly slipped away because of neglect and poor service. We can't suddenly turn our organization into an innovative powerhouse in six months because the market shifted. We can't radically and quickly reengineer years of sloppy habits and convoluted processes when revolutionary new technology appears. When cost pressures build, we can't dramatically flatten our organizations and suddenly empower all who've had years of traditional command and control conditioning. These are long-term culture, system, habit, and skill changes. They need to be improved before they're needed. In the words of an ancient Chinese proverb, "Dig a well before you are thirsty."

Problems that you, your team, or your organization may be having with change aren't going to be improved by some "change management" theory. To effectively deal with change, you don't focus on change as some kind of manageable force. You deal with change by improving you. And then your time must come. Successful change and continual improvement go hand in hand. In his book *The Age of Unreason,* London Business School professor and consultant Charles Handy writes, "If changing is, as I have argued, only another word for learning, then the theories of learning will also be theories of changing. Those who are always learning are those who can ride the waves of change and who see a changing world as full of opportunities rather than of damages. They are the ones most likely to be the survivors in a time of discontinuity. They are also the enthusiasts and the architects of new ways and forms and ideas. *If you want to change, try learning,* one might say, or more precisely, *if you want to be in control of your change, take learning more seriously* [my emphasis]."

Resistance to today's change comes from failing to make yesterday's preparations and improvements. When we, our teams, and our organizations fail to learn, grow, and develop at the speed of change (or faster), then change is a very real threat. If change finds us unprepared, it can be deadly.

IMPROVEMENT PLANNING:
TAKING CHARGE OF CHANGE

He who is not prepared today will be less so tomorrow.
—Ovid

Especially in groups or organizations, effective learning and capability development don't happen just because we want them to. Telling everyone to "initiate change," "be more innovative," "empower," or "improve service/quality" as the distribution company's CEO did is useless. Visions, goals, innovation, experimentation, pinpointing performance gaps, and everything else I've covered to this point won't take you far if you, your team, or your organization's capabilities are weak. For example, empowerment without enablement isn't just stupid; it's unethical. It's like putting a complete novice at the controls of a clunky old airplane and "empowering" this new pilot to land in the middle of a ferocious thunderstorm. If your organization's systems don't work well, if your skill levels aren't strong, if processes are out of control, if measurements are giving incomplete or false feedback, if communication channels are crossed, or if reward and recognition practices are not aligned, the clearest focus, strongest context, and best of intentions will be wasted.

What's needed is disciplined, rigorous improvement planning. The larger your organization, the more improvement planning and coordination you'll need to do. This is truly effective strategic planning. *Few things are more strategic than the capabilities of your organization.* Competitors can match or trump your capital investments, marketing campaigns, or new products and services. But few competitors have the foresight, discipline, and skill to build a strong and constantly improving organization. By building a highly capable organization—one that's continually learning, growing, and developing—you will develop an unmatched competitive advantage. You'll be able to move quickly to minimize the threats and capitalize on the opportunities change throws at you. You'll also be in a position to start creating that change. You'll be the "destiny controller" in your industry and chosen markets.

You'll notice that Improvement Planning is on the management side of the improvement map (page 53). Improvement planning certainly involves leadership. But it's on the management track to emphasize the disciplined, systematic, and rigorous processes involved. The next eight chapters (15 through 22) cover the eight major improvement areas needing close attention and development. These are improvement infrastructure, process, and discipline; process management; teams; skill development; measurement and feedback; structure and systems; education and communication; and reward and recognition.

Continually improving our capabilities means we have to go beyond planning. The goal of planning isn't plans, but action. However, before acting, you need to ensure you're acting on the right things. You need to find the leverage points that will give you the biggest payoffs. You must coordinate improvement activities so everyone's not heading off in all directions at once. You need to ensure that everybody sees and acts according to the bigger organizational picture. In other words, you need an improvement plan.

Tailor Your Improvement Process

> *They know enough who know how to learn.*
> —Henry Brooks Adams, nineteenth-century
> American historian

A dim-witted man went to a lazy tailor for a new suit. The first day he wore it, a friend pointed out that the right sleeve was far too short. So he went back to the lazy tailor. The tailor said, "Oh, it doesn't need alteration. Just raise your right shoulder, and then pull and hold the sleeve with that hand." The dim-witted man did as he was instructed although it caused him to hunch over and walk with a lurch. As he left the tailor shop, he met another friend. "How do you like my new suit?" he asked. "Very nice," the friend replied. "But, you know, I think your left pants leg is awfully short." So the dim-witted man headed back to the tailor shop. "Oh, that's because when you lean over to hold up your right sleeve, you pull up your left pants leg. What you need to do is bend your left leg just enough for your cuff to reach the top of your shoe." As the man hobbled down the street toward his office, he passed in front of two diners at a sidewalk cafe. "Look at that poor man," one diner said to her companion. "I wonder what happened to him?" "I don't know," was the reply. "But isn't it amazing how well his suit fits?"

Beware of pat formulas or off-the-shelf improvement packages. *Improvement tools, techniques, and approaches must be customized to fit our unique personal, team, and organizational circumstances.* That's why trendy programs like quality circles, excellence, customer service, quality improvement, teams, empowerment, reengineering, and the like have failed or fallen short in so many organizations. They're often sold as a one-size fits all, step-by-step process that you can drop right into your organization. When that doesn't work, some consultants try to alter the organization to fit the program rather than the other way around.

Most of these improvement programs are built on very sound principles and techniques that can have a profound impact on personal, team, and organization performance. The next eight chapters will dig below the buzzwords, jargon, and labels to get at and pull together these critical improvement underpinnings.

CHAPTER **15**

Infrastructure, Process, and Discipline

Cultivate only the habits that you are willing should master you.
Elbert Hubbard

Personal, team, or organization improvement doesn't happen just because you want to get better. You and everyone else might understand the pressing need for improving your ability to capitalize on rapid, unpredictable change. The picture of your preferred and vastly improved future may be strong. Your principles may embrace growth and constant improvement as a core value. Your customer/partner performance gaps may clearly show that big improvements are needed. Innovation and learning may be a top priority and even a strategic imperative. But unless you have the structure, processes, and disciplined habits for constant and ongoing improvement, it's all just useless, wishful thinking.

The high-performing "born leader" is a dangerous myth. Few highly effective teams just fall into place on their own because the right people were thrown together. High-performing organizations don't automatically emerge because somebody wanted them to, had a brilliant idea, or saw a great market opportunity. Outstanding leaders, teams, and organizations are the result of continuous and systematic improvement efforts. It's hard work. But, if you don't have a structure, processes, and disciplined habits to continue improving, you won't. You'll become a change victim, rather than a victor.

ORGANIZATION INFRASTRUCTURE
AND PROCESS

There is at least one point in the history of any company when you have to change dramatically to rise to the next level. Miss the moment, and you start to decline.

—Andrew Grove, chairman of Intel, quoted in a *Fortune* article
exploring why successful companies often fail

In *Firing on All Cylinders* I devoted more than 40 pages (Chapters 20 and 21) to the details of deploying an organization improvement process. Here's a summary of the keys to success:

- Establish an improvement infrastructure. It starts with a corporate or senior management steering council to lead and coordinate the improvement effort. Local steering councils then coordinate and focus operational and improvement teams.
- Give improvement as much weight as operations in management roles, responsibilities, and accountability.
- If your organization has more than a few hundred people in it, establish a full-time improvement coordinator.
- Develop strong internal support experts for training, process improvement, teams, and any other areas critical to your improvement efforts.
- Once a year, take your senior management team off site for 2 to 3 days of reviewing your organization improvement progress and planning what you will focus on for the next 12 months.
- Develop a detailed improvement plan. Use it to think through and involve everyone in deciding how you will deal with the areas covered in the next seven improvement planning chapters.
- Publish an annual improvement report. Use it to celebrate and widely broadcast progress to your internal and external partners.

YOUR PERSONAL
IMPROVEMENT PROCESS

The most important thing to report is that I have found that effectiveness can be learned—but also that it must be learned. It does not come by itself. It is a practice that must be acquired.

—Peter Drucker, *The Effective Executive*

Do you have the improvement habit? Are you a lazy learner? Do you act as if your formal education were an inoculation that's left you set for life? Are you a dedicated lifelong learner? Are you constantly on the grow? Do you devote at least 10 percent of your time to improving yourself? Where are learning and personal development on your list of time priorities? Are they luxuries that you get to occasionally, or are they a carefully scheduled and regularly planned activities?

These are critical performance questions. They are personal change management questions. Your answers determine your effectiveness in dealing with the fast-changing threats and opportunities that are popping in and out of your life. As I showed in Chapter 4, leadership and learning go together. Effective leaders aren't born that way. Strong leaders put learning and personal development high on their priority list. They have developed strong improvement habits that have built strong leadership skills.

So here's the most critical performance question of all—Do you have a process for continuous personal improvement? As I also showed in Chapter 4, there are dozens of learning styles and pathways to personal development (page 49). There is no one best way, no one right way to keep yourself growing and developing. You need to find the combination of personal improvement methods that keeps moving you forward toward your personal Focus and Context.

Developing a regular, systematic process and disciplined habits for personal improvement is hard work. One reason is because we're fighting against the Law of Improvement Displacement— short-term performance pressures drive out long-term improvement activities. But if we allow those short-term urgencies to tyrannize our time and displace long-term improvement, we're condemning ourselves to the treadmill of frantic, exhausting activities with decreasing performance levels.

DISCIPLINE: GETTING HOOKED ON THE IMPROVEMENT HABIT

The list of projects was always fresh, exciting, and new,
There were so many improvements to make and urgent things to do,
But little got done. There was no follow-through.

Discipline is the difference between the dreamer and the doer. Many people can visualize and tell a good story about what they are going to do. Some even set out to put their good intentions into practice. But few people are able to stick to their plans. Without the discipline to follow through, there can be no improvement. The depth of your discipline will determine the height and longevity of your improvement.

Discipline is as central to management as vision is to leadership. Like management and leadership, vision and discipline are interdependent. *Disciplined follow-through creates the results that move us closer to our visions.* Visions, in turn, provide the focus and energy that drives discipline. Without discipline, a vision is just a daydream. Without a vision, discipline is drudgery.

As with leadership, discipline is often talked about as something that we're born either with or without. "He is so disciplined," I've heard people say enviously of a high performer. But discipline isn't an innate characteristic. Strong or weak discipline is a habit formed by the hundreds of tiny choices we make every day. Choices like whether to raise that snack, cigarette, or drink to our lips. Whether to do the job ourselves or take the extra time today to help team members develop the skills so they can do the job tomorrow. Or whether to invest a few minutes in planning your day while focusing on the bigger context of your vision, values, and purpose. Each choice of and by itself is as insignificant and weak as a single strand of thread. But weave enough of these daily choices together and you've got a cable of habit that can lift you up or pull you down.

PATHWAYS AND PITFALLS

Organizational

The learning organization can mean two things; it can mean an or-
ganization which learns and/or an organization which encourages
learning in its people. It should mean both.

— Charles Handy, *The Age of Unreason*

- Ensure that your team has a good balance of active and re-flective learning. Active learning comes from exploring, searching, creating, and experimenting. Reflective learning comes from taking time out of daily operational pressures to review how well improvement activities are working and to plan further changes.
- Develop a two-track approach to your change and improve-ment efforts. One track is short term. You're looking for quick wins and immediate results, particularly from changes to operating processes (something I'll discuss in the next chapter). The other track is long-term culture change. You need to think through and establish the teams, skills, mea-surements, and structural and systems alignments, as well as the education and communication strategies, that will pro-foundly and permanently change "the way we do things around here" (how I define *culture*).
- Unless you're running experimental pilots or working with highly autonomous divisions or departments, involve the whole organization in the improvement effort.
- Spend as much time planning organization changes and im-provements as you do setting strategies, budgets, and other operational plans. Get unions, work teams, management, ex-ternal partners (like agents, distributors, and suppliers), and possibly board members involved in planning how to im-prove your organization's performance capabilities.
- Have an external consultant assess the effectiveness of your organization improvement effort (or at least use a rigorous, well-researched, self-assessment process). This should form the basis of your improvement planning. Do this annually or once every two years.

- Make sure every team's improvement activities are clearly aligned with business priorities.
- If you're an internal service/quality, organization development, or training support professional, cut the jargon and esoteric theories. Learn the business and the language of the people you're serving. Adapt your tools, techniques, and improvement processes to their situation as well.
- Hire and promote only highly self-disciplined, passionate, and continuously improving people into leadership roles. Otherwise, you'll be establishing (or continuing) a culture of stagnation and resistance to change.

Personal

The only difference between those who have failed and those who have succeeded lies in the difference of their habits. Good habits are the key to all success. Bad habits are the unlocked door to failure.

—Og Mandino, personal effectiveness author

- Join the Daily Reflect and Plan Club. This is the single most important improvement habit you can form. You need at least 15 minutes and ideally 30 to 45 minutes each work day. Use this time to read or listen to spiritual, inspiring, or educational material; write in your journal; daydream; review the previous day; set your priorities for the next day to sort out the urgent from the truly important; pray and meditate; continue developing your vision, values, and purpose, etc. Experiment with many of these activities until you find the ones most meaningful for you. You may need to juggle the time for reflection and planning to suit what's available to you, but try to find time during your peak performance hours. The payoff from this disciplined time investment accumulates over the years into an astronomical, incalculable return.
- Spend your time with optimistic and growing people. Unless you're trying to help them, avoid people with stunted personal growth, the victimitis virus, or the pessimism plague.

- If you're not one already, become a reader. This has been one of my most important sources of leadership reflection and learning. Many excellent books are available to inspire, instruct, and guide your personal, team, and organization improvement effort. I've found that most effective leaders are readers (as an improvement author, I will admit to some bias on the topic). Read with a highlighter and pen in hand. Make lots of notes to review again later.
- Become a teacher. Teaching has been another key source of personal leadership reflection and learning for me. It can (and should) start with people on your team. It can extend to giving internal or external presentations on your area of technical expertise, leadership or management topics, or "lessons learned" in your own improvement efforts. You could also volunteer to be a guest teacher at your community college, trade association meetings, or any upcoming management or leadership conferences.
- Become a writer. In his book *On Becoming a Leader*, Warren Bennis writes, "Writing is the most profound way of codifying your thoughts, the best way of learning from yourself who you are and what you believe." You can write in your own journal. You can write articles for your trade or association publications, local newspaper, or internal newsletter (many of these publications welcome such contributions). You could prepare a paper to deliver at a conference.
- Become a speaker. Do more than just on-your-feet speaking to a group. Reflect on your experiences and talk about your improvement plans with team members, the manager you report to, a close friend, or your spouse. I find that some of my best insights come from trying to articulate (or write) my thoughts.
- Become a listener. You can get hundreds of hours a year of education, inspiration, information, and instruction by listening to audiotapes in your car.
- Become a student. Attend workshops, seminars, and training sessions. Take college or university courses.
- Develop or join a network of colleagues who are as interested in personal learning and development as you are. This can be a powerful way to learn from other people's experi-

ences. It's also a great place for you to reflect on your own experiences and articulate your improvement plans. For the past few years I've run ongoing executive development sessions with groups of 20 to 25 senior managers in each one. They've proven to be powerful sources of learning and personal development for all of us involved in them.

A group that meets regularly is an excellent forum for making public declarations or even "contracts" regarding your personal improvement plans. Since I am so concerned about not being hypocritical, I've always found this approach makes it much harder to back away from forming the tough, new habits you know you need to develop.

- Develop the habit of stretching outside your comfort zone a bit at a time. It will never go back to its original size. You might try analyzing a problem in a new way, developing a new skill, meeting new people who operate at the performance level you're aspiring to, watching or listening to an educational television or radio program, or making that tough phone call right off the top. Daily or even just weekly small stretches accumulate into powerful new habits and ever stronger discipline muscles.

- Don't succumb to the victimitis virus by allowing senior managers to disempower you. Leadership is action, not position. Be a leader. Make things happen. If you know it's right for your team and the organization, learn how to play the system to get what needs to be done, done. Remember the Jesuit's Rule—It's always easier to get forgiveness than permission.

- Build your discipline by keeping your commitments. Call back when you promised. Meet your deadlines. Show up on time.

- Use Benjamin Franklin's "method for progressing." He identified thirteen virtues he wanted to develop. Each week he worked on one of the virtues for a total of "four courses (cycles) in a year." Each night before retiring Franklin reflected on and recorded his progress on that week's virtue.

As you read through the hundreds of Pathways and Pitfalls outlined in this book (and especially those in the next seven chapters concerning improvement planning), identify those that you would most like to develop (use your vision, values, and purpose to help set priorities for them). Then begin to systematically work on one at a time until they become habitual.

- Put quotes, goals, reminders, vision or purpose statements, and affirmations where you will see them a few times a day. Keep changing them and moving them around so that you don't start to look past them.

- Develop a personal improvement plan. Review the many learning styles and pathways to personal development I mentioned in Chapter 4 (page 49) and in this section. Choose those that fit you. Schedule time for your improvement as if your career and ability to master change depended on it. It does.

- Gather perceptions of your current performance levels from members of the team you lead, your peers, your customers/partners, and the person you report to (this is especially important if you're not a reflective person). Get both open-ended (blank-sheet approach) and specific, structured feedback. Your structured feedback should ask for performance perceptions across the areas you'll be covering in your personal improvement plan.

If you can't manage your time and discipline yourself to devote at least 10 percent of your time to personal improvement, you don't deserve to be a leader. You deserve to become a victim of the changes swirling around us. Get control of your time, priorities, and destiny. But you'd better do it soon. Tomorrow is arriving much more quickly than it used to.

CHAPTER **16**

Process Management

> *The building blocks of corporate strategy are not products and markets but business processes. Competitive success depends on transforming a company's key processes into strategic capabilities that consistently provide superior value to the customer.*
>
> —George Stalk, Philip Evans, and Lawrence Shulman,
> "Competing on Capabilities: The New Rules of Corporate Strategy"

A group of sailors were out in an old boat. The boat hit a rock and sprung a slow leak. The group began to argue over whose fault it was that they hit the rock. Then they argued over whose responsibility it was to fix the hole. Those on the starboard side shouted that those on the port side, where the hole was, should be responsible for fixing it. All the while, the boat filled with water and floundered in the increasingly heavy seas. As the shouting and finger pointing increased, a large wave swamped the boat. Everyone drowned at sea.

Our traditional functional or vertically managed organizations force the people in them to act like those foolish sailors. Individual departments (such as accounting, production, sales, service, or development) and areas (branch or field offices) work to optimize their own performance. Goals, objectives, performance measurements, and career paths move up and down within the narrow walls of these functional chimneys or silos. Managers and their teams focus on doing their own jobs, taking care of their own segment of the production, delivery, or support process. Everyone focuses on a narrow piece of the organization while losing sight of the big picture.

Functionally managed organizations reduce organization performance levels while increasing cycle times and costs by (1) fostering an "us-versus-them" approach to communications and fighting for organizational resources, (2) leaving unmanaged gaps between departments that disrupt cross-functional work processes, (3) making improvements or changes in one department that hurt the effectiveness of other departments in the process, and (4) losing sight of customer-partner relationships and meeting everyone's needs. With a narrow focus on their own departments or functions, people in a vertically managed organization easily forget that they're all in the same boat.

HORIZONTAL MANAGEMENT: GOING WITH THE FLOW

> *Major breakthroughs in time to market, investment, piece cost, and quality come horizontally across the organization, not vertically through individual, isolated functions. And it is our business schools that have not taught how to manage process across functions.*
> —Louis Lataif, Dean of the School of Management, Boston University

Although our organizations have been organized vertically, their operations depend on processes that flow horizontally (such as the flow of materials, customer interactions, financial transactions, product development, and the like). In the 1950s, 1960s, and 1970s, that didn't matter. Expensive layers of inspectors, coordinators, expeditors, supervisors, and managers plugged and patched the leaks to keep their organizations afloat. In the 1980s, manufacturers were forced by their superior-quality Japanese competitors to dramatically improve their production processes— or sink. Many manufacturers made huge gains in quality, productivity, cycle times, and cost reduction by rediscovering process improvement techniques developed in America by such pioneers as W. Edwards Deming and Joseph Juran (Chapter 1 of *Firing on All Cylinders* provides a more detailed account of the roots of the service/quality revolution).

By the late 1980s, the same cost and service/quality pressures were building in service organizations (and on the administrative side of manufacturing companies). The problem was amplified by the information technology revolution that was quickly gathering speed. Managers soon found that buying expensive computer systems and sophisticated software was money down the drain if all they did was automate existing processes. It just meant that things got messed up faster.

The timing was perfect for Michael Hammer's *Harvard Business Review* article "Reengineering Work: Don't Automate, Obliterate," published in the July-August 1990 issue. A former MIT professor and information technology specialist, Hammer "had been frustrated by how fixated many organizations were on using information systems merely to automate the business processes they already had in place." The popularity of Hammer's articles and related speaking engagements led to the publication of a bestselling book (written with consulting executive James Champy), *Reengineering the Corporation: A Manifesto for Business Revolution.*

In their book, Hammer and Champy define process reengineering as "the fundamental rethinking and radical redesign of business processes to achieve dramatic improvements in critical contemporary measures of performance, such as cost, quality, service, and speed. . . . Reengineering isn't about fixing anything. . . . Reengineering a company means tossing aside old systems and starting over. . . . Reengineering can't be carried out in small and cautious steps. It is an all-or-nothing proposition. . . . Tradition counts for nothing. Reengineering is a new beginning."

MANAGING THE REENGINEERING-INCREMENTAL IMPROVEMENT PARADOX

> *Grant me the patience to continuously improve some processes, the courage to radically reengineer others, and the wisdom to know when to do either.*

The call for revolutionary and radical process reengineering soon clashed with the continuous improvement techniques of the quality movement. This approach is based on the wide-spread use of teams to make incremental process improvements. Continuous improvement achieves its impressive results through "rapid inch up"—adding together hundreds or thousands of individual and team improvement efforts over many years. As the Greek poet Hesiod pointed out, "If you add a little to a little and do this often enough, soon it will become great."

But many quality improvement efforts failed to produce significant results because they were poorly implemented. So managers jumped on the reengineering bandwagon. However, choosing between process reengineering or incremental improvement is about as useful as deciding whether to use only addition or multiplication. Both are needed. How, when, and where each approach or combinations of both are used depends on the task to be performed. Like visions and goals, reengineering and incremental improvement is another and/also paradox to be managed (see chart).

Both reengineering and incremental improvement provide the vital process management so critical to the management and technology balance I argued for in Chapter 3. I've seen organizations provide an exciting Focus and Context that turns everybody on. They've provided education and training and reward and recognition and pinpointed their customer/partner performance gaps. But with ineffective processes and weak support systems (coming up in Chapter 20), their performance slipped, and the improvement effort was unsuccessful. Passionate leadership is vital. But it's just so much dissipated energy without disciplined management and effective technology. The strength and contributions of both these areas depend on process management.

Balancing Reengineering and Incremental Improvement

Reengineering	Incremental Improvement
Radical redesign and creation of new processes	Continuous improvements to existing processes
Broad, organization-wide	Single teams or functions
Destroy the old and begin fresh	Standardize and stabilize existing processes
Top down	Bottom up
Major structural changes force new behaviors	Training and culture change drive new behaviors
High investment and risk with little room for error	Moderate investment and risk by learning as you go

PATHWAYS AND PITFALLS

A process is only as strong as its weakest think.

- I call it the principle of bumbling bureaucracy—when left on their own, processes naturally turn inward to serve management and departmental needs rather than the organization's key customers and partners. *Improve processes from the outside in.* Draw a customer-partner chain (see Chapter 10, page 125) to get very clear about just whom the process should really be serving (customers and partners, not bureaucrats or management) and what the desired outcome is. Next determine the customers' most important measures of the process and how well it's performing. Use this performance gap data to establish breakthrough goals and/or continuous improvement targets.

- The broader and more comprehensive the process you're attempting to improve, the more senior management needs to be directly involved. Strategic processes (those few core or macro processes that span your organization) need a hands-on executive owner who is the champion of that process and accountable to improving it across its many vertical or functional chimneys. Major reengineering efforts demand huge blocks of key senior managers' time and attention.

- Give lots of time and attention to the diagnosis stage of process management. There's a huge amount of learning to be done here. If a process has never been diagrammed or "blueprinted," no one really knows who and what's all involved. The bigger (and, ironically, more important) the process, the truer that is. Most of these cross-functional processes were never designed in the first place. (How can you reengineer something that was never engineered to begin with?) Rather, they're a haphazard collection of personal steps, old habits, cultural holdovers, and local procedures. Most of the pieces exist in somebody's head and have never been mapped out and standardized. That's why there's so much variation, unpredictability, misunderstanding, errors, and rework as one group hands off its part of the process to the next group.

- Make sure everyone involved in outlining, managing, diagnosing, and improving the process is well trained. Managers and improvement teams need to know how to collect, analyze, and act on data so that decision making is based on facts and an accurate picture of what's really going on. And ensure that team leaders and members have strong interpersonal skills. These include facilitating successful meetings, managing conflict, confronting issues, leading a team, being a team player, and so on.
- Make sure that managers and improvement teams involved in process management are operating in a data-rich environment. Process management depends heavily on data and analysis to gather reliable information about the scope of a process, how it's performing (measurement), and what customers/partners expect of it. These data should be highly visual (lots of diagrams, charts, and graphs) and broadly available so that everyone can see the big picture. Data-based tools and techniques include cause-and-effect diagrams, flowcharts, check sheets, Pareto charts, histograms, scatter diagrams, affinity charts, tree diagrams, and the like.
- Most managers underestimate how much time, attention, and support process improvement teams need. Unguided process improvement teams can be detrimental to your organization's performance. They busily set about improving things that don't matter, make changes that (without their intending to) create problems somewhere else in the organization, or just squander precious organization time and resources. If your management team can't give improvement teams the support they need, reduce their numbers to a level that you can support. If you're not sure what that level of support is, ask.
- Choose processes you're going to radically reengineer very carefully. The changes will be disruptive and will tie up huge amounts of time and resources. Make sure you're leveraging those major investments in processes that will have a significant, strategic impact on your organization's performance.
- Make sure all your process improvement activities are clearly and tightly linked to your strategic imperatives. Each effort should also have highly focused and specific improvement

goals (that are an aggressive, major stretch) and measurements. Establish feedback and follow-up steps for each process management and improvement team.

- Keep everyone educated and updated on all your process improvement activities. Make it all as transparent and widely available as possible. Reduce apathy and resistance by increasing your education and communication efforts.

- Don't let specialists and consultants do theoretical reengineering in isolation and then launch it into the organization. A national retailer hired high-priced consultants to reengineer its logistics (ordering, warehousing, shipping, and invoicing) process. The new process made sense on paper, but those who had to make it work felt cast aside. Because they didn't own the new approach, it wasn't too hard to "demonstrate" that the consultant's process didn't work.

  Reengineering is becoming the new mantra for frustrated strategic planners who are putting this new label on their old ineffective approach. Elite groups of senior managers, hands-off staff people, technology specialists, and assorted experts study, analyze, and plan major changes. With more focus on theoretical planning than implementation, they go for big breakthroughs with radical organization changes and major investments in sophisticated technology. Getting wide-scale involvement in mapping out and dramatically improving (or developing a consensus to radically redesign) the existing process is seen as too slow and not bold enough. But those theoretical changes generally prove to be impractical in the real world. And those who aren't involved in planning the battle can be counted on to battle the plan. This elitist, expert, planning-driven approach rarely works.

- Don't develop your own internal, homemade version of process management. I've seen too many poorly designed attempts at process management. Designing your own makes about as much sense today as trying to manufacture your own computer system or write your own software programs. Like information technology, the science of process management has come a long way in a few short years. It's become an extensive field unto itself (hundreds of books are now available on various aspects of the expanding topic). A multitude of well-researched and well-designed process management training packages and consulting services is available. However, like an information technology system, process management packages and services do need to be tailored to your unique needs. And you need to develop the internal expertise to support and continue evolving your process management technology with your consulting firm's help.

- Successful process management demands priority setting, organization, discipline, and a systematic approach. How's yours? You can't build a team or organization that's different from you. Undisciplined and disorganized managers can't build disciplined and organized teams.

Process management is an invaluable part of disciplined management systems and effective technology use. Reengineering and incremental process improvements can have such a profound impact on organizations that many managers focus almost exclusively on these powerful tools and techniques. But experience clearly shows that if process management isn't well-integrated into a larger improvement effort, it will eventually wither and quite likely die. That bigger picture includes Focus and Context; pinpointing customer/partner performance gaps; exploring, searching, and creating new markets and customers; innovation and organizational learning; establishing goals and priorities; and extensive improvement planning covering the areas in the chapters that lie just ahead.

CHAPTER **17**

Teams

> It is obvious that teams outperform individuals. . . . Teams will be
> the primary building blocks of company performance in the organi-
> zation of the future. . . . If there is new insight to be derived from the
> solid base of common sense about teams, it is the strange paradox of
> application. Many people simply do not apply what they already
> know about teams in any disciplined way, and thereby miss the
> team performance potential before them.
>
> —Jon Katzenbach and Douglas Smith,
> *The Wisdom of Teams: Creating the High-Performance Organization*

A scout leader was trying to lift a fallen tree from the path. His
pack gathered around to watch him struggle.

"Are you using all your strength?" one of the scouts asked.

"Yes!" was the exhausted and exasperated response.

"No. You are not using all your strength," the scout replied.
"You haven't asked us to help you."

Good managers have always fostered teamwork. But highly
effective leaders are now showing the performance power of
building team-based organizations. When effectively organized
and led, teams:

- Multiply an organization's flexibility and response times
- Flatten vertical hierarchies and smash functional chimneys
- Provide a vehicle for wide-scale participation in organization
  change and improvement efforts
- Turn involvement and empowerment rhetoric into reality
- Expand jobs and elevate the sense of purpose and meaning
  they provide
- Foster a spirit of community, cooperation, and belonging
- Build the commitment of those people who will ultimately
  make—or break—any organization change or improvement
  effort

- Harness the improvement energy and ideas of everyone throughout the organization
- Become the key unit of organizational learning by sharing collective experiences and multiplying intellectual power
- Replace command and control discipline with far more powerful and lasting self- and peer discipline
- Improve communications and deepen understanding of change and improvement decisions being made
- Produce better problem solving and more thorough decision making

Where teams have been effectively organized and led, team outcomes have led to dramatic improvements in productivity, customer service, quality, process management, innovation, cost effectiveness, job satisfaction, morale, and financial performance.

TEAM TYPES AND FOCUS

If the organization is to perform, it must be organized as a team.
—Peter Drucker

Managers' growing understanding of the power of a team-based organization has created a teams explosion. Suddenly we're seeing a profusion of high-involvement teams, high-performance teams, corrective action teams, service and quality improvement teams, project teams, task forces, steering councils, process management and improvement teams, problem-solving teams, cross-functional teams, departmental teams, work teams, regional or branch teams, self-directed and self-managed teams, semi-autonomous teams—to name just a few.

But many so-called teams aren't. They're groups, committees, task forces, or councils. Managers are often confused by teamwork, "teaminess," or team spirit. They don't realize that groups can have a team spirit and show some teamwork, but still not be a true team. The best definition of a team I've come across is provided by Jon Katzenbach and Douglas Smith in their well-written and useful book *The Wisdom of Teams*. They define a real team as "a small number of people with complementary skills who *are equally committed to a common purpose, goals, and working approach for which they hold themselves mutually accountable.*" The two consultants then take their definition of *team* a step further to describe a high-performance team: "This is a group that meets all the conditions of real teams, and has *members who are also deeply committed to one another's personal growth and success.* That commitment usually transcends the team. The high-performance team significantly outperforms all other like teams, and outperforms all reasonable expectations given its membership."

The Whats and Hows of Teams

> *When teams work, there's nothing like them for turbocharging productivity. . . . Forget all the swooning over teams for a moment. Listen carefully and you'll sense a growing unease, a worry that these things are more hassle than their fans let on—that they might even turn around and bite you. . . . The most common trouble with teams: Many companies rush out and form the wrong kind for the job.*
> —Brian Dumaine, "The Trouble with Teams," *Fortune*

The dozens of team labels and types can be boiled down to two core types: operational teams that work *in* the business or process to produce, serve, or support and improvement teams that work *on* the business or process to multiply its capabilities and effectiveness. Effective operational teams are a hybrid of both types. They work in the process or business to meet production or service goals while also working on the process or business to expand its performance potential. Teams whose primary or sole purpose is improvement are usually cross-functional. They're often permanent process management teams or temporary project teams formed to solve a specific process problem.

Besides clarifying what a team's purpose and role is, the other important management decision is how it will operate. The team management choices can be plotted on a three-point continuum:

1. Management commands and controls the work group, with some consultation and involvement (this is not a team).

2. Management roles and responsibilities (such as scheduling, planning, meeting facilitation, and establishing measures) are shared between team members and the team leader.
3. The team is autonomous and manages itself.

The third point on the continuum talks to self-managed rather than self-directed teams. That's because teams do need direction from the rest of the organization. That direction usually comes from a manager who's guiding and coordinating their activities or from a management team they report to. Self-directed teams can too easily become self-serving teams. Without clear guidance and direction, their activities can drift away from the organization's overarching Focus and Context, its customers/partners, and its performance and improvement goals (strategic imperatives). That's the path to unproductive busywork and self-destructing teams.

If you look back at Katzenbach and Smith's description of real and high-performance teams, you can clearly see that only groups that can be classified as having shared management or self-management fit their definitions. This is consistent with a growing body of research and my own experience. A team's commitment and performance increases exponentially with the degree of power, control, and ownership *team members feel they have* (in their own—not management's—perceptions of their work).

Team Types and Focus

© The Clemmer Group Inc.

This diagram shows the What-How choices that need to be made with every team. Use it to plot each team's role or purpose and how it will be managed. It's not unusual for an organization to have a wide variety of teams that could fit within various points on this chart. But a large proportion of teams in a highly effective team-based organization are skewed toward the self-management end of the How continuum. These organizations also have a good balance of teams focused on working in the business or process as well as on the business or process.

LEADING TEAMS: YOU'VE GOT TO TAKE IT PERSONALLY

If you would create something you must be something.
—Johann Wolfgang von Goethe

Most managers grew up in a command and control era. In those days, a "strong leader" was a decisive problem solver who was a tough disciplinarian. He (most were men) "took control" and "made things happen." Teamwork was when everyone rallied and pulled together to meet the leader's goals and follow his direction.

It's tough to change those deeply ingrained values and approaches. In my workshops and consulting, some days it feels as if I see a never-ending stream of "old school" managers (some of the worst can be newer and younger managers) who are struggling to transform themselves into effective team developers and leaders. It can be done. It is being done. Your team's effectiveness depends largely upon your effectiveness as a leader. Your team leadership effectiveness hinges on:

- *Your level of self confidence.* Sharing power and developing others to do what you used to do is almost impossible if you're insecure. If you draw much of your self-worth from how well others "listen up and follow your command," you're going to have a tough time empowering and developing a real team (let alone a high-performance or self-managed team).
- A new view of your job. For example, in a team-based organization, management's job is not problem solving. It's

making sure the right problems are being solved by teams equipped and supported to solve them.

- Servant-leadership. Your job is to direct and guide your teams. But you're also there to serve them. They are your customers. So what's your performance gap? How do you know? What's your personal improvement plan for closing your biggest gaps?
- Strong team leadership skills. A *Fortune* poll found that being "a team player and team leader" was the most important skill CEOs felt an MBA should have. This is also the single biggest factor in your confidence levels with teams. There's a strong relationship between your skills at facilitating a team discussion, handling conflict, encouraging and capitalizing on diversity, keeping a meeting on track, building a team's effectiveness, etc., and your enthusiasm for teams. The same is true of all the managers in your organization.
- A strong, effective senior management team. If you're a senior manager, make sure your team is a model to the rest of the organization before you try to "do teams." If you're not a senior manager and your senior team is not a good example of team effectiveness, don't let that get in your way. Be a leader. Show them how it's done.

Chapter 5 of *Firing on All Cylinders* contains a more detailed discussion of the movement toward team-based organizations and management's role in them.

PATHWAYS AND PITFALLS

Building a Team-Based Organization

> A lot of the things that prevent teamwork are not in people's attitudes. They are in the design of the organization and management practices.
>
> —Rosabeth Moss Kanter, Harvard Business School professor

The following tips, techniques, and traps are aimed at senior managers and improvement professionals deploying dozens, hundreds, or thousands of operational and improvement teams across their organization.

- Lead by example. I am fed up with listening to strong individualists in senior management groups talk about teams—for everyone else. Stop trying to make your organization into something different from you. You're making yourself and everyone else crazy trying. Get focused, develop your skills, establish feedback loops—do whatever needs to be done to turn your group into a team.
- Developing team skills and changing team leaders' and members' behavior is central to senior management's critical coaching role. It can't be delegated. Outside experts or internal human resource development professionals can provide invaluable guidance, tools, and training processes, but they can't own the job of building team skills.
- Because effective teams clearly outperform any other method of organizing people, teams have become a management craze. But like quality circles in the early 1980s, many efforts to build a team-based organization are poorly planned and executed. Teams are given zippy new labels and better analytical tools, but the same weak implementation strategies and cultural conditions are still choking them off. A telecommunications company called my firm in to help it out of the teams traps it had fallen into. Dozens of team rallies and hype sessions were held all around the company. More than a thousand improvement suggestions were generated. But because little action was taken, enthusiasm had turned to cynicism. Hundreds of voluntary improvement teams were formed with no strategic focus or direction. They ended up spending much of their time devising strategies to get managers on their side and brainstorming how to deal with organization-wide system and process problems.

   The senior management team turned things around by re-forming all the teams into operational and process improvement teams with clear mandates and measurements. These were linked to the organization's four strategic imperatives. (Cost reduction, customer satisfaction, innovation, and cycle time reduction were that year's top priorities.)
- Use the diagram on page 210 with your senior management team to establish (or review) your implementation strategy for teams in your organization. Start by taking management levels, divisions, departments, or groups and plotting where

the teams in those areas would be on the graph today. Then plot where you would like them to be in 2 years.

- Use the Outstanding Teams Checklist (page 216) to ensure that every new team in your organization has all of the direction, guidance, and leadership identified there. You can also use the checklist to assess your current teams. But rather than guessing or projecting your own perceptions, practice servant-leadership and ask the teams. Have team members rate the leadership they would like to have on each point compared to what they feel they are currently getting.

- Too many teams are formed with vague goals of increasing "feel good" teamwork, job satisfaction, involvement, or empowerment. *Teams are a means, not an end.* They're a by-product of effective leadership focused on doing real and meaningful operational and improvement work. That's why most team-building exercises don't work. I've seen too many groups go off on wilderness excursions or use "structured team-building experiences" to try to turn a group into a team. These approaches don't work because they're not focused on business and performance issues or the broader organization context and focus. They don't get any real work done. I was asked to speak at an internal management conference for fifty middle and senior managers of a manufacturing company. An OD (organization development) consultant was running the management team through 2 days of visions and values work—in a vacuum. It was unconnected to the business strategy. There was no implementation planning and no goal setting. And a year later, there were no real teams or improved performance results.

  Don't promote teams; promote performance and results. Teams are a key vehicle for achieving higher performance. But it's the pressure of performance goals and the glue of a passionate vision and shared values that bonds group members and transforms them into a real team. That's providing they have the process, structure, leadership, skills, support systems, and culture to pull together and get results.

- You can tell that teams are operating within a fuzzy vision or unfocused strategy when progress is measured by activities rather than meaningful results. "Whoever dies with the most teams wins," joked one frustrated manager. So "measures" like the number of teams formed, projects underway, or people trained cloud the more critical question of whether all this team activity is making any real difference to the organization's performance.

Floundering teams are often disconnected from the burning strategic issues that are keeping senior managers awake at night. Teams work on minor or local issues while senior management worries about how to slash overhead, reduce cycle times, develop new products, or drive up customer satisfaction. So the teams implementation becomes a training, empowerment, involvement, or some other kind of "bolt-on" program operating outside of the managerial mainstream.

- Ensure that every team has clear performance goals and measures. These should:
  - Reflect the organization's goals and priorities or process management activities
  - Be developed and owned by the team with senior management's guidance
  - Provide plain and simple feedback and learning loops (only the vital few) so the team can monitor its own progress and take early self-corrective action
  - Originate in customer/partner performance gaps or be aimed at finding new markets, products, and services and at filling unmet needs
- Senior managers must be highly involved in building a team-based culture. That means that they work as hard as (or harder than) any team leader or member at building their personal team member and leadership skills.

Leading Your Team

Skilled team leaders transform a group from what they are into what they could be.

- The following Outstanding Teams Checklist reflects what we've covered (and have yet to cover) together in this book. These are the key elements of top-performing teams (and organizations). Use this checklist to assess yourself and your team. Even better, get your team to do this assessment:

__ A high-performance balance (analytical skills and disciplined management processes, technical skills and strong capabilities to use the latest technologies, and people leadership skills)

__ Strong self-determination with no tolerance for the victimitis virus or pessimism plague. (One team agreed, "you can visit Pity City, but you aren't allow to move there.")

__ Passion and high energy for rapid and continuous learning, developing, and improving

__ A clear and compelling picture of the team's preferred future (including desired team type and focus)

__ A clearly articulated set of shared principles outlining how the team will work together

__ A strong sense of purpose and unity on why the team exists

__ Solid agreement on whom the team is serving within the customer-partner chain and organization processes

__ Identification of, and an aggressive plan for, improving the team's customer-partner performance gaps

__ Relentless exploring, searching, and creating new customers and markets (if appropriate to the team's role)

__ A process for innovation and team learning

__ A handful of performance goals and priorities directly linked to the organization's strategic imperatives

__ A concrete process and discipline for continuous team improvement linked to the organization's improvement effort

__ Process management skills, roles, and responsibilities

__ High levels of team leadership and team effectiveness skills

__ Powerful feedback loops and measurements

__ A culture of thanks, recognition, and celebration

- If your meetings are a chore or have become a meeting of the bored, you've got a skill problem. Meetings should reenergize and refocus. Most don't. With the proliferation of practical resource materials, seminars, and training now available, there's no excuse for poorly run meetings. Here's a prime area where a modest investment in learning and skill development can pay incredible dividends in saved time and frustration. If your meetings were just 10 percent better (25–40 percent improvements aren't uncommon after good training in meeting leadership), how long would it take to repay your learning and skill-building time?

- Effective teams meet frequently. At the senior management level, I've found a direct correlation between how frequently a team meets and the amount of vertical management—departmentalism, territoriality, turfdom, etc.—in that team. I am amazed at the number of management teams that rarely meet. The senior management group of a company I worked with hadn't met since its last retreat two years earlier. As we reviewed an internal survey they had just conducted, not surprisingly, one of their biggest organizational problems was poor communications. If senior managers don't frequently get together and talk to one another, how can they expect the rest of the organization to do anything but follow their lead?

- Team learning and development is dependent upon team reflection (and ideally feedback from others who work with and for that team) and on how effectively the team members work together. But don't get too introspective, with everyone laying on conference room couches. The reflection needs to be within the context of the work the team is doing.

- If you're trying to move your team toward shared or self-management, you need to lead as if you were driving a car on an icy road. Guide and intervene with a light touch. Sudden, jerky changes will send the team into a skid.

- Build a series of small wins. That doesn't mean pumping up your team with a lot of hot air (you'll quickly send their phoniness meters over the red line). But look for ways to point out and celebrate the real performance progress the team is making.

See Chapter 14 of *Firing on All Cylinders* if you'd like a more detailed outline of the team leadership skills I've touched on here.

Most high-performing organizations use a wide variety of teams. But many managers underestimate what it takes to build a team-based organization. The improvement pathways and passages we've covered so far get teams started and focused. The route to ever higher performance lies just ahead.

CHAPTER **18**

Skill Development

If most people knew how hard I have worked to gain my mastery, it would not seem wonderful at all.

—Michelangelo

You can't do what you don't know how to do any more than you can come back from a place that you've never been. If people in your organization don't know how to use a new technology, what good is it? If you don't have strong communication skills, how can you inspire, energize, and arouse your team to high performance? If managers can't bring people together around a vibrant vision, core values, and powerful purpose, how can they provide the focus and context for organization improvement? If you don't have a clear picture of your organization's and team's customers/partners and their expectations, how can you increase your service/quality levels? If teams don't know how to pinpoint their performance gaps, how can they close them? If people don't know how to set goal and priorities, get organized, and manage their time, how can they do these things? If you don't know how to analyze and reengineer or improve processes, how can you boost your organization's effectiveness? If managers don't know how to lead teams effectively, how can they build a team-based organization?

Knowing what needs to be done and why is a major step in the climb to higher performance. Wanting to make the changes that lead to improved performance is also important. Next comes acquiring the ability to change. If you don't have the skills to change your behavior, then passion, visions, goals, improvement plans, and discipline won't take you very far.

I've spent the best part of two decades in the skill-building business. My library and files are full of examples and research showing the powerful payoffs that come from skill training. Large parts of my previous books are dedicated to this critical performance-improvement issue. It all shows that *top-performing organizations invest substantially more time and money in skill development than does the average organization.* It also shows that highly effective leaders dedicate much more time and effort to their own skill development than most other people do. They have developed themselves into effective leaders; they weren't born that way.

Skill development is at the center of mastering change. If you don't know how to operate in a team-based organization, teams are a threat. If you don't know how to enable and support people on your team, empowering them is out of the question. If your technical skills fall behind, technological changes are to be avoided. If you're not an effective coach, moving people toward shared or self-management is a hare-brained idea. If your people skills are weak, you'll spend time in back rooms, boardrooms, and your office (managing things) rather than out with customers and partners figuring out how to serve them better (leading people). If your meetings are where minutes are kept but hours are lost, having more of them would be absurd.

THE WHAT-HOW BALANCE

Skills are like tax deductions; we use them or we lose them.

Knowledge and skills are closely related, but different, improvement activities. *The Concise Oxford Dictionary* provides these definitions:

> Knowledge—theoretical or practical understanding; the sum of what is known
> Skill—expertness, practiced ability, facility in an action or to do something

To improve personal or organization performance, both knowledge and skills are needed. But many managers and training professionals (who ought to know better) get these two confused.

Knowledge generally increases with skill development, but skills don't always increase with more knowledge. Just because we know better doesn't mean we do better. Behavioral science research consistently shows that we act our way into new ways of thinking far more easily than we can think our way into new ways of acting.

Skills are built in a variety of ways. Most of them involve a cycle of practice or application, feedback, and then further application, more feedback, further practice, etc. These steps are basic to effective training. The same process is used by professionals such as physicians to develop their "hands-on" abilities. The foundation of such training is knowledge or education. But medical students don't become physicians just by regurgitating information on tests, analyzing cases, or writing a thesis. They go through a period of internship and practice to show that they have a balance of knowledge and skill. Unfortunately, business school training doesn't follow the same path of mixing theoretical understanding with real-world application.

Besides being too theoretical, the education that most managers get focuses heavily on management and lightly skims leadership. Both management and leadership knowledge and competencies are generally built on a base of technical skills that managers developed in their functional disciplines such as accounting, market-

Finding the Right Balance

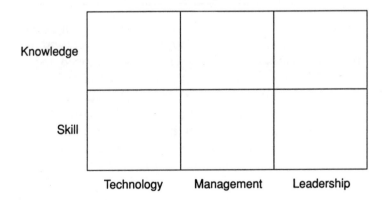

© The Clemmer Group Inc.

ing, production, and the like. All three areas—technical, management, and leadership—need to be covered. And everyone needs some mix of education and skills across the three components. It's a question of finding the right balance for the job to be done and direction you and/or your organization are moving. As you prepare your personal, team, or organization improvement plan, use the diagram to determine what area you need to improve and how you are going to improve it.

PATHWAYS AND PITFALLS

Skills to do come of doing.
—Ralph Waldo Emerson

Chapters 11 to 14 of *Firing on All Cylinders* are dedicated to general skill development and building personal, coaching, and team skills. Here's a summary and update of what I've since found to be some of the most critical tips, techniques, and traps to skill development.

Organizational

I have never found an organization in the world that overtrains its people.
—Charles Garfield, researcher and author on peak performance

- Despite clear evidence of the huge returns training provides, many organizations do far too little of it. Even within the training business, many companies are so wrapped up in operational pressures of maintaining today's cash flow that they neglect improvement efforts that build tomorrow's wealth. High-performing organizations consistently invest from 3 to 5 percent of their payroll expenses in training. Many lesser performing companies fall well below that (1.5 percent of payroll should be the minimum level). Training was a big factor in Achieve's growth. We consistently made the investment of taking all Achievers out of the field and flying them to a central location for a few days of sharing experiences, education, and training. Even when times were tough, we maintained our average of 12–15 days per year for everyone in our field force.

- A key contributor to ineffective training is weak evaluation. "Happy sheets" (rating of the training program, instructor, facilities, lunch, etc.) don't tell you if the training was any good. Instead, measure behavior change and impact on service/quality levels, process performance, leadership as seen by those being served, innovation, productivity, costs, or progress in reaching improvement goals.

- Match the development method to the objective. No amount of traveling on the wrong road will bring you to the right destination—no matter how many other misdirected travelers are also headed toward oblivion. For example, knowledge-based or theoretical approaches are the wrong road to developing practical skills and behavior change.

- A powerful and underused method for organizational skill development is training senior managers as trainers and having them deliver a number of the skill-development sessions. This approach usually means there are no attendance problems at training sessions. Participants don't show up asking, "How serious is management about these new approaches?" And senior managers are put on the spot to practice what they've been preaching. Teaching is also a potent learning experience for the teacher and leads to a deeper understanding and mastery of the skills being developed in others.

- A popular way of flushing training dollars down the drain is by failing to link training with strategic imperatives and organization Focus and Context. What happens in the classroom and what happens back on the job are worlds apart. Trainees learn which hoops to jump through, pledge allegiance to the current improvement fad, give their enthusiastic "commitment" to building "the new culture," get their diploma—and then go back to work.

Don't train just because it's a good thing to do. Skills are a means, not an end. Lasting skills aren't built in a vacuum. They're developed on the basis of clearly understood needs (performance gaps) and application to pressing threats or opportunities.

- Don't "sheep dip" people through training programs that give them skills they might eventually need. Use just-in-time training to provide the skills team leaders and members need at the time they're going to use them. For example, teach people how to lead or participate in process improvement teams just before they're going to form or lead one.
- Don't deal with skill deficiencies through changes to organization structure or reengineering processes. Both of those are vital to improved performance. But you need to dig deeper. When teams or individuals have performance problems, it may be because they don't know how to make the needed improvements.
- When organizations attempting to expand their use of teams are asked what they would have done differently, the response is often more training of team leaders. Too many team leaders are asked to deal with complex and difficult team issues without having been prepared for a new and vastly different role. As a result, meetings frequently become wasteful and ineffective. Healthy team diversity and differences degenerate into destructive conflict. These struggling teams often lose their momentum. Reaching agreement and taking action becomes difficult. Many poorly led teams also remain narrowly focused and miss the big picture. And these teams generally fail to look ahead and anticipate change.

Personal

We all want to know how to make other people effective. But that's not the place to start. The place to start is: "How do I make myself effective?"

—Peter Drucker, management professor, author, and consultant

- Skill building starts with assessment. Clarify your skills performance gap by identifying what skills you need to fulfill your vision. Then get feedback on your current skill levels. Because most managers overestimate their leadership skills, they underdevelop them. That's why feedback from those you are leading is so vital to keeping you grounded in their perceptions of your skill reality.

- Use the diagram on page 221 to plot which areas and activities should be in your personal improvement plan. Be especially careful of confusing knowledge and skills. Knowing isn't doing. I continually run into managers who use lots of "leader speak" about vision, values, purpose, innovation, service to others, and the like. They're often very knowledgeable about the theories of leadership. Then I talk to others on their team or who report to them. They give me vivid examples of technomanagement or bureaucratic actions that show anything but leadership behavior.

- Develop and continue improving your verbal skills, especially in front of groups. Without effective communication skills you may be a good technomanager, but you'll never be a strong leader. You won't inspire, arouse, and energize people. Your organization or team's Focus and Context will be just so many lifeless words and colorless ideas.

- Skills are developed through practice, application, feedback, more practice, and so on. Seek out and participate in training programs, coaching and mentoring experiences, or low-risk, live situations that provide this skill development cycle for you.

- Be first in line for any training your organization offers. Then become an instructor or at least get actively involved in follow-up coaching and support to your team members going through any training sessions. Developing your people development skills is one of the most important leadership improvement activities you can do.

A key element in learning and skill development is feedback. That's the next stop in our improvement planning process.

CHAPTER **19**

Measurement and Feedback

Ignorance is the starting point for the bliss that leads to oblivion.

Joan, a doughnut store manager, watched a customer get up and make his way to the pay phone beside the counter. "Hi. I'm calling about the ad you had in the paper for a regional manager a few months ago," Joan overheard her customer saying on the phone. "Oh, I see, the position's been filled. Are you happy with the new manager?" the man asked. "You are. OK, thanks."

As the customer went past the counter, Joan said sympathetically, "I couldn't help but overhear your call. Sorry that job wasn't available."

Somewhat puzzled, the customer replied in a voice different from that he'd used on the phone, "What? Oh, that. Oh, I have the job now. I was just calling to see how I was doing."

High performers actively seek feedback. They know that's the only way to change their course and improve their performance. Feedback and measurement identify the "here" that goes with vision's "there." Getting from here to there depends on a solid understanding of where "here" is. But in most organizations—if it's given at all—feedback is a distorted jumble of mixed messages and past results. It's almost impossible to draw connections between today's results and yesterday's behavior or today's behavior and tomorrow's results. It's as if we're archers being judged on our ability to hit the target with a few arrows each day. But the target is hidden in the mist. And the results of our daily shots are consolidated and given to us at the end of each month. Then we are rewarded or punished for the "accuracy" of our aim and exhorted to improve.

Feedback is central to learning. Faulty feedback is one of the biggest contributors to organization, team, and personal learning disabilities. If you don't know how you're doing, you can't improve.

The right measurements establish vital feedback loops that show whether the approaches being used are moving the organization toward its goals. They help separate the useful from the useless work. Effective measures show whether all the training, team activities, experimentation, and process management are producing results. They help managers see through the dust storms raised by furious flurries of enthusiastic "busywork" creating the illusion of progress.

The quality movement has played a key role in the development and refinement of measurements to give early warnings and balance the backward-looking, historical financial measures managers have relied so heavily upon. But the quality and quantity of nonfinancial performance measures being used is still far too low. There are two main reasons. First, many managers haven't done their homework and don't realize just how disciplined this field has become. They don't know that a vast array of effective tools measuring performance in the areas of customers/partners, process, organization improvement, and the like are now readily available. Second, managers aren't comfortable with feedback. They haven't learned how to get it and how to give it effectively. So measurements turn into "gotchas" to be avoided.

CORE STRATEGIC MEASUREMENTS

Crude measures of the right things are better than precise measures of the wrong things.

Chapter 18 of *Firing on All Cylinders* identifies and describes seven core measures for service/quality improvement. These are customer satisfaction measures, process measures, product measures, project measures, cost of quality, the quality improvement process, and benchmarking.

Those measurements are an important part of service/quality improvement. But they don't encompass all of the broader performance issues we've been covering in this book. Here are the five core measurement areas that provide much broader and more balanced feedback loops for assessing and improving organization performance:

- *Customers/Partners.* Measurements might include performance gap analysis for each customer and/or market segment, external partners (such as distributors and suppliers), and all your internal partners. This area might also include price/value perceptions, customer/partner turnover rates, market-share measurements, market perceived-quality levels, and competitive benchmarking.
- *Innovation and new markets.* Revenues generated from new products, services, or markets can be measured. You might also measure the number of experiments, skunkworks, and pilots underway.
- *Competencies and capabilities.* These measurements could include process accuracy and effectiveness, cycle times, project measures, reliability, on-time performance, cost effectiveness, rework, error rates, and other non-value-added work (using tools such as activity-based costing), knowledge and skill levels, or productivity levels (such as revenue per organization or team member).
- *Learning and improvement.* Rates of improvement in the other four areas could be tracked. You might also do self-assessments or bring in outside experts to examine the effectiveness of your organization improvement process. Another form of measurement could include quality audits and supplier certification.
- *Financial.* These traditional and historical measures might include profitability, cash flow, return-on-investment, sales levels, or shareholder value.

Across these five core measurement areas, hundreds of measurements and supporting submeasures are possible. That complex approach makes sense for some highly disciplined and measurement-experienced organizations. But *your overarching goal in developing measurement and feedback loops should always be simplicity.* Ideally, you want to identify the vital few measures within each area that have the biggest impact on performance. These come directly from your strategic imperatives, which in turn grow out of your Focus and Context. Your few core measures are then cascaded to all operational and improvement teams, who use them to develop their operating targets and/or improvement objectives. Once these teams have made changes and improvements, progress is assessed. This important time of reflection and learning becomes input to the next turn of the cycle.

This annual improvement cycle brings together many of the elements we've covered so far in this book (progress assessment will be covered in Chapter 24). It's a condensed version or another way of viewing this book's central improvement map (page 53). The annual improvement cycle starts with the vision, values, and

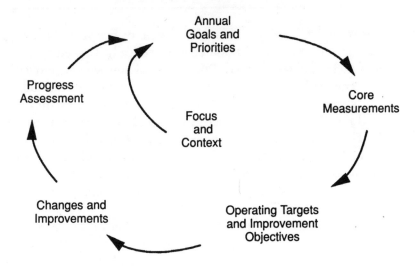

**Strategic Measurements Guide
the Improvement Process**

Annual
Goals and
Priorities

Progress
Assessment

Focus
and
Context

Core
Measurements

Changes and
Improvements

Operating Targets
and Improvement
Objectives

© The Clemmer Group Inc.

purpose that form the organization's Focus and Context. These establish the strategic imperatives, or key goals and top priorities. From these, core measurements around the five areas we've just covered are developed. Operating and improvement teams then use these imperatives and measures in setting their operating targets and/or improvement objectives. Based on this planning, changes are made and improvements initiated using process management, systems realignment, experimentation, pilots, and the like. All the while (and at periodic intervals), managers lead their teams through a series of progress assessments. These learnings are captured, celebrated, shared, and incorporated in the next year's cycle of strategic imperatives, core measurements, and so on.

FEEDBACK: AN ESSENTIAL ELEMENT OF LEARNING AND IMPROVEMENT

The major difference between the most and least successful executives is the latter's lack of awareness. Successful executives are critical of their own performance. Unsuccessful executives are critical of the performance of others.

—Harry Levinson, *The Exceptional Executive*

At our youngest daughter's sixth birthday party, five-year-old Ryan hit her on the head. As Vanessa cried hysterically, I asked him to apologize. He politely refused. When I asked him why, he replied, "Mr. Clemmer, I don't apologize unless I see teeth marks or blood."

Many managers don't realize the pain and problems they've created unless they see teeth marks or blood on those they work with. The most insensitive managers are generally the ones who don't have good personal feedback systems and refuse to seek input on how to improve their personal performance. Their "open door policy" is "if you don't like the way I do things, the (exit) door is always open."

You can't build an organization or team that's different from you. If your team or organization avoids or even resists performance measurement and feedback, take a hard look at your own approach to personal feedback. If you don't have a continuous system and practice of actively soliciting feedback on your behavior, your organization is reflecting your measurement values. Feedback-impaired managers are usually in favor of performance measurement and strong feedback loops—for everyone else.

I first noticed this connection when I was trying to understand why some teams or organizations had rich and powerful flows of performance data and rigorous measurements. But many other organizations that seemed equally determined to improve had very weak performance measurements. It didn't seem to be a knowledge issue. The organizations with weak measurement systems knew all about "360-degree" feedback systems, performance gap analysis, data-based tools and techniques, and the like. But it was a lot of talk. There was little application. Then I began to notice how people tiptoed around sensitive issues, especially problems that should have been raised with their immediate managers or further up the hierarchy. I began to take note of the number of conversations I was having about how people try to gauge a senior manager's mood to see if today is a good day to raise a sensitive issue or flag a problem. I also noticed how many managers claimed that they wanted to build a learning organization and then did little to learn how their behavior was perceived by people in their organization.

Personal feedback—especially about problems or faulty signals you've sent—can be very painful. But your frequency, sensitivity, and action (or lack of it) on personal performance feedback sets the pace and tone for the rest of your team and organization. Many of the best measurement tools and techniques are severely curtailed in a feedback-adverse culture. As consultant H. James Harrington puts it in *Business Process Improvement,* "Measurement is the lock, feedback is the key. Without their interaction, you cannot open the door to improvement."

PATHWAYS AND PITFALLS

Nothing requires a rarer intellectual heroism than the willingness to see one's equation written out.

—George Santayana, American philosopher, poet, and novelist

Organizational

- Far too many measures are designed to meet internal needs. They may satisfy management's command-and-control paranoia for "snoopervision" by tracking every activity and minute of the day. Or they're designed to serve accounting, information technology, human resources, or other support departments. Numerous measures are also highly technical, production- or product-focused. Many organizations are entangled in a multitude of such complex internal measures.

What's missing in this measurement mania is the customer. High-performing organizations measure from the outside in along the customer-partner chain. They begin by measuring what's important to customers and pinpointing the performance gaps. Next on the measurement pecking order are the needs of those external and internal partners serving customers. Then attention turns to the people producing products or serving the servers. The measurement needs of managers and support departments come last in the customer-partner chain.

- Discuss the five core measurements on page 228 with your management team. Which of the five are well covered in your organization now? Which need more work? What are you going to do about broadening, simplifying, and improving your measurements? Set measurement action plans.

- Most managers rely far too heavily on financial measures. They're clearly an important vital sign of the organization's health. But the bottom line is history. It shows today's consequences of yesterday's management decisions. However, it's often an unreliable predictor of how today's decisions will affect tomorrow's results. Results are the outcome: They can't be managed any more than you can turn back time. You can't manage results, you can manage only the causes of those results. Organization improvement starts by identifying and measuring the vital areas that have the biggest impact on your results. If you're driving with your eyes on the rear view mirror of bottom-line results, you won't see the swamp until you're sinking in it.

- As important as what's measured is how the information is used. In many organizations, team members and managers resist measuring accuracy rates, cycle times, rework, customer satisfaction levels, wait times, and the like because they've been beaten up with this information. Despite the mountain of evidence showing that 85–90 percent of errors and mistakes originate in the organization's structure, system, or process, all too many managers still look for *who* rather than *what* went wrong.

- Micro or local measures need to flow out of organization-wide, macro measures. To counter growing complaints from its distributors, one manufacturer began measuring its rate of incomplete orders. Mounting back-order levels, shipments of the wrong parts, and many clerical errors were discovered. More than 60 percent of the "pick orders" didn't match the distributor's invoices. Management's solution was to replace the shipping department manager. The new manager promptly disciplined, fired, and "motivated" clerks and shippers to "shape up the department." After a temporary improvement, error rates settled in slightly above their previous level. Only when measurement, root cause analysis, problem solving, and improvement activities focused across the entire sales, order entry, picking and packing, inventory control, accounting, and invoicing process did error rates plunge by nearly 300 percent.

- Weighing yourself ten times a day won't reduce your weight. No matter how sophisticated your measurements are, they're only indicators. *What the indicators say are much less important than what's being done with the information.* Measurements that don't lead to meaningful action aren't just useless, but they're also wasteful. Measurement is an essential tool for transforming and improving organization effectiveness. Choosing the right tool is the first step. How skillfully the tool is used determines its ultimate effectiveness.

- Measurements should never be used in isolation. As shown by the diagram on page 229, effective measures provide vital links between Focus and Context (vision, values, and purpose), strategy, improvement, and higher performance.

- When our son, Chris, was eight, we always knew exactly where we stood with him. Two notes, one saying "I love Mom/Dad" and the other saying "I don't love Mom/Dad" were posted on the bulletin board in his bedroom according to what he felt we'd earned at that moment. Eventually we convinced him that love was unconditional. But the example of highly visible and transparent measurement is right on the mark. Too many people in organizations (and relationships) spend a lot of time trying to read mixed messages or figure out what's being measured (and valued) and why.

- Get teams to develop their own measures. Make sure they're broad, balanced, and simple. Make measurements as close and immediate to the activities being performed as possible.

- Move your team and organization to a 360-degree performance-feedback system—starting with you. 360-degree feedback involves gathering data and performance perceptions from the people reporting to you, the people you serve in the customer-partner chain, your suppliers, and the manager(s) you report to. Your role in helping others on your team move to this approach is that of coach. You will provide your performance feedback as one of the many sources for your team and individual members. But your main job is to help your team and its members gather, understand, digest, and act on the feedback they get from their customers, partners, and anyone reporting to them.

- Be careful of using market share or competitive indicators too heavily. You could be making great gains in a shrinking market. Some high-performing leaders don't really care what competitors are up to because they're moving far ahead by blazing new trails, developing unconventional product extensions and uses, or opening up new markets. Competitors warrant attention and study to ensure that your company isn't falling behind in key areas or to figure out how to exploit their weaknesses. But too much attention to competitors keeps your focus inside traditional approaches and old (likely outdated) market models. Your company becomes defined and bounded by industry standards. If it comes down to a choice between studying, keeping up with, and trying to outflank your competitors or knowing your current and potential customer needs so well that you can anticipate market changes and new market opportunities, choose the latter.

- Benchmarking, a powerful and popular measurement and improvement tool, involves finding competitors, processes, or functions that you can use as a point of comparison and learning. Here are a few keys:
  - Get outside your industry and find comparable processes or functions that are many times more effective than yours.
  - Benchmarking isn't "corporate tourism"; you benchmark a process, function, or organization with your own set of measurements, process maps, and the like. You're there to compare and learn, not visit and poke around.
  - Send out the teams that will be making the improvements and changes.
  - Exchange information with the companies you're benchmarking so you can both learn.
  - If you're just starting on a rigorous, planned organization improvement effort, don't benchmark yet. You're not ready. You need to have well-trained teams, clear process maps, and core measurement data before you can effectively compare yourself with anyone else.
  - Have someone study and become an expert in benchmarking, hire a consultant, or use a well-proven approach to benchmarking.
  - Start small and increase the scope of your benchmarking with your experience.

Personal

To become different from what we are, we must have some awareness of what we are.

—Eric Hoffer,
American longshoreman and philosopher

Ironically, if you're a feedback-impaired manager, you're the least likely to realize it. You're not listening to what people have been trying to tell you. That's because you're too busy defending yourself. If someone suggests you're defensive, you'll become defensive about your defensiveness.

Following are some ways to develop your personal feedback skills. These leadership actions are also aimed at balancing hard organization measurements with soft feedback.

- Run extensive organizational climate surveys at least once a year. Review the results with the people that completed the survey to further clarify their feedback. Get them involved in making the improvements they're suggesting.
- Spend large amounts of time with people on the front serving lines, production lines, or support offices. You know you're visible and accessible enough when your presence isn't a royal visit or special occasion and people are comfortable in challenging your actions and flagging potential problems.
- Hold regular breakfasts ("muffins with management"), lunches, and celebration dinners with frontline teams. Take this time to ask for feedback, concerns, and suggestions. A simple question such as "What's the dumbest thing management asks you to do?" can produce powerful insights.
- Invite frontline teams to management meetings to show off their accomplishments, provide input to new directions and plans, or give their views on the state of your organization.
- At the end of your meetings, spend 10–15 minutes getting participant feedback on the process used to run the meeting. Find out what went well, and how future meetings could use everyone's time and involvement even more effectively.
- Use focus groups (a cross section of typical frontline performers) to test new management directions before making grand announcements to everyone. Even if you press on against the advice of the focus groups, you'll have deeper insights regarding how to address the issues the new direction may raise.
- Develop systems, practices, and skills to get continuous feedback on your leadership effectiveness from the people you lead.
- Get your team into the habit of committing to personal plans and reporting on the leadership actions each member takes to visibly signal the values or priorities your group is espousing. For example, if customer service improvement is a key goal, each team member should report on the amount of time he or she spends with customers.

- Be very careful about how you receive bad news or problems that are raised. If those who bear bad news feel you blame them, they'll shy away from giving you this feedback in the future. People shouldn't have to try and gauge your mood or sugarcoat problems and issues in front of you.
- Hold yourself visibly accountable to the same standards and measures you apply to anyone else. This is an extension of a basic leadership principle—never ask anybody to do anything that you haven't done or aren't willing to do yourself.
- Get rid of management perks and privileges, such as special parking spots. You want to knock down the walls and minimize the differences between you and people on your team or in your organization. You will be approached with feedback, ideas, and input only if you're approachable. Separating yourself with special perks and privileges makes you less approachable.
- When giving or receiving feedback, keep it in balance. Point out the strengths or things going well. Use your own blessings and brag list to keep your perspective if you've been given some painful personal feedback.
- Don't assume that no news is good news. Your customers, partners, peers, or team members may have given up on trying to tell you anything. Silence or purely positive comments probably indicate feedback impairment. The problems haven't gone away; they've just gone underground—for now.

Improving personal and organizational performance without constant feedback is like trying to pin the tail on the donkey when you're blindfolded. Only through knowing where you are can you change where you are going.

CHAPTER **20**

Structure and Systems

Structure influences behavior. When placed in the same system, people, however different, tend to produce similar results.

—Peter Senge, *The Fifth Discipline:*
The Art and Practice of the Learning Organization

The CEO of a national retailer was frustrated. His face grew noticeably redder as he told me how he had set up each store as a profit center and was attempting to hold store managers and their regional managers accountable for profitability. But when a store underperformed, the store manager would demonstrate that head-office buyers were forcing the store into stocking the wrong merchandise for its particular mix of customers. Or the managers would claim that the marketers hadn't put together the right campaign for their local markets. When the CEO tried to hold the buyers accountable for the slow-moving merchandise, they would blame the stores for not displaying it well enough. Or the buyers would point their fingers at the marketers for not moving the merchandise. When the marketers were confronted, they blamed the stores or the buyers.

Another organization in the office equipment business had started an intense focus on customer service and quality improvement. As team members finally began listening to their customers, they kept hearing how bureaucratic their company was. One day a customer in one of the biggest cities they served pointed out that they had thirty-three phone numbers in the phone book. "We don't know whom you should talk to. Here, you figure it out" is what the company was essentially saying to its customers. "Maybe you should give us an organization chart so we have a fighting chance of getting to the right department," the customer suggested. When improvement teams tried to map out some of the service processes in these departments, they had to follow the bouncing customers as callers were sung a few verses of "No, that's not my department." Service providers were just as frustrated by all the interruptions from "all those idiotic customers who keep calling us when we're obviously not the right people for them to talk to."

Both of these examples illustrate the behavior-shaping role of structure and systems. It's like the strange pumpkin I once saw at a county fair. It had been grown in a four-cornered Mason jar. The jar had since been broken and removed. The remaining pumpkin was shaped exactly like a small Mason jar. Beside it was a pumpkin from the same batch of seeds that was allowed to grow without constraints. It was about five times bigger. Organization structures and systems have the same effect on the people in them. They either limit or liberate their performance potential.

YOU'RE GETTING THE BEHAVIOR
YOU DESIGNED

A jillion smart, energetic people submitting to the "right" incentives won't get you a micrometer closer to the customer unless the dead weight of a vertical hierarchy is lifted—almost entirely—off their backs. There's no liberation when much more than a semblance of the superstructure remains.

—Tom Peters, *Liberation Management*

If you're not happy with the behavior of people on your team or in your organization, take a closer look at the system and structure they're working in. If they behave like bureaucrats, they're working in a bureaucracy. If they're not customer-focused, they're using systems and working in a structure that wasn't designed to serve customers. If they're not innovative, they're working in a controlled and inflexible organization. If they resist change, they're not working in a learning organization that values growth and development. If they're not good team players, they're working in an organization designed for individual performance. Good performers in a poorly designed structure will take on the shape of the structure.

Many organizations induce learned helplessness. People in them become victims of "the system." This often comes from a sense of having little or no control over their work processes, policies and procedures, technology, support systems, and the like. "You can't fight the system," they'll say with a shrug as they give the clock another stare, hoping to intimidate it into jumping ahead to quitting time. These feelings are amplified by a performance management system that arbitrarily punishes people for behaving like the system, structure, or process they've been forced into. "Empowering" helpless people without changing the processes, structure, or systems they work in is worse than useless. It increases helplessness and cynicism. It's like "empowering" that seed in the Mason jar to become a full-grown, well-rounded pumpkin—but leaving it in the jar.

Improvement planning, process management, teams, skill development, and the like are either constrained or boosted by your organization's structure and support systems. If they're poorly aligned with your Focus and Context, strategies, and goals, your performance will never come close to its full potential. One of the key cylinders in *Firing on All Cylinders* is devoted to systems. These include human resource systems (featuring promotion and job assignments and performance management), supplier management, accounting systems, technology, customer systems, distribution systems, information systems, and control systems. I treated structure as just one more subsection of systems. I've since realized that was a mistake. Structure plays a much bigger role in performance. That's why I've focused most of this chapter on structure.

THE SHAPE OF HIGH PERFORMANCE

Any intelligent fool can make things bigger, more complex. It takes a touch of genius—and a lot of courage—to move in the opposite direction.

—E. F. Schumacher, twentieth-century German
economist and conservationist

The evidence is clear and overwhelming. Centralized, hierarchical organizations work about as well as the old Soviet Union. Despite all the evidence, I am still appalled by the number of variations on the centralization theme I still keep smacking into. What makes things even worse is how senior managers in these dysfunctional organizations proclaim empowerment, participation, teams, leadership, trust, and the like. Then they take partial measures while expecting total success. They liberate parts of their organizations while limiting other parts. They push hard with one foot on the accelerator while also pushing hard with their other one on the brake. Their words say "You're empowered." Their actions say "You're empowered as long as you get approval first." Like that national retailer, these dysfunctional organizations end up trying to go in two opposing directions at once. I once halted an executive retreat and everybody went home after the group of seven division presidents and corporate staff vice presidents couldn't agree on whether their values were centralization or decentralization. Trying to do both at once was ripping the organization apart. The CEO never could decide which direction he wanted to commit to. He was eventually fired as frustrations and infighting rose while organization performance fell.

Most centralists don't set out to deceive anybody. In their heads they know that high degrees of involvement, participation, and autonomy are key elements in high-performance organizations. But in their hearts, they still crave orderliness, predictability, and control. That's why they cling to such anachronisms as strategic planning. It's part of their futile search for a master plan that can regulate and bring a sense of order to our haphazard, unpredictable, and rapidly changing world. Our equally outdated accounting systems give centralists plenty of reinforcement. For example, hard financial measures can clearly show that consolidating and centralizing support services and functions saves money and increases efficiency—at least on paper. What don't show up are the alienation, helplessness, and lack of connections to customers or organizational purpose that mind-numbing bureaucracy brings. The energy-sapping and passion-destroying effects of efficiencies may save hundreds of thousands of dollars. But traditional accounting systems can't show the hundreds of millions of dollars lost because of lackluster innovation, mediocre customer service, uninspired internal partners, and unformed external partnerships.

I am an extreme (some might argue dangerous) decentralist. Since I began my management career, I've given people high degrees of autonomy. I've run even small organizations to the point of such inefficient decentralization that people are running their own show. It works. Here are some of the reasons:

- Everyone can see and manage his or her work as part of a whole, interconnected system, not as one in a bunch of parts and pieces.
- People are trusted and treated as responsible, caring, and committed adults—which is how they then behave.
- A collection of small, self-contained teams or business units is many times more flexible and responsive at meeting threats and capitalizing on opportunities.
- Ownership, commitment, energy, and passion levels are much higher.
- Everyone focuses on meeting customer/partner—not the internal bureaucracy's—needs.
- People have more control over their work. The vicious cycle of learned helplessness is replaced with a virtuous cycle of hopefulness and leadership.
- Bureaucratic committees become entrepreneurial teams.
- Feedback loops are much clearer, shorter, and closer to the customer and markets.

High-performing organizations that are thriving in today's chaotic world are adapting and pioneering a wide variety of highly decentralized structures. They are giving up control of people so that people can control their own and the organization's destiny. This is creating an explosion of organization structures and models with such names as network, shamrock, pulsating, jazz combos, adhocracy, horizontal, hollow, spider's web, flat, meritocracy, modular, cellular, cluster, inverted, starburst, federal, pancake, and virtual.

The search for an ideal or perfect structure is about as futile as trying to find the ideal canned improvement process to drop on the organization (or yourself). It depends on the organization's Focus and Context, goals and priorities, skill and experience levels, culture, team effectiveness, and so on. Each is unique to any organization. We are also in the midst of a major transition from organization and management practices that began around the turn of the twentieth century. My cloudy crystal ball won't allow me to see which organization structure or model will dominate the twenty-first century. Because we're no longer in an age of mass production and standardization, I'm sure there won't be just one type. Rather, we'll see our top organizations grow and shed a variety of structures and models to suit the changing circumstances.

However, the shape and characteristics of a high-performing organization structure is coming clearly into view:

- *Intense customer and market focus.* Systems, structures, processes, and innovations are all aimed at and flow from the voices of the market and customers. The organization is driven by field people and hands-on senior managers in daily contact with customers and partners.
- *Team-based.* Operational and improvement teams are used up, down, and across the organization. A multitude of operational teams manages whole systems or self-contained subsystems, such as regions, branches, processes, and complete business units.
- *Highly autonomous and decentralized.* Dozens, hundreds, or thousands of mini-business units or businesses are created throughout a single company (I've split business units of twenty five people into smaller business units). Local teams adjust their company's product and service mix to suit their market and conditions. They also reconfigure the existing products and services or develop new experimental prototypes to meet customer/partner needs.
- *Servant-leadership.* Senior managers provide strong Focus and Context and strategic direction to guide and shape the organization. But very lean and keen head-office management and staff also serve the needs of those people doing the work that the customers actually care about and are willing to pay for. Support systems are designed to serve the servers and producers, not management and the bureaucracy.
- *Networks, Partnerships, and Alliances.* Organizational and departmental boundaries blur as teams reach out, in, or across to get the expertise, materials, capital, or other support

they need to meet customer needs and develop new markets. Learning how to partner with other teams or organizations is fast becoming a critical performance skill.

- *Fewer and more focused staff professionals.* Accountants, human resource professionals, improvement specialists, purchasing managers, engineers and designers, and the like are either in the midst of operational action as a member of an operational team, or they sell their services to a number of teams. Many teams are also purchasing some of this expertise from outside as needed.

- *Few management levels.* Spans of control stretch into dozens and even hundreds of people (organized in self-managing teams) reporting to one manager. Effective managers are highly skilled in leading (Focus and Context), directing (establishing goals and priorities), and developing (training and coaching).

- *One customer contact point.* Although teams and team members will come and go as needed, continuity with the customer is maintained by an unchanging small group or individual. Internal service and support systems serve the needs of the person or team coordinating and managing the customer relationship.

PATHWAYS AND PITFALLS

Farming looks mighty easy when your plough is a pencil, and you're a thousand miles from the corn field.

—Dwight Eisenhower

- Effective systems follow, serve, and support rather than control, direct, and dictate. I continue to find that the key structure and systems alignment question is "for whose convenience is your organization designed?" Is it to serve customers and those producing for or serving them? Or is it designed to make life easier for management and staff support groups? Look at your planning, accounting, invoicing, telephone, information technology, and human resource systems. Just whom are they serving? Systems either enslave or enable. How do people in your organization feel systems are helping or hindering them?

- Organization structure and systems are clear indications of management's true values (regardless of what might be printed on pretty parchment paper). How far do you really trust people? What size fishtank have you put them in? When people miss performance targets, do you develop and improve them or get somebody else to do the job? The answers to these questions are found in the degree of decentralization and autonomy in your organization. How's yours? What do the people in your organization think about the control and autonomy they have?

- To what extent is your system and structure aligned with your team's or organization's vision, values, and purpose? You need to agree on the philosophy and approach underpinning any changes to your structure and systems. Look at the eight characteristics discussed in the previous section. Get your team to discuss and agree on which might be dropped from or added to this list. Discuss each of the remaining characteristics individually. How far do you want to go with each one? What are the implications for changes and improvements in your team and the organization? How can you ensure that the structure and system conclusions you arrive at are reflected in your improvement plan? This critical team discussion needs to take place before you go off and reengineer or restructure your organization.

- Flatten your organization. Aim for no more than two levels of management. There're few excuses for anything over three.

- Form follows function. Let the structure evolve from your strategy, process, and systems. A strong Focus and Context will provide the glue that keeps everyone together. And keeping everyone focused on goals and priorities will allow more fluidity in organization design. Organize around good people and highly skilled teams. Your structure needs to fit the people it supports, rather than force people to fit your structure.

- Don't let "experts" or staff people design organization structure (playing shuffle-the-organization-charts-and-boxes) any more than you let them develop formal strategic plans or do theoretical reengineering in isolation from those being reengineered. Line managers should develop structures around processes, strategies, customers, and teams. Stop trying to box people into organization charts. They don't show key relationships and the way your organization really works anyway.

- One of the biggest barriers to decentralization is the skill levels of those being given more autonomy. The more you push authority and operating responsibilities to operating teams, the more training and coaching support they'll need.

- Another major barrier to decentralization is management values and skills. How are yours? As James Brian Quinn puts it in *Intelligent Enterprise*, "The old management concept of 'if I'm not in control, it's out of control' has to give way to genuine delegation and rewards for 'coaching' and 'coordination.'"

- Turn your head office into a lean and keen field service center. Move all staff and support functions out into the real world. Train and hold staff people accountable for being coaches rather than controllers. They exist to provide expertise and support. Don't let them ask for reports or get in the way of people doing the work that customers are paying for. Better yet, put them on a fee-for-service basis competing with external experts.

- Structure, systems, and processes are intertwined. You can make a fair degree of progress by changing processes only. But eventually (and often quickly), process improvement teams will slam into unaligned systems and structures. However, you'll also get nowhere changing systems and structure without changing processes. Start with process mapping and improvement. System and structural changes will follow.

- Don't split your sales or customer service force along division or product lines. It's too confusing and frustrating for clients to have to organize your service processes for you. If you're providing complex or multiple products and services, turn your key sales or customer contact people into generalists or project managers (that means lots of training and support). Their role is to manage the customer interface and coordinate all the experts, specialists, and other team members who will be brought in when needed.

- Make sure everyone in your organization understands that your structure is fluid and must continually change in a fast-changing world. There is no such thing as "once we get past this change (such as a reorganization), things will return to normal." Constant change and improvement is normal.
- Experiment, pilot, and learn. Continually look for new and better ways to align your structure and systems.
- There is no such thing as overcommunication in organization improvement efforts. But try to overcommunicate why changes are being made and where they fit into your larger Focus and Context and strategic imperatives.

You have to keep pulling out the weeds of bureaucracy (such as staff groups, controls and constraints, policies and procedures that get in the way). It's a never-ending job.

CHAPTER **21**

Education and Communication

The increasing availability of new information and communication technology is one of the key ingredients that makes a high-involvement management approach possible. This capability, more than any other, makes it possible for individuals to become self-managing, to be involved in the business, and to control processes and operations.
—Edward Lawler III, *The Ultimate Advantage: Creating the High-Involvement Organization*

Shortly after Vanessa, our second daughter, was born, my wife, Heather, was talking with six-year-old Chris, our only son, about how much she liked having a boy in the family. "If you like little boys so much, how come you brought home another girl?" Chris tearfully rebutted.

The less we know, the more we suspect. Like Chris, people in your organization will make up their own explanations for events and actions they don't understand. These can be fanned by the winds of rumor and innuendo into scary scenarios of impending doom. At times of dislocating change, those breezes quickly become blustery gales that create raging infernos if trust levels are low. *Managers routinely underestimate the amount and quality of education and communication required to make improvement efforts successful.* They fall victim to our human tendency to judge others by their actions, but to judge ourselves by our intentions. Because most managers intend to make nothing but beneficial changes and improvements, they often fail to appreciate the explanations others are giving for their actions.

If people don't buy into why changes or improvements are necessary, they will fight and resist them. Before people will want to improve, they need to agree with why they need to improve. Then they are ready to learn how to improve. To reach this stage, you need to treat everyone on your team and in your organization as a partner. Strong partnerships are built on keeping each other informed. Effective partners communicate frequently and clearly. If you want people on your team or in your organization to behave like business partners, treat them that way. Treat them like responsible adults and give them a deep and continuous understanding of what's going on in the business. They can't become self-disciplined and self-managed without it. With little knowledge and scanty information people won't—in fact, they can't—take responsibility. Because information is power, the only way of empowering or sharing power is by sharing information.

Much of what we've covered in this book is useless if you or the people in your organization who will make it all work don't understand what's to be done and why. For example, having a clear Focus and Context isn't worth much if people don't understand it. If your Focus and Context isn't well communicated, it will be dead and lifeless—and unfulfilled. Commitment and understanding go hand-in-hand. Only by understanding (and feeling aligned with) the organization's larger Focus and Context will people thrive and grow. Powerful leaders constantly clarify team or organization Focus and Context and keep people excited about working within it.

A constantly improving and highly effective team or organization is transparent. The why, who, what, and how of decisions made and actions taken are obvious to everyone. The culture is marked by openness and informality. Information is widely shared. That means lots of education combined with powerful communication systems, processes, and practices. It's one of the keys to organizational learning and innovation.

EDUCATION: YOU CAN'T IMPROVE
WHAT YOU DON'T UNDERSTAND

Order and simplification are the first steps toward the mastery of a subject.

—Thomas Mann

Learning is a central theme of my life, my work, and this book. Education is a key component of learning. Both are broad, comprehensive topics. However, within the narrower focus of improvement planning in this chapter, *education* refers to the understanding and information people on your team or in your organization need about your improvement effort.

Once your management team has established an improvement plan and process, there are many ways to help everyone in the organization understand what's going on and why. These include one-on-one discussions, group presentations, workshops or seminars, videos, printed materials, and the like. The best approaches are personal and interactive. Rather than just presenting the improvement plan and process, effective improvement education engages everyone in discussions that deepen understanding and provide feedback, options, and further ideas to the team guiding the improvement effort. That's why workshops or seminars featuring presentations and discussions by senior managers are such an effective educational tool in the improvement process.

Developing an Education Improvement Plan

Because this book is built around a central improvement map, it shouldn't surprise you that the education plan I suggest you build follows the routes charted there. Following are the key components in roughly the order you might use them in an educational workshop or seminar. You need to stress or focus on those points that will be the most important to the audience you're working with, your organization's culture, and the direction you're trying to move in.

- *Why should we change or improve?* This step is the first and most critical. Changes and improvements that don't seem to have solid reasons behind them appear to be the whimsical fancies of management. They will (and should) be resisted. Reasons you give should talk in terms of the audiences'—not your own—interests.
- *Balancing leadership, management, and technology.* Everyone needs to understand this critical balance. They might pinpoint where they are now, and what needs to change in order to move to a better balance.

- *Self-leadership.* Leadership is an action, not a position. The organization needs everyone to take the initiative and become a thermostat leader.
- *Focus and Context.* The team or organization vision, values, and purpose need to be clear and compelling. You can also help everyone develop a personal Focus and Context and look for ways to align it with those of the team and the organization.
- *Customers/partners.* Understanding and drawing a customer-partner chain (with performance gap data if you have it) puts the audience you're working with into the middle of the big picture.
- *Organizational learning and innovation.* Outline and discuss how your organization is searching for deeper latent/unmet needs, exploring new markets, experimenting, and learning from clumsy tries. Then clarify the role and involvement of your audience.
- *Team and organization goals and priorities.* Present and discuss your team and/or organization's strategic imperatives, improvement targets, and key measures. Outline and discuss the cascading goals and objectives along with the ongoing review process your audience will be involved in.
- *The improvement model, plan, and process.* Introduce, update, or clarify the improvement model you're using and why. Walk through all the subcomponents and the plans that have been developed (or are developing) for this planning period. These should include improvement structure and process, process management, teams, skill development, measurement and feedback, organization structure and systems, continuing education and communication strategies, reward and recognition, and your plans for regularly reviewing, assessing, celebrating, and refocusing the improvement process.
- *Improvement tools, techniques, principles, and practices.* Introduce or review the methods that your team and/or organization will be using. Discuss how this group will be trained and expected to use the improvement tools and approaches.
- *Next steps.* Explain what's going to happen next and how your audience can expect—and will be expected—to become further involved in the improvement effort.

COMMUNICATION STRATEGIES, SYSTEMS, AND PRACTICES

Before you say what you think, be sure you have.
—Malcolm Forbes

Communication is both a symptom and a cause of organization performance problems. Over the years, I've heard hundreds of managers use communication as a vague catchall for every type of organization and team problem imaginable. Generally, the root cause of many "communication problems" could be traced to poorly designed organizations; ineffective processes; bureaucratic systems; unaligned rewards; unclear customer/partner focus; fuzzy visions, values, and purpose; unskilled team leaders and members; cluttered goals and priorities; low trust levels (another symptom); and weak measurements and feedback loops. Whenever a manager calls our firm to solve a "communication problem," we always know we have some digging to do.

However, communication strategies, systems, and practices do play a central role in personal, team, and organization performance. Information, understanding, and knowledge form the lifeblood of the organizational body. *A thoughtful and comprehensive communication strategy is a vital component of any organization improvement plan.* It sets the tone and direction of improvement efforts. Communication strategies influence the energy levels for change and improvement. Strong communications keep everyone focused on goals and priorities while providing feedback on progress and the course corrections needed. Effective communication strategies, systems, and practices have a huge and direct effect on organization learning and innovation.

Effective communication strategies, systems, and practices

- Deliver clear and consistent messages to all parts of the organization
- Are simple, direct, and fast, with a minimal number of filters and interpreters
- Inspire and energize
- Are user-friendly, human, and personal

- Move information, experiences, learning, ideas, direction, and feedback equally well in all directions—up, down, and across the organization
- Provide multiple channels
- Are possible only in an atmosphere of trust and openness

Despite all their talk about communication, many managers don't appreciate the highly strategic role communication plays in their improvement efforts. Consequently, they don't spend enough time thinking through what they want to say and the best ways to say it. But the amount and type of your communication speak volumes about how much you trust people and whether you see people as partners or "subordinates" who "work for you." Your communication strategies, systems, and practices set the dimensions of the environment or fishtank you are putting people in.

Up Close and Personal

A vision is little more than an empty dream until it is widely shared and accepted. Only then does it acquire the force necessary to change an organization and move it in the intended direction.
—Burt Nanus, *Visionary Leadership*

The best information and communication systems, strategies, and technology can actually make things worse if you don't have strong communication skills. With today's technologies, a much bigger audience can conclude much faster that you don't have your act together. A powerful Focus and Context, clear goals and priorities, and a well-designed improvement plan won't look that way if they're poorly communicated. So, many technomanagers devise slick internal marketing campaigns and invest in expensive information technologies. They're on the right track. But although customers and partners appreciate and (when well-trained and supported) will use these technologies, they want to break through the mechanical alienation these tools and approaches can bring. People want a personal touch. They want to feel the passion, energy, and human side of their leaders before they can partner with them.

Leadership and communication are inseparable. Your ability to energize, inspire, and arouse people to ever higher levels of performance is directly related to your ability to communicate. Strong leaders are strong communicators. If your communication skills (especially verbal communication) are weak, you'll never be much of a leader. You may be a passable administrator, director, technician, team member, or technomanager. But without strong verbal communication skills, you'll never be an effective leader. As organizations move toward shared and self-management, you'll be left behind. Unless you improve your communication skills, you'll become a victim of the shifting balance between managing things and leading people.

Effective communication is no more a natural skill than leadership is a born trait. Very few powerful communicators just open their mouths and let the words naturally flow out. Most leaders have learned, developed, practiced, and refined their communication skills through a lot of hard work and conscientious effort. They have learned how to sell and persuade.

PATHWAYS AND PITFALLS

Communications help to keep people feeling included in and connected to the organization. . . . Give people information, and do it again and again.

—William Bridges, *Managing Transitions: Making the Most of Change*

Organizational

- In Chapter 13 I argued for consolidating all the potential goals and improvement opportunities your team and organization could pursue into three or four strategic imperatives. This was similar to my advice in Chapter 8 on reducing lists of potential values into three or four core values. The same is true for education and communication. *You need to establish the few core messages you want to communicate throughout your organization.* They must flow directly from your values, strategic imperatives, and the points of your Education Improvement Plan (pages 250–251).

Once you've established your core messages, use any and every communication channel you can to review, remind, and reinforce them. These include:

- Newsletters
- Videos
- Voice and electronic mail updates and dialogues
- Recognition and celebration events
- Annual shareholder reports
- Annual improvement reports
- Visits to, from, and among customers and partners
- Special improvement days and fairs that allow teams to display their activities and results
- Orientation and training sessions
- Teleconferences
- Information technology systems such as interactive computer databases
- Toll-free hot lines and telephone information centers

- Get out and talk to people. Multiple communication channels can and should be widely used to reinforce and support your core messages. But *the best way to communicate is in person*. Over the years I've found that the most effective communication approaches used by large organizations (and smaller ones that are geographically dispersed) are like political campaigns. Leaders are out actively "pressing the flesh" and standing up to present their change and improvement themes and core messages. During times of major change or refocus, I've seen senior managers at some large organizations spend well over a hundred days per year delivering these vital communication messages. That's leadership.

- Get your story together among your management team before any of you head out to give your version to the rest of the organization.

- Get people together. Double or triple your travel budget. Get teams together weekly, monthly, and certainly no less than quarterly. That's especially important for management, operational, or improvement teams that aren't in the same building. At Achieve, we found frequent face-to-face communications were the most important when we could least afford the time or the money to hold them. I continually find that most misunderstanding, mistrust, and misdirection can be turned around by getting the key players together. But this method works only—and here's the "big if"—if the meetings are well run.

- Develop highly visible scoreboards, bulletin boards, or voice mail, electronic or printed announcements of progress toward team and organization goals and priorities.
- Share all core strategic measurements (including "confidential" financial, and operating data) with everyone in your organization. Treat people like full-fledged business partners and they'll act that way (put them in big fishtanks). But don't snow them under with a blizzard of meaningless reports and numbers. Train everyone to read these data. Show them how to relate the measurements to their daily operations and improvement activities.
- Team education, learning, and communication can be kept simple. In my early management years I got a lot of mileage from having my team sit around a conference table reading, discussing, and debating selected book passages or articles. This dialogue established a common values and knowledge base that enhanced mutual understanding, teamwork, communication, and context for further training and work together.
- Establish an internal "best practices and good tries" communication system, clearinghouse, or network. A free flow of information and active communication is the lifeblood of a learning organization. Use videos, visits, fairs, databases, electronic and voice mail, meetings, reports, hot lines, teleconferences, information technologies, and the like.
- Keep your organization flat, lean, and decentralized.
- Develop an Education Improvement Plan covering the areas I outlined on pages 250–251. If your organization is doing work in this area now, get feedback from the people involved in delivering and receiving it on just how complete and effective the educational process is.
- Get feedback from your customers and partners on the characteristics of your education and communication strategies, systems, and practices. How close is your approach to the

characteristics listed on pages 252–253? How many communication channels are you using? Are they clogged or working well? What others could you be using?

- Just when you're sick of repeating the same core messages over and over again, that's when people in your organization are starting to hear you. First, they didn't understand. Then, they didn't believe. If you stop repeating yourself now, they'll conclude that you weren't serious after all.

- Don't trust the management hierarchy to deliver your core messages. It's full of filters and personal agenda that twist and distort your messages. Yet you can't go around your managers. They need to be central in communicating, reinforcing, and repeating your core themes. So start with them and give them that responsibility. But don't assume it will get done as you want. That's why personal meetings and multiple communication channels are so important.

- Keep moving your best people to the teams, positions, and parts of the organization that will spread their experience and leadership as broadly as possible. It's also a great way to continue their development.

- Reward and thank people who bring you bad news before it festers into a catastrophe.

- Trust and communication levels go together. Find out how high your organization or team trust levels are. If they're low, find out what's causing the problem. This may be painful. The source of misunderstandings and mistrust is often in a manager's behavior.

Personal

> *In general, those who have nothing to say contrive to spend the longest time in saying it.*
>
> —Abbott Lowell, early-twentieth-century American lawyer and president of Harvard University

- There is no one best communication style or magical speak-by-the-numbers formula that will make you a compelling verbal communicator. However, if you master the following

steps, you'll become an above-average communicator and
leader:

- Steven Covey's principle "seek first to understand" is an
  important starting point. In *The Seven Habits of Highly
  Effective People,* he writes, "If you want to interact effectively with me, to influence me . . . you need first to understand me."
- Everyone is tuned into the radio station WIFM—What's
  in It for Me. Talk in terms of my—not your—interests.
- Keep it simple, direct, and conversational.
- Never hide behind a written speech; don't read when
  you're supposed to be speaking. We want to see and hear
  from the real you.
- Be clear what your communication objectives and main
  points are before you open your mouth. Start by giving
  them to me.
- End by summarizing what you've told me and outlining
  what I should do next.
- Illustrate your presentation with personal anecdotes, examples, and stories. Talk in the first person. Go light on
  generalities, theories, and philosophies.
- Where possible, support your main points with facts,
  data, or research
- Use occasional touches of relevant humor (but don't tell
  old jokes) to lighten things up and show your humanness.
- Prepare an outline of your key points.
- Use short, action-oriented words. Don't perpetuate poly-
  syllabic obfuscation!
- Put passion and energy into your presentation. Keep link-
  ing back to the team, organization, or personal Focus and
  Context that's most meaningful to your audience.
- Get reactions to what you've presented. Try to lead a discussion around your main points.
- Continually get feedback on your presentation skills,
  style, and approach.
- Take training in public speaking. Find safe environments and
  forums for practicing and being coached on your presentation skills. Increasingly, your speaking and presentation abil-

ities (verbal communication skills) will determine just how effective a leader you will become.

- Do you keep your spouse or life partner informed? Would he or she call you a good communicator? You use the same pattern, frequency, and quality of communication with work partners. Set this as one of your improvement goals if it's an area that needs work.
- Use electronic or voice mail, meetings, notes, and conversations to keep people informed. Keep doing it until people tell you you're overdoing it.
- Return phone calls the same day or immediately the next morning. When you don't have an answer yet, call and say that you don't have an answer but you'll get back with one by a certain time. Then do it. On such leadership examples trust and strong communication cultures are built.
- How much do you communicate? What do you mainly communicate? What portion of your communications reflects your Focus and Context, strategic imperatives, and core measurements? Who says so besides you?

George Bernard Shaw once observed, "The greatest problem in communication is the illusion that it has been accomplished." It's an important reminder. Education and communication—like so many aspects of personal, team, and organization improvement—are never finished.

CHAPTER **22**

Reward and Recognition

A chronic record of mediocre performance may indicate, among other possibilities, that there is something wrong with the job itself or with an organizational structure that holds employees responsible for things that they are powerless to control. Turning the workplace into a game show ("Tell our employees about the fabulous prizes we have for them if their productivity improves . . .") does exactly nothing to solve these underlying problems and bring about meaningful change.

—Alfie Kohn, *Punished by Rewards: The Trouble with Gold Stars, Incentive Plans, A's, Praise, and Other Bribes*

It seemed like a good idea at the time. As Achieve was rapidly growing and hiring new people, I put together a sales incentive and recognition program. It had increasingly bigger prizes, bonuses, plaques, and awards with each sales level or "club" achieved. At one of our quarterly meetings, I excitedly unveiled my new reward and recognition program. It was welcomed with about as much enthusiasm as a thunderstorm at a picnic. "These are the very motivational gimmicks I've been so glad to get away from," said one newly hired sales and consulting veteran. "Yeah. I joined this company to make a difference and prove to organizations that they can succeed by treating their people with dignity and respect. I like money and recognition as much as anyone else, but that's not the reason I am excited about working here," added another participant. "This doesn't fit our values of working together and treating each other as adults. How can we partner with you to build the business if you're dangling carrots in front of us like we're donkeys?" asked a third.

They were right. I humbly put away the plaques and flashy announcements. I had put a lot of time and energy into hiring partners, Achievers, associates whose personal vision, values, and purpose were strongly aligned with the company's. I didn't want just employees, I wanted people who cared deeply about the business because of what we stood for, where we were going, and why we existed. My proposed reward and recognition program contradicted all that. It was too shallow and crass—even insulting. It threatened to swing attention away from the deep, meaningful issues of principles and purpose and move them to the hollow level of self-interest and selfishness.

YOUR VALUES ARE SHOWING

Well, Jones, according to our policy manual you're about due for a compliment.

I've always felt that managers and leaders use rewards and recognition in very different ways. But I've had trouble understanding what those differences actually were. Chapter 16 of *Firing on All Cylinders* is loaded with strategies, techniques, and examples of successful reward and recognition programs and strategies. As I wrote the original chapter for the first edition, rewrote it for the second edition, and watched managers and organizations use the approaches I'd outlined, I was puzzled. Why were the same methods highly successful in one organization and dismal flops in others?

Then I came across Alfie Kohn's book *Punished by Rewards*. This controversial book takes the dangers and effects of reward and praise to a negative extreme. I don't agree with all of his conclusions. But his thoughtful arguments are based on a massive review of research covering this topic. As so often happens with a good book, Kohn clarified and articulated the issues I'd been struggling with:

All rewards, by virtue of being rewards, are not attempts to influence or persuade or solve problems together, but simply to control. . . . Control breeds the need for more control, which then is used to justify the use of control. . . . Punishment and reward proceed from basically the same psychological model, one that conceives of motivation as nothing more than the manipulation of behavior. . . . Good management, like good teaching, is a matter of solving problems and helping people do their best. This takes time and effort and thought and patience and talent. Dangling a bonus in front of employees does not. In many workplaces, incentive plans are used as a substitute for management: pay is made contingent on performance and everything else is left to take care of itself. . . . If it does make sense to measure the effectiveness of rewards on the basis of whether they produce lasting change, the research suggests that they fail miserably.

As with so many improvement tools and techniques, the big differences with rewards and recognition approaches have to do with how they're used.

FINANCIAL REWARDS, COMPENSATION, BONUSES, AND INCENTIVES

Managers tend to use compensation as a crutch. After all, it is far easier to design an incentive system that will do management's work than it is to articulate a direction persuasively, develop agreement about goals and problems, and confront difficulties when they arise.
—Michael Beer, Harvard professor of business administration, researcher, and author of papers and books on organization change

Decades of research and dozens of studies show again and again that while the perceived lack of money can be a demotivator, the

Using Rewards and Recognition

Traditional Management Approach	Leadership-Based Approach
Lead with to manipulate, control, and direct behavior	Follow with to support organization change and improvement
Used *on* employees to push motivational buttons	Used *with* people to develop meaningful systems and practices
Paternalistic pats on the head	Participative, respectful partnerships
Management decides who gets rewarded and recognized for meeting their goals	Customer input helps management and partners decide whom and how to reward and recognize
Assumption that performance problems are from lazy, unmotivated, and uncaring people	Knowledge that poorly designed systems, structures, and processes leave people feeling powerless and uncaring

chance to earn more is not a motivator. Money always shows up as fourth or fifth on any list of motivational factors. Pay gets people to show up for work. But pay doesn't get many to excel. More important is interesting, challenging, or meaningful work, recognition and appreciation, a sense of accomplishment, growth opportunities, and the like. But the big problem is that managers have consistently listed money as the number one factor that they think motivates people. So they keep fiddling with pay, bonus, and financial incentives in a futile attempt to find the elusive combination that will motivate people to higher performance.

Bribing people to perform turns them into mercenaries. It debases, degrades, and demeans work. It sets a vicious, self-perpetuating cycle into motion—incentives, inducements, rewards, and the like leave people feeling manipulated and overly focused on what they get for complying with management's goals and direction (tuned only to WIFM—"What's in It for Me"). The emptier work is, the more people look elsewhere for fulfillment; so we demand more money and incentives to continue working in such a meaningless, unfulfilling job (which then "proves" to managers that people won't improve their performance unless they're bribed to do so). Money is never an effective rallying point for high performance. It can't be. Money doesn't create energy and excitement in a bigger cause and purpose.

I believe in paying people very well. I agree with the wag who said "If you pay peanuts, you get monkeys." I have long believed in, and practiced, profit sharing and organization or team performance bonuses. The people who helped create the profits should share in the rewards in proportion to their contribution (which can be very tough to establish). But more important than the money are the messages profit and performance bonuses can send. They should make people feel like partners, not puppets on a string. That means rewards should follow, not lead, high performance. It also means that education and communication, measurement and feedback, skill development, and many of the improvement steps we've covered so far must be tightly melded to any reward programs.

A high-performing organization is filled with higher performers who are highly paid. Pay people well. But once you're sure they feel their compensation is fair and equitable, don't even mention money again until next year. Fix everyone's attention on the bigger and more meaningful issues of Focus and Context, customers and partners, innovation, goals and priorities, and growth and improvement. Concentrate on building a culture of success and forward momentum with lots of recognition and appreciation for everyone's contributions.

RECOGNITION AND APPRECIATION: INSPIRING, ENERGIZING, AND AROUSING

Just as it is easier for some parents to show love with gifts than with hugs, it is often easier for organizations and managers to show gratitude with money than with words.

—Andrew Lebby, senior partner, The Performance Group

I've found that managers' approaches to recognition can be divided into three categories:

1. **Management by Exception.** One manager proudly used this term to describe his approach. "If you haven't heard from me, that's a good sign," he explained. "That means I think you're doing just fine. I only deal with the exceptions. I look for problems and people that need correcting. Those are what I jump on." In a later conversation that same manager talked about his failed first marriage. "What really drove me crazy were her constant complaints that I never told her I loved her," he complained. "I married, her didn't I? Obviously I loved her. Why did I need to keep saying it, then?" Personal and organization consultant John Scherer calls this approach Gap-Zap. When things are going well, nothing is said—we leave a gap. When things get off track or there's a problem—we zap.

Variations of management by exception are leading causes of the demoralization and fear that's rampant in so many groups and organizations. People feel criticized, ignored, unappreciated, and even used. They feel like a piece of equipment or just so many "human assets with skin wrapped around them."

2. **Flattery and Manipulation.** Flattery is a negative form of praise that does more harm than good. It's used to control and

dominate. At the personal level, this sickly (and sickening) form of recognition is practiced by people who "lay it on thick." Generally the compliments they pay are overblown and out of proportion to the deed or person they're addressing ("we could never survive without your contributions"). Or their phony flattery is vague and general ("you do great work").

Many manipulative managers have built extensive recognition programs and practices around "doing their recognition thing." They hand out flattery, compliments, awards, prizes, and "atta boy's" just as they would control and reward the family dog with a biscuit and a pat on the head. One company actually handed out stickers, awards, plaques, and merchandise as part of their "Atta Boy/Girl" program of "recognition." Another "motivational speaker" makes this approach the centerpiece of his suggested management methods. Using the training approach for teaching killer whales to jump high out of their tanks as his model, he gives out "Good Whale" stickers that are to be stuck on deserving people or their work.

3. Recognition and Appreciation.   Only two groups of people thrive on sincere recognition and genuine appreciation—men and women. Reflecting on a life of pioneering work, the nineteenth-century American philosopher and psychologist William James said, "I now perceive one immense omission in my psychology— *the deepest principle of human nature is the craving to be appreciated* [my emphasis]." Sincere recognition and genuine appreciation are highly energizing. Accomplishment and achievement should be their own reward for high performance. But it feels even better when other people notice and appreciate what we've done. Recognition and appreciation continually show up near the top of most lists of motivational factors. They are key sources of the fun and excitement, will to win, desire to belong, and passion so vital to continually improving performance.

Highly effective leaders use a multitude of ways to build an atmosphere of success, accomplishment, and pride through recognition and appreciation. But these leaders aren't central figures in control of the "goodies." Rather, these leaders model, encourage, and support people giving recognition and appreciation up, down, and across the organization and within and among teams and team members. Chapter 16 of *Firing on All Cylinders* outlines a series of programs, techniques, and practices for team, individual, and personal recognition programs. As I reflect on and compare organization and team cultures, it's clear that the high-energy, high-performance culture radiates sincere recognition and genuine appreciation. That's why the same recognition programs that fizzle out in other organizations thrive in these. It's also clear that these vibrant, successful cultures are led by managers who have well-developed personal recognition skills and appreciation habits.

PATHWAYS AND PITFALLS

No one is apathetic except those in pursuit of someone else's objectives.

—Henry Ford

Organizational

- Don't use money to try to shape behavior or boost performance. It doesn't work. (If you think it has in the past, what happened when you took the carrot away? No doubt, performance slipped and you were left with stimulus-dependent people looking for progressively bigger carrots.) Unless people feel your compensation and bonus systems are a major block, leave them alone. Get on with all the much higher leverage performance and improvement activities we've covered in this book. When you do need to review or adjust your financial rewards, get the people you're compensating involved. They should give you feedback on your current approach and improvement ideas. Ideally, they would design and own the compensation system.
- Keep reward programs simple and direct. They should be easily understood. People should also see a direct connection between what they and their team do to serve customers or partners and their compensation. That argues for shared management or self-managed teams operating in a decentralized structure. I've found that simple three-tiered compensation systems work well: (1) personal, (2) team, division, or plant, and (3) corporate profit sharing. Base the rewards on an open-

ended percentage of earnings, not performance to a budget or projections (that just invites game playing at budget time).

- Whose needs are your recognition and reward systems designed to serve? What are the goals? Are they to manipulate, control, and "motivate"? Or do they build an atmosphere of helpfulness, appreciation, and high energy. How do you know? As with beauty, quality, or customer service, reward and recognition are in the eyes of the beholder. So *get all your partners involved in designing meaningful reward and recognition systems and practices for each other.* Involvement can happen through combinations of gap analysis, focus groups, teams that study and recommend, or teams that design and implement the reward system.

- Get clear about what is to be rewarded and recognized and by whom. Move management out of the role of deciding who gets rewarded and recognized for what behaviors. Work with your partners to blend customer/partner input with your team's or organization's vision, values, purpose, strategic imperatives, and improvement goals. Set up systems, programs, and training, and provide a personal leadership example that gets customers and partners involved in giving frequent recognition and appreciation to each other.

- Make sure there's a good balance between rewarding and recognizing both current performance and improvements. People who do well today but aren't improving won't help your team or organization get better. Anyone who's not continually improving will become a liability.

- Don't set up competitions for limited rewards—unless teamwork isn't important to you. Fear of failure and losing don't create energy. Find ways to meaningfully recognize and energize as many people as possible.

- Don't use suggestion systems. They reward people for lobbing ideas at others to implement. They work best in a paternalistic culture where they reinforce traditional management control rather than shared or self-management.

- Never use promotions as a reward. People should be put into larger leadership roles only because they have demonstrated the capacity, vision, values, skills and so on for ever higher levels of leadership. Using promotions as rewards puts an unhealthy focus (and competition) on position, rank, and titles as a means of measuring worth. It also sets the promotee up for failure in his or her new position.

- Traditional performance appraisals are dangerous and detrimental to performance. They don't work. Why are you using them? If it's to manipulate and control behavior, you're paying a big performance price to indulge your unhealthy fetish. If it's to develop people, replace appraisals with frequent performance discussions and coaching based on 360-degree feedback.
- Separate compensation and performance discussions. They serve two different (and often opposing) purposes. Over 85 percent of the factors affecting individual performance are in the system, process, or structure of the organization.
- Build jobs around people. Align good people with what they like to do and what needs doing. Helping people to grow, expand, and move to new challenges and opportunities is one of the best ways to show sincere recognition and genuine appreciation for their improvement efforts.
- Keep measurements, improvement progress, and recognition highly visible. Use scoreboards, bulletin boards, voice mail, electronic or printed announcements, and the like.
- As your reward and recognition program and practices take shape, use the full array of education and communication strategies, systems, and approaches outlined in the last chapter.
- Recognize and reward both individuals and teams.
- Use a wide variety of methods to recognize and appreciate contributions.

Personal

> *Brains, like hearts, go where they are appreciated.*
> —Robert McNamara, former U.S. Secretary of Defense and president of the World Bank

Whether your team or organization develops a healthy recognition and appreciation culture depends to a large extent on the personal example you set. If you manage by exception or Gap-Zap people, most others will follow your lead. Energy and morale will be low. In this uncaring environment, recognition programs will be contrived and out of place. They won't work for long. The same is true if you use a lot of flattery and manipulation. Well-designed recognition programs may create a sharp spike of excitement and energy, but eventually the culture you've established will drive down their impact.

- Get feedback on your personal recognition skills and appreciation habits. Look for the connections between that feedback and the team or organization recognition programs you're using. Are they aligned?
- Here are some keys to giving sincere recognition and genuine appreciation:
  - Recognize or show your appreciation as immediately as possible after the event or action you want to acknowledge.
  - Be specific. Avoid general platitudes and global statements.
  - Mention how the action or behavior was personally helpful or fits within the bigger team or organization vision, values, and purpose.
  - Keep it brief. Long, detailed compliments can be uncomfortable and sound overdone.
  - Ask if there's anything you can do to provide further support or service to that person or team.
  - Ask yourself whether that exchange helped enlarge the team's or individual's self-determination and self-motivation or whether it increased dependence on your approval?
- Don't recognize only top performers and superhuman efforts. Eighty percent of your people aren't shining stars, but their solid day-to-day performance keeps your team and organization alive. Even small increases in their energy and enthusiasm will have a dramatic cumulative effect. Develop the habit of looking for incremental performance or improvements that deserve to be recognized. Make this part of your personal improvement plan to strengthen this vital leadership habit.

- Never compare or contrast teams or individuals.
- Sincere recognition skills and genuine appreciation habits aren't turned on at work and turned off when you go home (flattery and manipulation can be). Develop the habit of pointing out the positive at home, with friends and neighbors, at social activities, and so on.
- Show appreciation for good tries, pilots, and mistakes that advance organization learning, especially if that experience is shared openly and widely for all to benefit from and build upon.
- Heather has taught me the value of sending each other cards for every occasion (birthdays, anniversaries, Mother's/Father's Day, Valentine's Day, Thanksgiving, Christmas, Easter, etc.). It's a powerful appreciation habit. She's also shown how important and valued a short personal note of thanks can be. Put those occasions on your calendar. Send notes to team members' homes. It's those little things that make a big difference over time.
- Lead the applause for any individual or team who makes a presentation to your team.
- Where it fits, recognize people in public or in front of others. Always deal with performance problems in private.
- Say "thank you."
- As with communications, use every channel you can—public and private, oral and written, to reinforce and support success, accomplishments, and progress.

Like improvement efforts, effective reward and recognition is an integrated process, not a bolt-on program. Because you can't make your team or organization into something different from you, it starts with you.

CHAPTER 23

Change Champions and Local Initiatives

Today's successful business leaders will be those who are most flexible of mind. An ability to embrace new ideas, routinely challenge old ones, and live with paradox will be the effective leader's premier trait. . . . Leaders will have to guide the ship while simultaneously putting everything up for grabs, which is itself a fundamental paradox.

—Tom Peters, *Thriving on Chaos:*
Handbook for a Management Revolution

Beware of formal organization improvement plans. Like strategic plans, organization improvement plans can reduce your organization's effectiveness. They can lead to rigidity, bureaucracy, and resistance to change.

"What are you talking about?" I can hear you fairly screech at me. "You've just spent the last nine chapters outlining the key elements of improvement planning. Now you're telling me to ignore it all?" Hold on. I am certainly not suggesting that. Constant and ongoing personal, team, and organization improvement planning is vital. And as Chapter 15 and more than forty pages of *Firing on All Cylinders* attest, I am a big believer in organization improvement plans.

But too many change and improvement plans are built on the same faulty premise as strategic planning—that there is a right path which can be determined in advance and then implemented. I often hear managers declare that they have the right strategic or improvement plan, but the reason things aren't going according to plan is because of "execution problems." A deadly assumption. Although there are many reasons for execution problems, one of the key problems is a top-down improvement plan or change program. Because of their insecure need for order and control, many technomanagers try to use improvement planning to regulate and

271

direct the random and chaotic events swirling around them. They aren't comfortable with letting their improvement plan and path to higher performance unfold and evolve toward their vision, values, purpose, goals, and priorities. In other words, they think they can start with the answers. They're not comfortable with learning.

Other organizations and consultants may have been down a road similar to the one you're on. You have much to learn from their experiences. But you can't follow their path. And because you've never been down this road before, you don't really know what the best paths and approaches are. Your improvement path evolves as you get to each fork in the road and get those people closest to the action to help make the most appropriate choices. You need an unwavering strategic focus on where you're going. But exactly how you get there can only be roughly sketched. Details get filled in as you go. Most of the problems and opportunities can't be anticipated and planned for in advance. You have to take advantage of the unforeseeable opportunities that will quietly present themselves as your journey unfolds. In other words, strategic opportunism.

FOLLOW THEM, FOR YOU ARE THEIR LEADER

Grass-roots change presents senior managers with a paradox: directing a "nondirective" change process. The most effective senior managers in our study recognized their limited power to mandate corporate renewal from the top. Instead, they defined their roles as creating a climate for change, then spreading the lessons of both successes and failures. Put another way, they specified the general direction in which the company should move without insisting on the specific solutions.

—Michael Beer, Russell Eisenstat, and Bert Spector,
"Why Change Programs Don't Produce Change"

Improvement planning is on the management track of the improvement map (page 53). Like performance gap analysis (also on the management track), organization improvement planning calls for systems, processes, and discipline. These are often top-down, organization-wide approaches. Developing change champions and supporting local initiatives is on the leadership track of the improvement map. Like innovation, many change and improvement paths are discovered accidentally by change champions blazing new trails (strategic opportunism again). These can then be structured and made passable for the whole wagon train. This is an important part of organizational learning. Improvement processes evolve and change to fit the shifting environment and what's being learned about what works and what doesn't. Both top-down and local, or bottom-up, approaches are needed. The challenge is finding the right balance.

Over the years I've written and spoken extensively about the pivotal role senior managers play in the success or failure of any organization improvement effort. Their behavior is the single most important variable in the process. But among those senior managers who work hard to visibly and actively lead their organization improvement effort, many fill only half their role. They personally signal values, plan, direct, and coordinate. That's vital. But what most fail to do as well is follow and serve. They don't manage (or may not even have thought about) the servant-leadership change and improvement paradox.

The leadership component of the change and improvement paradox consists of all the strategic components we've covered so far. It's managing the Focus and Context, identifying customers/partners and the gaps to be closed, and cultivating the environment for innovation and organization learning. Improvement leadership means establishing goals and priorities and setting the improvement planning process and framework. However, the service side of the paradox is about followership. This starts with a recognition that the organization is full of current or potential change champions. As members or leaders of operational and improvement teams, these people are much closer to the action than is anyone in senior management. So they have a much better sense of which change and improvement tactics will work. But perhaps even more importantly, they hold the balance of implementation power. Without their commitment, the best-laid plans will fail (another major cause of "execution problems").

Think Corporately, Act Locally

Balancing top-down improvement planning with local initiatives involves identifying and supporting the change champions, innovative teams, and other efforts that are already underway. At the corporate or organization-wide level, improvement planning includes establishing strategic imperatives, and improvement objectives, setting the broad improvement map (such as the infrastructure and process to be used), and developing preliminary plans. Part of that planning entails connecting to and incorporating the existing pockets of change and improvement. These teams and champions have often gone through the first two steps of the four-step exploration-experimentation-development-integration process I outlined in Chapter 12. Their (often unorthodox and unofficial) approaches and experiences can be a gold mine of learning for the organization improvement process. As these early innovators are educated to the full organization improvement plan, they're shown how to adapt the new process and tools. They can use them to build on their earlier experiences and move ever closer to their improvement goals.

DEVELOPING CHANGE CHAMPIONS

Whenever anything is being accomplished, it is being done, I have learned, by a monomaniac with a mission.

—Peter Drucker, *Adventures of a Bystander*

When I look back at the successful team or organization changes I've been involved in, most—and certainly all major ones—were always driven by a "monomaniac with a mission." Sometimes that was me. Other times I was working with, or sponsoring and running interference for, a passionate person pushing hard for a change or improvement. The change could have been in an accounting or human resource system. It could be a product or service, telephone answering procedure, training program, or work process. Sometimes it was to the organization structure, marketing strategy, or the very business the company was in. My consulting experience and research into the nature of innovation and organization change have made clear *the key role change champions play in team and organization change.* They are needed to overcome the bureaucratic response of "we've always done it this way" (which almost guarantees it's no longer relevant today). Champions push against the inertia, passive resistance, or outright opposition that resists many changes.

Good champions are passionate about their cause or change. They are staunch, zealous fanatics. Great champions are emotional, irrational, irreverent, impatient, and unreasonable. They want the change—no matter how big—to happen this week, this month, or certainly by the end of this quarter. To impassioned change champions, the sky is often falling and the situation is desperately urgent. Or the improvement opportunity they're advocating is the one and only key to the organization's future. Highly effective change champions don't just rock the boat, they're determined to capsize it. They want to disrupt and demolish the status quo. Many of the best champions don't just want change; they want a revolution.

With their focus on ordered, controlled, and planned "change management," many managers suppress or drive out champions. In an oppressive environment numerous would-be champions become good little bureaucrats conforming to the official plans and obediently following "the system." Others subversively continue to make changes out of sight of management or the bureaucracy. Some leave to start their own businesses or join a less stifling, more entrepreneurial organization.

Champions are vital learning leaders for your organization. You need their energy, ideas, and creativity today more than ever. But you have to learn how to coordinate their unbounded and disruptive zeal. Their energy needs to be gently directed toward your Focus and Context, strategic imperatives, and improvement process. They have great strengths, but many also have glaring weaknesses. For example, they may refuse to see or try to understand the need for a delicate balance between change and stability. You can't harness or manage champions (remember, you manage things and lead people). Point them in the right direction and get out of the way. Then sponsor and protect them from the bureaucracy when they need it. Once your change champions have found the new trail, pave it over and make it official. Now you can set the relevant teams or parts of your organization on this new road to higher performance.

PATHWAYS AND PITFALLS

> *Unfortunately, it's the rare company that understands the importance of informal improvisation—let alone respects it as a legitimate business activity. In most cases, ideas generated by employees in the course of their work are lost to the organization as a whole.... This important source of organizational learning is either ignored or suppressed.*
>
> —John Seely Brown, "Research That Reinvents the Corporation"

- You can't encourage and support what you don't know is happening. The most interesting and useful local change and improvement initiatives rarely make it into reports or formal channels. That may be because they're "illegally" breaking corporate rules, deviating from the standard process, or failing to follow the official plan. It may be because local champions or teams (skunkworks) don't realize the significance of their innovation to the rest of the organization or a potential new market. So get out and poke around. Find out what's happening in all the nooks and crannies of your organization. Look for people and teams who are solving problems in creative new ways. Then, fulfill the critical leadership role Walt Disney was talking about when he said, "I am like a bee, buzzing from one part of Disney to another spreading the pollen of creativity and stimulation."
- Don't let training, quality, or other improvement professionals impose a top-down organization improvement plan on everyone. One size does not fit all. However, people can't go off simply doing their own thing. There needs to be some organization-wide coordination and consistency in your improvement effort. Another part of senior management's leadership role involves clarifying what is mandatory and what is optional in your improvement effort. The organization's destination and priorities shouldn't be optional. But the best route to get there should be open for exploration,

customization—and local ownership (the most critical element of building commitment).

- One non-negotiable is that all improvement activities focus outward. All changes either serve an external customer or partner or serve somebody who is leading or will lead to new markets and the filling of unmet needs. Changes that make internal life easier but reduce customer service, quality, or innovation aren't improvements. Current and potential customers and/or the partners serving them should be at the center of, or key members on, the local learning teams. They need to be "mucking around" to find new and improved ways of producing, delivering, or supporting your products and services.
- Demonstration or pilot projects are powerful learning, change, and improvement tools. Opening a new plant, branch, division, or office is a great opportunity to set up a "greenfield site." This is where you can test new structures, tools, and techniques (such as self-managed teams or horizontal management).
- A highly effective leader can have 20 years of rich learning and experience. But many mediocre performers have one year of experience multiplied twenty times. The same learning disability afflicts organizations that haven't developed the systems and practices for transferring and communicating the rich learning that comes from local initiatives. You need an internal "best practices and good tries" system, clearinghouse, or network. You should have electronic databases; frequent meetings; active voice or electronic mail systems; team visits, fairs, or other share-and-compare forums. Measurement systems and feedback loops should make the results every team is getting highly visible and widely available to everyone. Your education, training, and communication activities should continuously keep people throughout your organization in touch with what's working and what isn't.
- Celebrate, publicize, recognize, honor, thank, applaud, and otherwise encourage champions and local teams who take the initiative to change and improve their part of the world.
- Senior managers need to uncover and coordinate local improvement initiatives to ensure they are pointed in the right

direction and are focused on the goals and priorities that really matter. You don't want teams working flat out to make changes that hurt some other part of the organization or are trivial and meaningless. That calls for an improvement process or infrastructure. But be careful that it doesn't turn into a stifling bureaucracy that kills any initiatives that aren't part of the official plan. One way to avoid that pitfall is to make sure the infrastructure is run by operational teams and managers, not staff support professionals (they should act as consultants to management). Another is to ensure that improvement planning's main goal is to produce education, change, and improvement, not plans. The plan should be an outcome of the more valuable and ongoing improvement planning process.

- Look for the existing leaders and champions who are making improvements and changes. Shape your improvement plan and process by building on their energy and experience. Because change champions won't be covering all areas as completely as possible, they are also the logical starting point for making the changes and improvements that will better round out and balance your long-term effort.
- Develop change and improvement momentum by building around the champions who are most likely to make the effort succeed. They will help to bring the others on side. They are also the ones you and everyone else can learn the most from. But don't try to impose their successful approaches on others. Ownership and personalization are the keys to local adoption of changes and improvements. Sell, persuade, educate, and communicate.
- A key measure of managers and teams should be how much they've changed, improved, and innovated. Continuous personal improvement and the ability to live with and manage paradox should be a central factor in hiring and promoting managers. Managers who aren't personally improving pay lip service (sometimes even passionate lip service) to the importance of change and improvement. But it stops there. Give them education, skill development, coaching, a role in the improvement planning process, and your own personal improvement example. If they still aren't personally improv-

ing and leading change initiatives, you can't afford to keep them. Leaving them in a management position will cost you the commitment and trust of everybody who's watching to see how serious you really are. Help these stagnant managers find career opportunities elsewhere.

- Discuss with your management team how your successful change champions (some of whom will be present) have emerged and been supported in the past. What can you learn from those experiences? How does your bureaucracy suppress or drive out emerging champions? How can you ensure that change champions get the mentoring, sponsorship, and management support they need to buck the system? What do your champions think?

- If you're not a senior manager, your organization change and improvement choices are (1) do nothing but complain and hope "they" smarten up; (2) quit; (3) make as many changes as you can in your own area. Help others to change and try to influence the system. In other words, act like a leader!

ON A PERSONAL NOTE

Example is contagious behavior.
—Charles Reade, nineteenth-century English novelist

You can't develop change champions if you're not one. You don't need to be irrational, irreverent, or unreasonable. In fact, you may provide more of the steady and stabilizing balance that every team and organization needs. You do need to be passionate. Even more importantly, you need to be personally changing and improving. If you're not, you'll feel overwhelmed by the changes and revolutions champions will be inciting. You'll come to see these activities as "out of control" threats to your stable and protected world. You can't build a team or organization that's different from you. If you're not on a steep personal growth curve, any change champions or local improvement initiatives on your team or within your organization will be forced to slow down to your sluggish improvement pace. Establish a personal improvement plan and get to work on you.

CHAPTER 24

Review, Assess, Celebrate, and Refocus

Nothing in the world can take the place of persistence. Talent will not; nothing is more common than unsuccessful people with talent. Genius will not; unrewarded genius is almost a proverb. Education will not; the world is full of educated derelicts. Persistence and determination alone are omnipotent.

—Calvin Coolidge

Our performance results are determined by what we finish, not by what we start. But whether it's diet and fitness, investments, leadership development, or organization change and improvement efforts, many people search for the quick and easy technique or approach. When the latest improvement fad doesn't create a magic transformation, the next hot book, guru, theory, or change program beckons. Improvement faddists are like the medieval alchemists who searched in vain for a formula to turn base metals into gold. But what's most important to improvement isn't what's new. It's what works. It's more than just your improvement process and plan. It's ultimately your improvement action that determines your performance results. The effectiveness of that action hinges on your follow-through and stick-to-it-iveness.

Our learning and development are highly dependent on our habits of performance review, assessment, and reflection. Many individuals, teams, and organizations have a limited or faulty understanding of what's working, what's not, and why. Like the rooster who came to believe that his crowing produced the sunrise, cause-and-effect relationships get distorted. Learning and understanding are highly dependent on performance review, assessment, and reflection.

Our energy and enthusiasm for continual growth and improvement is strongly influenced by whether we feel like winners, taste success, and are having fun along the way. It's all too easy to let what's wrong and what yet needs to be improved overshadow what we've accomplished and how far we've come. The pressure of continuous performance improvement can be draining. If we're going to maintain high energy levels, we need to develop the habit of periodically taking the celebratory pause that refreshes.

Review, assess, celebrate, and refocus are essential elements of a vital step in the improvement process. It's a step that I now realize I glossed over too quickly in past writing and consulting. I've come to realize that missing this step causes many organizations and management teams to drift off their improvement track. Because they don't review and assess, they can't recognize celebration opportunities nor effectively refocus to move on to the next leg of their journey. That's why I've given this step such a pivotal and prominent place on the improvement map (page 53). It's the step that both completes and restarts the endless improvement cycle. Without this essential component, learning, energy, and momentum dwindle.

REVIEW AND ASSESS: STEP BACK TO STEP AHEAD

In the fast-moving New Economy, you need a new skill: reflection. . . . The sort of reflection that's gaining popularity aims at learning that results in increasingly effective action by individuals and groups. It requires facing reality within an individual psyche and in the outer world of markets and customers—and then thinking and communicating honestly about that understanding.

—Stratford Sherman, "Leaders Learn to Heed the Voice Within," *Fortune*

Throughout this book I've emphasized getting feedback from customers, partners, and team members. I've tried to stress the importance of periodic progress reviews and suggested numerous ways you do that on your own and with your team. We've looked at how central experimenting, reviewing, revising, and retrying is to innovation and organization learning. I've recommended quarterly reviews to assess progress toward goals and priorities. We've looked at the value of personal time logs and daily reflection and planning sessions to increase personal effectiveness. I've tried to convince you to develop and use your own version of Benjamin Franklin's "method for progressing" by identifying all the tools, techniques, and habits you want to form and then establishing a systematic plan and process to make them part of your nature. We've looked at measuring your rate of improvement as one of five core strategic measurements.

All of those steps are essential to learning and improvement. Without these and related actions, improvement plans and activities quickly drift off track and become meaningless. *When you don't know how you're doing you can't improve.* Yet so many managers fail to periodically review and assess their progress. Their approach makes about as much sense as setting off on the high seas for a far-away destination and then ignoring instruments, stars, or maps to determine that the ship is still on course. I've come to realize that failing to periodically review and assess is one of the major reasons so many improvement efforts lose their way.

I hope you're convinced by now that reviewing and assessing progress is a critical daily, weekly, monthly, and quarterly activity. But there's a danger to constantly reviewing and assessing your personal, team, and organizational performance in the midst of hectic operations and performance pressure. At least once a year you and your team need to get away from the daily flurry of activities, step back, and look at the bigger picture. You need to reassess whether you're on the right track or whether you're making good time—in the wrong direction. You need to look at your full improvement effort and discuss, debate, and decide if it has the right focus, priorities, approaches, and the like. You need to celebrate progress and reenergize everyone to push forward even harder. And you need to set new plans and directions for the next stage of your improvement process. It's that bigger, more formalized review, assessment, celebration, and refocus that this section of the improvement map (and this chapter) is all about.

CELEBRATION: THE PAUSE THAT REFRESHES

Success is every minute you live. It's the process of living. It's stopping for the moments of beauty, of pleasure; the moments of peace. Success is not a destination that you ever reach. Success is the quality of the journey.

—Jennifer James, *Success Is the Quality of Your Journey*

After 45 years of hard work, the grizzled old rancher decided it was finally time to sell the ranch, retire, and enjoy the rewards of his toil and sweat. So he called a real estate agent to list the place for sale. The agent spent most of a day with the rancher riding the range and getting a feel for the ranch he would be selling. A few days later, the agent returned to finalize the listing and get approval for an ad he'd prepared. It was written to attract a city dweller from the large metropolitan area less than 100 miles away. The ad described the freedom of the open range. It talked in poetic terms about the river that happily babbled to the lush green hills as it meandered by. The ad described heartbreakingly beautiful sunsets that painted the big open sky with an awesome array of reds, oranges, and crimsons. It spoke of the deep satisfaction and contentment of sitting on the big front porch and watching the young colts play in the corral. After reading the ad, the seasoned old rancher walked over to the huge picture window and silently gazed out. A few minutes later, he softly whispered, "This ranch isn't for sale after all." As the rancher turned to face the agent, a tear ran down his wrinkled, leathery cheek. "All my life I've dreamed of a place just like this. Now I finally realize what I've got here."

The relentless drive for ever higher performance and reaching our next goal often leaves us too numb and exhausted to enjoy what we have achieved. Rather than pausing to appreciate what we have accomplished, we become narrowly focused on what we haven't yet attained. Dale Carnegie once observed, "One of the most tragic things I know about human nature is that all of us tend to put off living. We are all dreaming of some magical rose garden over the horizon—instead of enjoying the roses that bloom outside our windows today." I've been as guilty of this as anyone. When we don't slow down to savor successes along the way, each accomplishment becomes less fulfilling. When I have paused to savor and celebrate, life becomes richer and much more satisfying. I also find that it's a great "battery recharger." Savoring and celebrating is highly energizing. Paradoxically, it's when things are darkest and our goals seem farthest from reach that a focus on what's gone right and what we have to be thankful for can be the most invigorating.

Radical change and aggressive breakthrough targets are often daunting. Continual change and constant improvement can be exhausting. That's why effective leaders break the endless improvement journey into a series of short exciting trips. A key element in each short trip is celebrating and savoring success. It's how effective improvement leaders reenergize everyone to strive for the next goal. Energizing leaders employ a multitude of creative ways to foster appreciation and recognition giving among all team and organization members. They also find numerous ways to hike energy and enjoyment levels by marking and celebrating milestones along the way. Energizing leaders constantly search for ways to make change and improvement fun and rewarding. They know that the laughter index is a key indicator of the health and vitality of a team or organization.

Taking on this important leadership role means you'll need to overcome decades—if not centuries—of training and conditioning that business is very serious stuff. Tom Peters has speculated on the cause of this energy-sapping view of organizational life. He claims that over the entrance to most business schools there's a giant stone lintel with these words deeply inscribed in it, "All ye who enter here shall never smile again." If suppressed laughter does spread the hips and produce gas, that may explain a few things.

REFOCUS: THE CYCLE BEGINS ANEW

It's easy to be a starter, but are you a sticker, too? It's easy enough to begin a job. It's harder to see it through.

—Margaret Thatcher

Reviewing, assessing, celebrating, and refocusing should be ongoing activities. But once a year, if you're leading an organization improvement effort, your management team needs to get away for a few days and take a concentrated look at where you've been and where you're going. Once you've retraced the path you've taken, you need to reaffirm, correct, or completely change your future course. As the improvement map shows (page 53), that leads back to your Focus and Context. It means revisiting your vision, values, and purpose. Are they still relevant? Do they need refining, updating, or redesigning? How could you make them more clear and compelling?

The same process is used for the rest of the pathways and passages on the improvement map. Are new customers and partners emerging? What about your approaches to innovation and organization learning? What action should you take to improve this key determinant of your future success? What are this year's key goals and top priorities? What part of the eight improvement areas (Chapters 15 to 22) need the most attention in this cycle? Who will be involved and how will you pull your improvement plan together? How can you further develop change champions and support local improvement initiatives?

PATHWAYS AND PITFALLS

The heights by great men reached and kept/Were not attained by sudden flight,/But they, while their companions slept,/ Were toiling upward through the night.

—Henry Wadsworth Longfellow

Organizational

- Prepare an annual improvement report. This is a collection of all the positive changes and improvements of the past year throughout your entire organization. It doesn't have to be glossy or slickly produced. It could be just a simple collection of summaries, stories, improvement charts, lessons learned, accomplishments, and the like. I have yet to see an annual improvement report that wasn't a source of enormous energy (and surprise) to everyone in the organization. When they read through the report, most people are stunned and then inspired by the amount of change and improvement that has been made. Yet many organizations don't bother to put a report together. Don't miss this golden opportunity.

- Use annual improvement audits or assessments from external improvement experts, self-assessments using a well-established improvement framework (quality award criteria can be quite useful, but most are narrower in scope than we've covered in this book), benchmarking, and other such methods of reviewing your improvement progress.
- A key step in the annual improvement cycle is a two- to three-day off-site senior management team meeting to review, assess, celebrate, and refocus. I've found that when management teams fail to hold such a meeting, they invariably lose energy, focus, and momentum. Here are some of the agenda items for that session:
  - Review of last year or the original Focus and Context, performance gap data, innovation and organizational learning strategies, goals and priorities, improvement plans, and strategies for change champions and local initiatives
  - Assessments of team and organization progress (ideally external, hard measurements and/or customer/partner perception data)
  - Review of all the improvements and positive changes of the past year (either from the annual improvement report or as a step toward compiling it)
  - Team celebration activities
  - Planning organization-wide appreciation, recognition, and celebration events and activities to build momentum by stringing together small wins (along with any big ones)
  - Identifying performance gaps and setting improvement priorities using discussion and planning questions like those outlined on page 285
- If you're a large diversified organization, network and bring together your improvement coordinators and support staff at least once a year.
- Make the final step of every major improvement or change project a one-half to one-day assessment of what went well, what would be done differently if the project were starting over, and the major lessons learned. This should be docu-

mented, video- or audio-taped, written up, presented in meetings, or in some way shared with the rest of the organization.

- Every improvement and operational team should follow a similar review and assessment process as part of its quarterly review. These should be disseminated and shared as well.
- During your reviews and assessments be especially vigilant for unexpected and unplanned successes. Dig deeper to understand the unanticipated results. Often you'll find "happy accidents," chance changes, or highly effective championing behavior. These are key sources of innovation. Study, learn, and understand what's going on. Time spent figuring out how to replicate and spread the causes of these results can be just as productive as problem solving, gap analysis, or improvement planning.
- Reflection, learning, communication, and openness go together. The more transparent your organization, team, and personal decision making, the more everyone else will learn and be directed to think more deeply about what they do and how it fits within the bigger picture.

Personal

> Reflection may be the pivotal way we learn. Consider some of the ways of reflecting: looking back, thinking back, dreaming, journaling, talking it out, watching last week's game, asking for critiques, going on retreats—even telling jokes. . . . Because reflection is vital—at every level, in every organization—and because burnout is a very real threat in today's hectic atmosphere, all executives should practice the new three R's: retreat, renewal, and return.
>
> —Warren Bennis, On Becoming a Leader

- If applicable, you and your life partner should get away at least once a year to review, assess, celebrate, and refocus the progress toward your vision, values, purpose, and goals.
- Using a journal to reflect on and record your deepest thoughts is especially important if you're going through a tough period and you don't have someone or a group of close people whom you can talk and reflect with. At this

point in the annual improvement process, look back through your journal entries to review and assess your progress.

- You can't recharge anyone else if your own batteries are low. Develop ways to maintain your energy and passion. How you can best do that is unique to you. You might try frequent reviews of your vision, values, purpose, and blessings and brag list. Daily affirmations can help. Jennifer James suggests taking a "bliss break" by making a list of all the little things that "give you a thrill." It's a fun exercise (the list can run to many pages once you get started). Setting aside four or five periods of 30 to 45 minutes per week for inner reflection, meditation, and spiritual renewal has been a major recharger for me over the years. Seek, find, and continually draw from your personal energy source.
- Learn how to be quiet and listen to your voice within. Follow where it leads.
- If you're not one already, become a celebrator. Celebrate birthdays, anniversaries, the kids going back to school, a friend's promotion or new business opening, and Thanksgiving (and give plenty of thanks). On Valentine's Day, Mother's and Father's day, and other special occasions, do more than send flowers and a card. Use these times to celebrate, appreciate, and recognize the special people in your life and the contributions they've made.
- Getting 360-degree feedback and other personal data on your performance can be very useful, especially if you're in denial (which you'll deny) or not very reflective (the less time you've taken to reflect over the years, the more you need this feedback). But keep the feedback and data in perspective. They're being given to you through the eyes and ideals of the person or people delivering it. They may not understand—or even agree with—your vision, values, and purpose. So the feedback could be leading you toward compliance with what others want from you or with how they see rather than toward self-leadership.

Reviewing, assessing, celebrating, and refocusing is an important check and jumping-off point in your improvement journey. Do it well, and you'll redirect and reenergize yourself and others to continue learning, changing, and improving.

CHAPTER **25**

Change Checkpoints, Improvement Milestones, and Ringing True to You

---

There are no smooth, direct, or certain roads to high performance. Success is mostly via detours. The routes are always under exploration and reconstruction.

We've traveled a long way together. Because you've stayed with me this long, my optimistic nature leads me to assume that *Pathways to Performance* (or at least portions of it) has been a good fit for you. My objectives in writing this book were irritation, inspiration, and instruction. I hope you have indeed been irritated, inspired, and instructed in all the right places. But if all you've done is read this book, I've failed. My overriding and primary objective throughout has been to get you to act. Without action, without your changing and improving your approaches to personal, team, and organizational leadership, reading this book has been only a recreational or intellectual exercise for you.

As I've stressed many times in these pages, one of the keys to learning is feedback. Another is learning about, sharing, and building upon the improvement experiences of others. You could be a big help to my own learning and in turn help others improve by giving me some feedback. At the end of this chapter (on page 298), you'll find my address and phone and fax numbers. Let me know about your improvement process. What's worked and what hasn't? What path have you carved for yourself, your team, and your organization toward higher performance? What additional Pathways and Pitfalls would you add within each of the chapters I've covered in *Pathways to Performance*? Have I missed or underemphasized important improvement areas? As with giving any

289

feedback, balance your suggestions with what you've found useful about this book's content or the way it's been written. That lets me know what I need to keep doing as well as what I could do, say, or write differently in the future.

Your feedback will help improve the workshops, seminars, retreats, and development materials produced and delivered by me and my associates at The Clemmer Group. We will also keep you informed of new improvement materials, publications, and services.

STEPS ON YOUR PATHWAY TO HIGHER ORGANIZATION PERFORMANCE

When you arrive at a fork in the road—take it.
—Yogi Berra

Many paths lead to higher performance. Throughout *Pathways to Performance* I've emphasized that the high performance route is individual and unique for every person, team, and organization. There is no one or best way. And what works for me or anyone else may not work for you. So you can't follow someone else's path. You need to blaze your own trail.

Although no route is exactly the same, successful organization change and improvement efforts cover similar territory. Highly successful organizations have passed most of these change checkpoints and improvement milestones as they move toward ever higher performance levels:

Change Checkpoints and Improvement Milestones

___ Clear and compelling reasons for changing and improving

___ Balanced focus on people, management, and technology

___ Strong ethic of self-determination

___ Comprehensive and balanced improvement model

___ Clear and compelling picture of your preferred future

___ Three or four core values

___ Definitive statement of purpose, business you're in, or why you exist

___ Rich and continuous customer/partner performance gap data

___ Intense exploring and searching for new markets and customers

___ High levels of experimentation, pilots, and clumsy tries

___ Robust process for disseminating team and organization learning

___ Three to four strategic imperatives for each annual improvement cycle

___ Direct links between all improvement activities and strategic imperatives

___ Comprehensive and balanced improvement plan

___ Improvement planning structure, process, and discipline

___ Well-designed, proven approach to process management

___ Clear understanding of the preferred types and focus of all teams

___ Well-trained team leaders and members

___ Intense levels of technical, management, and leadership skill development

___ Simple customer/partner, innovation, capabilities, improvement, and financial measurements

___ Active feedback loops that foster learning and improvement

___ Flat, decentralized, and team-based organization structure

___ Systems that serve and support customers and partners

___ Extensive and continuous education programs

___ Effective communication strategies, systems, and practices

___ Partner-designed reward and recognition programs within a vibrant appreciation culture

___ Strong development of change champions

___ Support for local initiatives

___ Annual progress reviews and improvement assessments

___ Frequent celebrations of major breakthroughs and small wins

___ Annual refocus and planning for the next year's improvement cycle

This list reviews the territory we've covered in the last twenty-four chapters. You and your management team can use the list in a variety of ways. It could be a simple checklist for the development of your improvement strategies and plan. You might have everyone on your team rate how well your organization and/or team is doing in each area now. Or you might have everyone rate the improvement urgency of each of these thirty-one areas. Another possibility is to have everyone do both rating exercises to give you performance gap data. Whatever approach you use, you'll want to get your partners (especially your internal ones) involved in identifying the areas needing the most improvement. Use these data to put together your change and improvement strategies and plans.

RINGING TRUE TO YOU: ARE YOU ON A PARALLEL IMPROVEMENT TRACK?

The cruellest lies are often told in silence.
—Robert Louis Stevenson

By now it's a familiar refrain (sing along, you know the words)—you can't build a team or organization that's different from you. You can't make them into something you're not. I've relentlessly hammered and incessantly beaten on this point because it's the single biggest reason that so many team and organization change and improvement efforts flounder or fail. The changes and improvements you try to make to others must ring true to the changes and improvements you're also trying to make to yourself. So here's a personal improvement questionnaire that runs in parallel to Change Checkpoints and Improvement Milestones:

Are You Trying to Make Your Organization or Team into Something You're Not?

To what extent are you:

___ Attempting to change your organization or team without changing yourself?

___ Prodding your organization to be more people (customer/partner) focused when you're a technomanager (driven by management systems and technology)?

___ Driving for industry or market leadership when you're afflicted with the pessimism plague and/or victimitis virus?

___ Striving to stimulate and energize others when you aren't passionate about your own role and life's work?

___ Promoting organization or team vision, values, and mission when your own picture of your preferred future, principles, and purpose isn't clear and/or well aligned with where you're trying to lead others?

___ Pushing for a customer-driven organization while controlling and dominating, rather than serving (servant-leadership)?

___ Aspiring to develop new markets and fill unmet needs while spending limited time with customers, partners, or those serving them?

___ Trying to build a learning organization when your own rate of personal growth and development is low?

___ Declaring the urgency of higher levels of innovation while you stick to familiar personal methods and traditional command and control management approaches?

___ Aiming for disciplined organization or team goal and priority setting when you're not well organized, a poor personal time manager, and fuzzy about your own goals and priorities?

___ Setting organization improvement plans without an improvement process of your own?

___ Promoting teamwork and a team-based organization without providing a personal model of team leadership and team effectiveness in action?

___ Supporting high levels of skill development—for everyone else?

___ Forcing accountability, performance appraisal, and measurement on others while you defend, avoid, or halfheartedly gather personal feedback?

___ Proclaiming empowerment and involvement while controlling and limiting people with a centralized structure and systems that constrain rather than support?

___ Talking about the need for better communications without becoming a strong and compelling communicator?

___ Establishing formal reward and recognition programs when your personal habits of giving sincere recognition and showing genuine appreciation are weak?

___ Espousing support for change champions while suppressing "off the wall" behavior and pushing people to follow your plans and stay within in your established system?

___ Advocating reviews and assessments while doing little personal reflection and contemplation?

Rate yourself on each of these nineteen questions. What do your answers tell you about your leadership? Does this exercise help explain the positive, negative, or so-so results of the team and organization improvement efforts you've led? Your reflections are important, but an even better source of feedback is the people on your team or those in your organization who know your leadership behavior well enough to give you some feedback. Ironically (and tragically), managers who need it most—the weakest leaders—are the least likely to ask for this kind of feedback. How about you? Are you ready to turbocharge your improvement process by getting this feedback?

Both the organization and improvement checklist and the personal leadership questionnaire are "fingers to the wind." They're not scientifically designed data collection instruments. But on their own as a simple checklist, or used more extensively to gather and focus feedback, they can provide you with a framework and some input for personal, team, and organization improvement planning. They identify the points we've visited throughout this book. You need to forge your own unique course that covers this ground if you're going to move to ever higher levels of performance.

PAY THE PRICE AND REAP THE REWARDS OF LEADERSHIP

Go confidently in the direction of your dreams. Live the life you've imagined.
—Henry David Thoreau

Do You Really Want to Be a Leader?

As you look at all that's involved in becoming a highly effective leader, you may be tempted to wonder if it's worth it. A good question. For some people it's not. Unfortunately, many of those people remain in management positions. They make themselves and everybody around them miserable. An important question is, Are you in the right job? Management roles are undergoing a major shift in emphasis. Technical expertise and managing processes and systems will continue to be vital to managerial success. But tumultuous times call for high levels of innovation, breakthrough thinking, and rapid responsiveness. Uncertain and unpredictable changes are successfully mastered through strategic opportunism, experimentation, continuous learning, and constant improvement. That means that even more important than managing things (systems, processes, and technology) is leading people. That demands well-developed and perpetually improving leadership skills. Do you really want to be a leader? Are you ready to continually build those skills and habits?

Blaze Your Own Leadership Path

Following the path of least resistance is what makes individuals and rivers crooked. Few people drift to success.

There are about as many views and definitions of what encompasses "leadership" as there are experts in this field. This book brings you the elements I've found to be the most critical. But there is one point that most leadership researchers and developers agree on: Leaders are made not born (a key point of Chapter 4). Leaders are rarely naturals. Certainly, some are innately better at some aspects of leadership than others. For example, they may be more verbal or naturally "people-oriented" than their technical or administratively inclined management counterparts. But most highly effective leaders have invested countless hours and long years in numerous forms of self-improvement.

What seems to confuse lesser performing onlookers is that these leaders—like highly skilled athletes—have developed their skills to the point of making it look easy and natural. It's like good writing. I can tell you, from thousands of hours of painful personal experience, that my most easy to read and "spontaneously flowing" pieces were often the most agonizing to write. I've often taken hours to write a few sentences or a paragraph (and then sometimes deleted or rewritten it later). The goal is conversational writing that sounds as if I just sat down at my keyboard and effortlessly banged out a chapter "off the top of my head." If I am successful, I appear to be a "natural born writer." The same is true of "gifted" speakers. Many have spent years polishing, practicing, and presenting what sounds like an "off the cuff," spontaneous delivery. The "naturally witty" Mark Twain once revealed, "It usually takes me three weeks to prepare a good impromptu speech."

Are you ready to pay the price of leadership? The pathways to outstanding performance and ever higher leadership levels are lengthy and difficult. The time, energy, and discipline to be successful are intense. It starts with a clear and constant focus on where you're going, what you believe in, and why you exist (your picture, principles, and purpose). But it also demands another important "p" word—persistence. Studies of high performers—from Nobel prize-winning scientists, to top athletes, to highly effective corporate leaders—show that their perseverance and "bull dog determination" was a key factor in their eventual success. As the vaudeville and film star Eddie Cantor put it, "It takes twenty years to make an overnight success."

Rather than focusing on the price to be paid, concentrate instead on the rewards to be reaped. Your time and your life are better organized. You—rather than competitors, the economy, your boss, or "the system"—can control your own destiny. Exciting new markets, products, and services have others scrambling to catch up. Your sense of mastery and confidence grows as you continuously improve your knowledge, skills, and experience. Relationships with those you care most about take on a new depth and richness. You feel more "centered" and in touch with your deep inner, spiritual being—your soul. Your group becomes a truly cohesive, stimulating, and continuously improving team. Your energy, passion, and respect for the person who stares back at you in the mirror flourish when you are true to you. The boy or girl you were would be proud of the man or woman you've become.

I hope our paths will cross again.

What's Worked for You?

Your feedback, ideas, experiences, and suggestions could be very helpful. Please mail or fax me with:

- What did you like best about or find the most useful in *Pathways to Performance*?
- How could this book have been even more useful?
- What personal, team, organization, or improvement process has worked best for you?
- What additional Pathways or Pitfalls would you add that haven't been mentioned in this book? Have I completely missed any improvement areas?

Send or fax your feedback to me at:

The Clemmer Group Inc.
476 Mill Park Drive
Kitchener, Ontario
Canada N2P 1Z1
Fax: (519) 748-5813
Phone: (519) 748-5968

Thanks! Your feedback will help improve the workshops, seminars, retreats, keynote presentations, and development materials produced and delivered by me and my associates at The Clemmer Group. We appreciate your contributions to our learning. We will also keep you informed of our new improvement materials, publications, and services.

NOTES

Chapter 1

2   Wallace Donham quoted in "Strategic Humor," *Harvard Business Review,* January–February 1994, p. 138. His comment originally appeared in the October 1932 issue.

2   *Atlantic Journal* quotation is from a presentation by Don Dewar, president, Quality Circle Institute.

3   "hinge of history," Alvin Toffler, *Powershift* (New York: Bantam, 1990), p. xix.

3   "what is emerging...," Alvin Toffler, *Powershift* (New York: Bantam, 1990), p. 238.

3   Warren Bennis quoted by Marilyn Norris in "Warren Bennis on Rebuilding Leadership," *Planning Review,* September–October 1992.

5   "Though forecasting specific events...," Ted Levitt, *Thinking About Management* (New York: The Free Press, 1991), p. 70.

Chapter 2

11   "Our tendency is to try things...," Richard Tanner Pascale, *Managing on the Edge* (New York: Simon and Schuster, 1990), pp. 20 and 21.

Chapter 3

19   Charles Handy quoted by Martha Nichols in "Does New Age Business Have a Message for Managers?" *Harvard Business Review,* March–April 1994, p. 60.

Page

23   Ted Levitt, *Thinking About Management* (New York: The Free Press, 1991), p. 46.

25   "IT assumptions about people and learning . . . ," Edgar Schein, *Organizational Culture and Leadership* (San Francisco: Jossey-Bass, 1992), p. 282.

27   "Morale began to lag . . . ," James Brian Quinn, *Intelligent Enterprise* (New York: The Free Press, 1992), p. 319.

27   Thomas Stewart, "Rate Your Readiness to Change," *Fortune*, February 7, 1994, p. 106.

29   "The results of our surveys . . . ," Jim Kouzes and Barry Posner, *Credibility* (San Francisco: Jossey-Bass, 1993), p. 13.

30   "Recent research . . . ," Brian O'Reilly, "Reengineering the MBA," *Fortune*, January 24, 1994, pp. 39, 44, and 46.

30   "It is not enough . . . ," *Credibility*, pp. 16 and 17.

30   Robert Half communication studies reported in *Training and Development Journal*, July 1986, p. 9.

30   "Without exception, visionary leaders . . . ," Burt Nanus, *Visionary Leadership* (San Francisco: Jossey-Bass, 1992) p. 182.

Chapter 4

39   "The defining characteristics of pessimists . . . ," Martin Seligman, *Learned Optimism* (New York: Knopf, 1990), pp. 4–5.

40   "Learned helplessness . . . ," *Learned Optimism*, pp. 15–16.

40   "Pessimism is self-fulfilling . . . ," *Learned Optimism*, p. 113.

40   "The management of self is critical," Warren Bennis and Burt Nanus, chapter titled "Leading Others, Managing Yourself," *Leaders* (New York: Harper and Row, 1985) p. 56.

41   "Organizational change begins with leaders . . . ," Stratford Sherman, "Leaders Learn to Heed the Voice Within," *Fortune*, August 22, 1994, p. 93.

44   "All of life is a series of choices . . . ," Zig Ziglar, *Top Performance* (New York: Berkley Books, 1986), p. 22.

45   Doug Snetsinger, *Learning Leaders: Perspectives From Canadian CEOs,* Institute of Market Driven Quality, Faculty of Management, University of Toronto, pp. *v* and 9.

45   "It seems clear that the leaders . . . ," Edgar Schein, *Organizational Culture and Leadership,* pp. 391–392.

46   Charles Garfield's comments taken from a presentation he gave at the National Speaker's Association conference in New Orleans in February 1985.

Page
46   University of Virginia research from Anne G. Perkins, "The Learning Mind-Set," *Harvard Business Review,* March–April 1994, pp. 11–12.

47   "They all agree that leaders . . . ," Warren Bennis, *On Becoming a Leader* (Reading, Mass.: Addison-Wesley, 1989), pp. 3 and 5.

Chapter 6

60   "Preference with a passion . . . ," Charles Garfield, *Peak Performers* (New York: Morrow, 1986), p. 62.

63   "Organizations exist to enable . . . ," Ted Levitt, *Thinking About Management* (New York: The Free Press, 1991), p. 64.

67   "In the National Career Development Project . . . ," Richard Bolles, *The Three Boxes of Life* (Berkeley: Ten Speed Press, 1978), p. 267.

Chapter 7

71   "Picture the force . . . ," Claude Bristol, *TNT* (Englewood Cliffs: Prentice-Hall, 1954), pp. 22, 25, 70, 186.

72   "The world has a way . . . ," Zig Ziglar, *See You at the Top* (Gretna, La.: Pelican, 1975), p. 196.

72   "You merely picture in your mind . . . ," Og Mandino, *The Choice* (New York: Bantam Books, 1984), p. 5.

73   "A railroad worker was repairing . . . " is based on a video by American Media in West Des Moines, Iowa.

73   "Exceptional patients refuse to be victims . . . ," Bernie Siegel, *Love, Medicine and Miracles* (New York: Harper and Row, 1986), pp. x, 24, 35, and 69.

74   "Peak performers, particularly in business . . . ," Charles Garfield, *Peak Performers,* p. 146.

74   "PEAR study" from Srikumar Rao, "Envision Success," *Success,* June 1992, p. 80.

79   "All of the leaders to whom . . . ," Warren Bennis and Burt Nanus, *Leaders,* p. 101.

80   "the ability to remain focused . . . ," Daniel J. Isenberg, "The Tactics of Strategic Opportunism," *Harvard Business Review,* March–April 1987, p. 92.

81   "the visionary approach is more flexible . . . ," Henry Mintzberg, *The Rise and Fall of Strategic Planning* (New York: The Free Press, 1994), p. 209–210.

Page
86   "Whatever you need to fit . . . ," Claude Bristol, *TNT,* p. 72.
87   Sanaya Roman citation and quote from "Envision Success" p. 80.

Chapter 8

92   "Values are directly relevant . . . ," Jim Kouzes and Barry Posner, *Credibility,* p. 60.
92   "Among the people I know . . . ," Donald Seibert, *The Ethical Executive* (New York: Simon & Schuster, 1984), p. 37.
93   "Leaders who establish cooperative relationships . . . ," *Credibility,* p. 130.
94   "The values gap . . . ," Andrall Pearson, "Corporate Redemption and the Seven Deadly Sins," *Harvard Business Review,* May–June 1992, p. 67.
97   "if a manager's . . . ," J. Sterling Livingston, "Pygmalion in Management," *Harvard Business Review,* July–August 1969. Reprint No. 69407.
98   "Plants that managers think . . . ," Regina Fazio Maruca, "Manufacturing Flexibility," *Harvard Business Review,* November–December 1993, p. 10.
98   "In almost all cases . . . ," John Kotter and James L. Heskett, *Corporate Culture and Performance* (New York: The Free Press, 1992), p. 96.
103   "making the right people decisions . . . ," Peter Drucker, quoted by Joe Flower, *Healthcare Forum Journal,* May/June 1991, p. 56.
103   "We stand at the crossroads . . . ," Benjamin Franklin, *The Art of Virtue,* edited by George L. Rogers, (Eden Prairie, Minn.: Acorn, 1990), p. 88.

Chapter 9

107   "is intended to serve leaders . . . ," Stephen Covey, *Principle-Centered Leadership* (New York: Summit, 1990), pp. 295 and 296.
108   "You're not ready to live . . . ," Charles Jones, *Life is Tremendous* (Harrisburg, Penn.: Executive Books, 1968), p. 65.
109   "From my eleventh year . . . ," Carl Jung quoted in Richard Leider, *Life Skills* (San Diego: Pfeiffer, 1994), p. 76.
110   "Acres of Diamonds" was repeated by Earl Nightingale in his radio addresses, audio presentations, and columns. This description was drawn from Alan M. Webber, "Acres

Page

of Diamonds," *Harvard Business Review,* May–June 1990, pp. 222–223.

111 "An overemphasis on profits . . . ," James Brian Quinn, *The Intelligent Enterprise* (New York: The Free Press, 1992), p. 324.

115 "Someone who knows his desires . . . ," Mihaly Csikszenthmihalyi, *Flow: The Psychology of Optimal Experience* (New York: Harper and Row, 1990), p. 217.

Chapter 10

118 Russ Conwell, "Acres of Diamonds," quoted by Alan M. Webber, *Harvard Business Review,* May–June 1990, p. 223.

119 O'Toole quoted by John Huey, "The New Post-Heroic Leadership," *Fortune,* February 21, 1994, p. 42.

119 "Despite the recent media coronation . . . ," Rosabeth Moss Kanter, "Even Closer to the Customer," *Harvard Business Review,* January–February 1991, p. 10, and "Think Like the Customer: The Global Business Logic," July–August 1992, p. 9.

122 "Rank is an appointed position . . . ," Ted Levitt, *Thinking About Management,* p. 44.

122 "It's difficult to say to someone . . . ," Srully Blotnick's book *Ambitious Men: Their Drives, Dreams, and Delusions* is excerpted in *Success,* March 1987, p. 54.

123 "A new morale principle is emerging . . . ," Robert Greenleaf, *Servant Leadership: A Journey into Legitimate Power and Greatness* (New York: Paulist Press, 1977), pp. 10 and 13.

126 Elderly couple's fiftieth wedding anniversary, Zig Ziglar, *Top Performance,* p. 119.

127 "Market-perceived quality . . . ," Brad Gale, *Managing Customer Value* (New York: The Free Press, 1994), page *xiv.*

Chapter 11

132 "No one will pay good money . . . ," The King of Prussia quoted by Peter Drucker in *Innovation and Entrepreneurship* (New York: Harper and Row, 1985), p. 127.

132 News item in an 1868 New York paper from Ashton Applewhite, William R. Evans III, and Andrew Frothingham, *And I Quote* (New York: St. Martin's Press, 1992), p. 467.

Page

135   "Above all, the machine organization...," Henry
       Mintzberg, *The Rise and Fall of Strategic Planning,*
       p. 400.

135   "the planning school's grand fallacy...," *The Rise and Fall
       of Strategic Planning,* page 321.

135   "If every valuable idea is logical...," Edward De Bono, *Serious Creativity* (New York: Harper and Row, 1992), p. *ix.*

137   Clayton Christensen study reported by Glenn Rifkin in
       "Wrestling with the S-Curve," *Harvard Business Review,*
       January–February 1994, p. 10.

138   Mercer Management Consulting study quoted by Myron
       Magnet, "Let's Go For Growth," *Fortune,* March 7,
       1994, p. 72.

139   "Above all, we know that an entrepreneurial strategy...,"
       Peter Drucker, *Innovation and Entrepreneurship,* p. 252.

140   "The need for innovation...," Tom Peters, *Liberation
       Management: Necessary Disorganization for the
       Nanosecond Nineties* (New York: Knopf, 1992), p. 480.

143   Darrel Rhea's teen research was taken from "The Nosy Art
       of Knowing Customers," *The Globe & Mail's* "Change
       Page," April 25, 1994.

                                                      Chapter 12
145   "We need a new way of thinking about...," Charles
       Handy, *The Age of Paradox,* (Boston: Harvard Business
       School Press, 1994), pp. 11–12.

146   James Brian Quinn, "Managing Innovation: Controlled
       Chaos," *Harvard Business Review,* May–June 1985, p. 73.

146   Henry Mintzberg, "Crafting Strategy," *Harvard Business Review,* July–August 1987, p. 68.

147   "Now, more than ever...," Rosabeth Moss Kanter, "Best
       of Both Worlds," *Harvard Business Review,* November–December 1992, p. 9.

151   "No one can predict...," James Brian Quinn, *Intelligent
       Enterprise,* p. 301.

152   "Experimentation involves the systematic searching...,"
       David Garvin, "Building a Learning Organization," *Harvard Business Review,* July–August 1993, pp. 82 and 85.

152   "An inventor is simply a person...," Charles Kettering
       quoted in *Bits and Pieces,* November 1987.

Page
153   "A new idea is delicate . . . ," Charles Brower, *Advertising Age,* August 10, 1959.

154   "Every highly innovative enterprise . . . ," James Brian Quinn, "Managing Innovation: Controlled Chaos," *Harvard Business Review,* May–June 1985, p. 79.

154   "Adhocracy is any organization form . . . ," Bob Waterman, *Adhocracy* (New York: W. W. Norton, 1990), p. 16.

154   "I learned the never-to-be-forgotten importance . . . ," Don Frey, "Learning the Ropes: My Life as a Product Champion," *Harvard Business Review,* September–October 1991, p. 52.

154   "It is no longer sufficient . . . ," Peter Senge, *The Fifth Discipline: The Art and Practice of the Learning Organization* (New York: Doubleday, 1990), p. 4.

157   "We don't do things right the first time . . . ," *The Stuff Americans Are Made Of,* American Quality Foundation, New York, 1993, p. 16.

158   "Every three years or so . . . ," Peter Drucker, *Innovation and Entrepreneurship,* p. 151.

160   "Because many professionals . . . ," Chris Argyris, "Teaching Smart People How to Learn," *Harvard Business Review,* May–June 1991, p. 100.

Chapter 13

163   "Effective executives know that . . . ," Peter Drucker, "First Things First" in *The Effective Executive* (New York: Harper and Row, 1966), p. 103.

165   "Things are little different . . . ," Ted Levitt, *Thinking About Management,* p. 95.

168   Yale study on written goals from "Get Your Wings—Soar to Success on your Attitude," a review of *Tune in to Success,* by Robert M. Unger and John H. Kupillas Jr., in *Success,* April 1991, p. 46.

173   "Concentration—that is, the courage . . . ," *The Effective Executive,* p. 112.

176   "People expect us to be busy . . . ," Stephen Covey, Roger Merrill, and Rebecca Merrill, *First Things First,* (New York: Simon and Schuster, 1994), p. 35.

180   "Any goal that forces you . . . ," Og Mandino, *A Better Way to Live* (New York: Bantam, 1990), pp. 110–111.

Page   Chapter 14

185   "Leaders in learning organizations . . . ," Peter Senge, "The Leader's New Work: Building Learning Organizations," *Sloan Management Review,* Fall 1990, p. 9.

186   "If changing is, as I have argued . . . ," Charles Handy, *The Age of Unreason* (Boston: Harvard Business School Press, 1990), p. 56.

                                           Chapter 15

191   "There is at least one point . . . ," Andy Grove quoted in Carol J. Loomis, "Dinosaurs?" *Fortune,* May 3, 1993, p. 39.

192   "The most important thing . . . ," Peter Drucker, *The Effective Executive,* p. viii.

194   "The learning organization can mean . . . ," Charles Handy, *The Age of Unreason,* p. 225.

195   "The only difference between . . . ," Og Mandino, "The Scroll Marked 1," *The Greatest Salesman in the World.*

196   "Writing is the most profound way . . . ," Warren Bennis, *On Becoming a Leader,* p. 48.

                                           Chapter 16

199   "The building blocks of corporate strategy . . . ," George Stalk, Philip Evans, and Lawrence Shulman, "Competing on Capabilities: The New Rules of Corporate Strategy," *Harvard Business Review,* March–April 1992, p. 62.

200   "Major breakthroughs in time to market . . . ," Louis Lataif, quoted in "MBA: Is the Traditional Model Doomed?" *Harvard Business Review,* November–December 1992, p. 129.

201   "had been frustrated by how fixated . . . ," quoted by Robert M. Randall, "The Reengineer," *Planning Review,* May/June 1993, p. 18.

201   "the fundamental rethinking and radical redesign . . . ," Michael Hammer and James Champy, *Reengineering the Corporation: A Manifesto for Business Revolution* (New York: Harper Business, 1993), pp. 2, 5, 31, 32, and 49.

                                           Chapter 17

207   "It is obvious that teams outperform . . . ," Jon Katzenbach and Douglas Smith, *The Wisdom of Teams* (Boston: Harvard Business School Press, 1993), pp. 1, 2, and 173.

Page

208 "a small number of people . . . ," *The Wisdom of Teams,* p. 92.

209 "When teams work . . . ," Brian Dumaine, "The Trouble with Teams," *Fortune,* September 5, 1994, p. 86.

212 "a team player and team leader," "Re-engineering the MBA, *Fortune,* January 24, 1994, p. 40.

216 "Pity City" comment from "Managing Change: The Art of Balancing," Jeanie Daniel Duck, *Harvard Business Review,* November–December 1993, p. 114.

Chapter 18

222 "I have never found . . . ," quote from Charles Garfield, speaking at the Canadian Public Personnel Managers Association conference in Regina, Saskatchewan, May 1990.

224 "We all want to know how to make . . . , Peter Drucker quoted by Joe Flower in "Being Effective," *Healthcare Forum Journal,* May/June 1991, p. 53.

Chapter 19

231 "Measurement is the lock . . . ," H. James Harrington, *Business Process Improvement* (New York: McGraw-Hill, 1991), p. 184.

Chapter 20

238 "Structure influences behavior . . . ," Peter Senge, *The Fifth Discipline,* p. 42.

239 "A jillion smart, energetic people . . . ," Tom Peters, *Liberation Management,* p. 131.

246 "The old managerial concept . . . ," James Brian Quinn, *Intelligent Enterprise,* p. 378.

Chapter 21

248 "The increasing availability of new information . . . ," Edward Lawler III, *The Ultimate Advantage* (San Francisco: Jossey-Bass, 1992), p. 224.

253 "A vision is little more . . . ," Burt Nanus, *Visionary Leadership,* p. 134.

254 "Communications help to keep people . . . ," William Bridges, *Managing Transitions* (Reading, Mass.: Addison-Wesley, 1991), pp. 27 and 41.

Page
258   "If you want to interact effectively . . . ," Stephen Covey, *The Seven Habits of Highly Effective People* (New York: Simon and Schuster, 1989), p. 238.

Chapter 22

260   "A chronic record of mediocre performance . . . ," Alfie Kohn, *Punished by Rewards* (Boston: Houghton Mifflin, 1993), p. 61.

261   "All rewards, by virtue of *being* rewards . . . ," *Punished by Rewards,* pp. 16, 27, 33, 37, 51.

262   "Managers tend to use compensation . . . ," Michael Beer, "Rethinking Rewards," *Harvard Business Review,* November–December 1993, p. 39.

264   "Just as it is easier for some parents . . . ," Andrew Lebby, "Rethinking Rewards," *Harvard Business Review,* November–December 1993, p. 42.

Chapter 23

271   "Today's successful business leaders . . . ," Tom Peters, *Thriving on Chaos* (New York: Knopf, 1987), p. 391.

272   "Grass-roots change presents senior managers . . . ," Michael Beer, Russell Eisenstat, and Bert Spector, "Why Change Programs Don't Produce Change," *Harvard Business Review,* November–December 1990, p. 159.

274   "Whenever anything is being accomplished . . . ," Peter Drucker quoted by Tom Peters and Nancy Austin in *A Passion for Excellence* (New York: Random House, 1985), p. 135.

276   "Unfortunately, it's the rare company . . . ," John Seely Brown, "Research That Reinvents the Corporation," *Harvard Business Review,* January–February 1991, p. 109.

Chapter 24

281   In the fast-moving New Economy . . . ," Stratford Sherman, "Leaders Learn to Heed the Voice Within," *Fortune,* August 11, 1994, pp. 92 and 94.

Page
283   "Success is every minute you live . . . ," Jennifer James, *Suc-
          cess Is the Quality of Your Journey* (New York: Newmar-
          ket Press, 1983), p. 38.
284   "All ye who enter here . . . ," Tom Peters and Nancy Austin,
          A Passion for Excellence, p. 252.
287   "Reflection may be the pivotal way . . . ," Warren Bennis,
          On Becoming a Leader, pp. 115 and 186.

INDEX